SAINTS ALIVE!

SHEILAH WARD LING

SAINTS ALIVE!

 St Paul Publications

St Paul Publications
Middlegreen, Slough SL3 6BT, United Kingdom

Copyright © St Paul Publications UK 1991

Cover photograph: Edmund Nägele FRPS

ISBN 085439 367 6

Printed by The Guernsey Press Co. Ltd, Guernsey, C.I.

St Paul Publications is an activity of the priests and brothers
of the Society of St Paul who proclaim the Gospel through the
media of social communication

For Vicky, Katy, Ted and Ellie
– our pilgrim children –
with love

AUTHOR'S NOTE

The contemporary characters depicted as preface and conclusion to each of these lives are imaginary, but I hope they may reflect those unknown members of the congregation of the faithful, who keep alive in their hearts the spirit of the Saints.

'St Therese of Lisieux' is an expanded version of a C.T.S. pamphlet that has already been published, and is reproduced by kind permission of the Incorporated Catholic Truth Society.

Contents

Foreword

The Second Vatican Council has reaffirmed the Church's veneration of the saints. In *Lumen Gentium*, the Council's Dogmatic Constitution on the Church, we are exhorted to follow the saints in their imitation of Christ. The lives of the saints, which bear witness to the Gospel, are God's reminder to us that we too can, in our varied walks of life and in the changing conditions of society, practise the Christian virtues and attain holiness. Indeed, God speaks to us through the saints and offers us a sign of his kingdom in the communion of saints, whose brothers and sisters we are in the body of the Church.

Our place in the communion of saints is nowhere better clarified than in the liturgy. Redeemed by the same blood of Christ and united in the same act of worship in the celebration of the eucharistic sacrifice, we renew our fellowship of communion in honouring the Virgin Mary, St Joseph, the holy apostles and martyrs and all the saints.

In *Lumen Gentium* the Second Vatican Council accepts the early Church's faith in the communion which exists between the faithful and the saints in heaven. The Council further endorses the decrees of the Councils of Nicea, Florence and Trent. At the same time we are urged to correct any abuses, excesses or defects in the practice of our devotion to the saints.

The authentic cult of the saints does not consist in exaggerated external acts, but in the practice of love by which we seek from the saints the example of their way of life, the fellowship of their communion and the help of their intercession. The Council also reassures us that such practice of devotion to the saints in no way detracts from divine worship. For the saints are our signposts to God.

The Publishers

Preface

It was while listening to a radio-programme about St Therese of Lisieux that I realized there was something terribly wrong with it. Everyone – even people who were devoted to her – talked about her as if she were dead. Therese, of all people – the saint who was spending her heaven doing good on earth! Yet every time we pray the Litany of the Saints, or participate in the Mass of their feasts, we are compelled to pay lip-service at least to the idea that they are endlessly, triumphantly alive. And we are assured, by their response to our attempts to communicate with them, that they wish to share with us the delights of their vision of God.

All of them were endowed with special talents in their service of him. Some had been gifted with a mystical union, like St Catherine of Siena and St Teresa of Avila, and left records of their journey in the life of prayer. This did not mean that they did not have practical and busy lives, in which they showed all the dynamism that activates modern women in their careers. Some, like St Bernadette, were vessels of grace, reflecting the beauty of their visions. Incidentally, St Bernadette was quite scathing about the biographies of the saints that were available to her, complaining of their over-zealous piety: she wanted to see the saints, warts and all, so she could identify with their humanity, and learn how they had cured their faults.

That they are human makes them accessible to us. The very fact that St Patrick's temper was on a very short fuse, and St

Monica was prone to emotional blackmail, gives us hope that we too can win heaven in spite of our addiction to similar vices.

I have tried to choose out of the great richness of the calendar, those saints that may most easily be encountered on a holiday trip to the cultural centres of Western Europe, because that is where the world comes to view the treasures of Christian civilization. It is my hope that a statue or a tomb, however dusty, may awaken curiosity about the saint commemorated there; and that this book, while placing them in their own time, will also pull them firmly into our lifetime, showing how we can use devotion to them as a means of following Jesus, as they did.

Perhaps the nearest of all in the imitation of Christ is everyone's favourite, St Francis of Assisi, who together with his spiritual friend St Clare, has so much help to offer in our present dilemmas. We may be sure that they, and all the others, pray for our impoverished world; so let us thank them by responding in the words of the divine praises:

'Blessed be God in his angels and his saints.'

19 November 1990

Sheilah Ward Ling

St Joan of Arc

 woman in her middle sixties, wearing her good black dress, was watching the crowds of young people in T-shirts and jeans sitting on the grass of the hillside at Taizé, waiting for the mass to begin. There was a great deal of laughter; they looked well-fed, judging by the brightness of their eyes in firm-fleshed, sunburnt faces. It occurred to her that it was just the sort of crowd that might have waited two thousand years earlier in the Holy Land, to listen to the words of the man who was heralded as the Messiah, and for whom the miracle of the loaves and fishes had been wrought.

It was a long time since she had been as young as that, and believed in miracles. She hardly knew what had brought her to Taizé. When the poster advertising a parish visit to the place had appeared on the church door, she had barely glanced at it. International gatherings did not attract her. 'France for the French' was the cornerstone of her creed. She didn't even like the foreign tourists who came into the bank where she worked, pestering to change their travellers' cheques. She served them unwillingly, never smiling. They spoke French badly, and without grace – when they bothered to try at all. France could have done without them.

Her country possessed a rich and fertile land, and had the best engineers, the finest craftsmen, the greatest artists in the world. In 1940, France had been betrayed by politicians and incompetent generals, and had pulled herself out of defeat into the prosperity these young people took for granted.

When she was seventeen, she had joined the Resistance in her home village, hiding in the forest by day, and coming out at night to ambush the columns of trucks marked with the hated swastika. It wasn't only because she loved her country passionately and couldn't stomach the idea of invaders on her soil. She had enjoyed the sleeping rough, and the comradeship of her fellows, and outwitting the enemy. She'd been prized and looked up to for her courage and cunning. And when she was picked up and beaten senseless many times over, she had given nothing away. She bore the scars still – honourable scars; she fingered the Cross of Lorraine pinned to her dress and felt the pain and the pride all over again.

Nothing in her life since had come up to it.

She thought, not for the first time, that she should have died then, in her youth – like her heroine, the patron of France – the Maid of Orleans – Joan of Arc.

* * *

In the early fifteenth century France had been riven by war with the English for over seventy years. Even during a respite when the Black Death in England decimated the population, and left it too weak for foreign invasion, civil war between rival dukes, most persistently waged by those of Burgundy and Orleans, took its place. In France, as weak king followed weak king, England took advantage of their powerlessness to seize large tracts of the country. When it suited them, they allied to Burgundy, with whom inter-marriage had given them strong ties.

The effect of these turbulent times on the burghers and peasants can be imagined. Their towns and villages were sacked, not once, but many times over, and all their meagre possessions taken. Anything they managed to acquire from their labours was taxed by their feudal masters. Only in Paris were the Guilds strong enough to rise against them, but they were ineffective because of inexperienced leadership, and a tendency to fall out among themselves.

14

Domremy, a village on the banks of the Meuse in Lorraine, was typical of many others of the time. It was divided in its allegiance between loyalty to the king, and the dukes of Burgundy. Apart from a certain amount of stone-throwing amongst the children, common interest in the fate of the village itself made the inhabitants tolerant of one another. There were some fifty households, farming their bleak lands, and obeying the summons of the church bells that marked the services – Mass and vespers, matins and compline – as well as marriages, baptisms and funerals. They sounded warnings, too, of bad weather and fire, and marauding bands, and on winter nights the wolves that came from the forest of Bois Chenu close by, up to the edge of the village.

Like many French settlements, it had grown up round a great Roman highway that led from Flanders down through Burgundy to the emperor's lands in the east, and south to Italy. Along this road came the travellers who kept the inhabitants of obscure Domremy in touch with the outside world. There were a great many of them in this age before nations retreated behind national boundaries, and the papal legates, as well as the preaching and mendicant friars, formed an international network; merchants from the rich wool lands of the north exported freely all over Europe.

One of the village elders was a man called Jacques d'Arc, who with his wife Isabelle lived in the part of the village that belonged to the French king. They had three sons and two daughters; the youngest child, Joan, was born on the feast of the Epiphany in 1412. Her sister Catherine married and died young, but Joan thrived, learning early the tasks that her mother did – beating hemp, spinning wool and tow, cooking and cleaning and washing. When harvest time came she worked in the fields, and tended her father's livestock on occasion. Childhood did not last long in those days. The status Jacques d'Arc had among his neighbours indicated that– though they were not by any stretch of the imagination rich – they were certainly not the poorest inhabitants of Domremy.

One of the projects that Jacques d'Arc carried through for the succour of his fellow sufferers from the warring factions was the leasing of a small chateau on an islet in the Meuse, as a refuge. He did this in 1417, when Joan was five. She must have known every inch of this miniature fortification. On peaceful days the land would be used for grazing livestock. When the alarm bells sounded, everyone hurried to its shelter and the drawbridge would be secured against intruders.

At seven, Joan witnessed her first battle, which took place at the neighbouring village of Maxey, across the Meuse. Her godmother's husband was captured, and was only released on the payment of a large ransom. For three years more, Domremy and the castellany of Vaucouleurs, of which it was part, were at the mercy of wandering bands of English and Burgundians, until 1422 when the Peace of Troyes was signed.

It was peace at a price. The mad king of France, Charles VI, weary of defeat, gave his country into the hands of the English Henry V, naming him as his heir and allowing him to marry his daughter. The luckless dauphin, his son Charles, had his legitimacy put in doubt by his mother, the German Ysabeau, a woman of notoriously easy virtue. Only two years later, both kings were dead, and the crown of France lay between Henry VI of England, a child of a few months, for whom his uncle the Duke of Gloucester was regent, and the dauphin – isolated in a pocket of unoccupied territory, and unable to get to his cathedral of Rheims, the traditional site of French coronations. Until he did so, there was no hope that he would ever be anything more than 'King of Bourges' – the derogatory title by which he was known.

The dauphin had no hope of accomplishing anything himself. He seems to have been an abnormally apprehensive character, a quality entirely understandable. As a child he found his favourites murdered, his uncle killed bloodily before his eyes. He had narrowly escaped death when a floor collapsed beneath his feet in La Rochelle. He sought divine guardianship by being assiduous in hearing three masses a day, and also hedged his bets by consulting astrologers. He had a hairless face, weak eyes, a bulbous nose, and was of meagre stature – a singularly unprepossessing prince. But the day was approaching when he would be swept on against his will to take up his royal burden. God had decided to take a hand in the fortunes of France.

Back in Domremy, Joan d'Arc had seen a vision – the face of an angel, and his winged shoulders. His voice came

16

through the church bells that sounded so often in the little village. He called her at first to live a spiritual life and earn God's protection: nothing remarkable in that. Pious virgins had seen visions since the dawn of the early Church.

There was nothing hysterical or attention-seeking about Joan. She told no one; not even when the vision returned and revealed himself as St Michael the Archangel, who had often been invoked by Frenchmen for his aid. His dealings with Joan were brief, and introduced her to the two female saints who were to become her life-long companions – St Catherine and St Marguerite. At first they appeared in brilliant light, wonderfully dressed and bedecked with jewels, as if they had determined to fascinate the unsophisticated country girl. Later, as she got to know them, she could distinguish between them by the mere sound of their voices.

They brought a message – simple, direct and preposterous – that she should raise the siege of Orleans, and have the dauphin crowned in Rheims Cathedral. There followed a dialogue in which Joan put forward her objections to this scheme. She was poor, she was a girl – thirteen at the time of the first apparition – she had no horse, nor could she even ride one. The voices reassured her; she must have confidence in herself. She would be doing the will of God, to whom nothing is impossible. The details became more specific. She must go to Robert de Baudricourt, captain of the castle of Vaucouleurs, and he would give her an escort of soldiers to take her to the dauphin. This was no sudden inspiration, immediately acted upon; the dialogue continued over four years, until the timorous adolescent, who burst into tears at the magnitude of the task before her, had become a young woman conscious of her mission.

Did the voices come from inside or outside? The question must be asked. It is crucial to our understanding of Jeanne d'Arc. Schizophrenics hear voices and see visions, and sometimes have the power to predict events, as Joan predicted the siege of Orleans before it happened. But the voices of schizophrenics urge them to destructive acts, and their para-normal knowledge of coming events seems pointless and arbitrary. It's as if they tune in to the eternal music of the spheres, but hear it as harsh and inharmonious, making no sense.

Joan's voices made admirable sense. She seems to have a great deal in common with the great figures of the Old Testament: Elijah and Samuel, and especially David, the warrior king of Israel, whose call came as hers did when he was tending his father's flock. But she was a child of the New Testament too, and there is something in her practical questioning, and final total obedience, that must remind us of Our Lady's reception of the Annunciation.

All through this strenuous inner life was woven the outer life of a peasant paying with hard work for the means of existence. But we may be sure that she kept her ears open for scraps of news that might concern her mission. Her resolution was firm; only the opportunity to put it into effect was lacking. It came in 1428, when her aunt, her mother's sister, was expecting a child and Joan went to live in her house to help with the extra work which the confinement would occasion. It was at Petit Burey, five miles from Domremy and the supervision of her parents, and only two miles from her objective, Vaucouleurs.

She must have confided something of her intentions to one member of the household: Durand Laxart, her cousin by marriage. He was twice her age, and she called him 'Uncle'. Whatever she said must have been convincing enough to make him consent to be her companion on her first visit to the Captain of the castle, a man her father had dealings with in his capacity as a village elder. She and Laxart started out at Ascensiontide in the fair weather of early May.

They had no difficulty in reaching the great hall of the castle. Joan ignored the crowd that thronged it, and went straight to Sir Robert de Baudricourt, stated her business bluntly, and waited for his reply. Young girls did not usually speak to him so directly, and he was curious to know who was the mysterious 'Messire' on whose orders she claimed to be speaking.

'The King of Heaven', was the ringing answer.

It was too much for Baudricourt, a good man of business, who had feathered his nest by smart negotiation all his life. He ignored Joan and told Laxart to take her back to her father, recommending him to administer a good thrashing and marry her off. On the face of it, a complete defeat; yet the voices had warned her that three attempts would be needed to gain Baudricourt's co-operation. And the seed had been sown.

The deadline that the voices had set was mid-Lent of the following year. It was a hard nine months. Vaucouleurs was in danger from armed attack, and the citizens of Domremy, always bound up in the fate of the castellany, were forced to flee to the shelter of a neighbouring town. Joan went with them, her light growing dimmer in an alien environment, consumed by the frustration of being unable to move in her cause. There was a dreadful day when it seemed that her father had got wind of her plans. He dreamed that he saw her riding in the company of soldiers. To him it meant one thing – the loss of her virginity– and he said if it came true he would rather see her drowned. He made an attempt to get her married, but the only result was an action for breach of promise. Joan argued her own case, and won.

Then Laxart's wife became pregnant. It proved an excuse for Joan to go to Petit Burey again. By this time the siege of Orleans was a reality that strengthened her arguments.

Once more she and Laxart sought out Sir Robert. He remembered her earlier visit very well; like everyone who met her – and that included her most violent opponents – he was intrigued by her personality, and had long and certainly not one-sided talks with her. Joan, with her intelligent directness, gave as good as she got from this rough entrepreneur. While she was with him, she impressed other members of the garrison; three of them offered to serve the dauphin with her. Still Sir Robert hesitated, and once more refused to help.

In her frustration, she made an attempt to go by herself, donning male dress for the first time. She got as far as the Chapel of St Nicholas in a wood about two miles from Vaucouleurs, then explained to the faithful Laxart that it was not honest to go in this underhand way, and turned back. Hearing of the exploit, two of the soldiers (Jean de Metz and Bertrand de Poulengy, her champions among the garrison) gave in their resignations to Baudricourt and offered themselves as her escorts to the dauphin at Chinon. This did something to move Sir Robert, but before he agreed to write to Charles and introduce Joan, he took the precaution of having her exorcised by the curé to whom she had often

19

confessed. She is on record as having been extremely indignant.

News came of further French disasters, outside Orleans. Joan had predicted them, and Baudricourt, once his doubts about her veracity had been set at rest, sent a letter to Chinon. While the reply was awaited, Joan made her preparations, dictating a letter to her parents, informing them of her intentions. Seeing her dressed in old clothes borrowed from Jean de Metz's body-servant, the good citizens of Vaucouleurs subscribed enough money to equip her for the journey. She had her hair cropped, and in a simple black doublet and hose, with a black woollen cap, she looked like a young squire – unlikely to raise any sexual desire amongst the bandits she might meet on the road.

These preparations only took up part of her immense energy. She fretted endlessly, with her goal just beyond the horizon. At last the courier came from Chinon, with two men-at-arms to join the party. The dauphin – the 'gentle dauphin', she always called him – had agreed to see her. Sir Robert advised caution and deliberation over what she should say to him. Her voices bade her go boldly and promised her that she should give him a sign of God's favour. The little party set out on the 23rd of February, at dawn, to avoid the whole town turning out in its enthusiasm. It was a muted beginning to an adventure that was to lead to both her victory and her death.

On the advice of her companions, who were more aware than she was of the dangers of the journey, they slept by day and travelled by night. Even that had its perils because the numerous rivers they had to cross were swollen by winter rains. But Joan was sure and confident, and the only thing that troubled her was that she was not able to hear a mass every day. They passed unscathed through the hostile territory, and reached Chinon on the Fourth Sunday in Lent: the respite between its rigours, and the drama and suffering of the final weeks.

The dauphin was awaiting her, his superstition reinforced by an old prophecy that France would be saved by a virgin of Lorraine. At the very gates of Chinon a horseman saw her approach the steep hill that led her to the castle where the man she hoped to inspire to be king lay frightened and intimidated. The anonymous rider asked if it was the Maid, and boasted that she would be a maid no longer if he had a night with her. Joan's reaction was swift and ruthless: she told him that it was an unworthy thought for one near death. About an hour later he fell into the river and drowned. Whether it was coincidence or not, the story flew through Chinon, and only added to the legend that had already grown up around her. People in those days were as susceptible as we are to rumour and hearsay, though they had no mass media to feed on.

Her reception at the castle of Chinon was sumptuous. A gathering of noble lords and knights was lit by fifty torches. She made her way unerringly to the dauphin, who was more shabbily dressed than many in the brilliant company, and fell to embrace his knees. He tried to draw her attention to a more impressive member of the assembly, but she would not be fobbed off, saying:

'In God's name, it is you and none other who are the king.' This was enough for Charles, and he drew her aside and talked to her with more animation than he had ever shown in his chequered career. But he was not so entirely convinced of her powers that he took them without question.

There followed six weeks of examination by the most learned clerics that were available, even sending her off to Poitiers where the Parliament was sitting, for a further array of bishops and inquisitors to examine her. They sought to trap her into admissions of witchcraft, then demanded signs of the divine nature of her mission. She refuted the one, and refused to budge on the other. The only sign she would give was before the walls of Orleans. A final indignity – an examination for virginity – was made by a band of reliable women, including the king's mother-in-law. Needless to say, she passed the test. Neither then nor later did any charge of unchaste behaviour ever stick to her. It was not that she was unattractive. She had enormous attraction of personality for both men and women, but it was one that transcended human sexual desire.

At last she got permission to go to Orleans. A small retinue was mustered to be her companions: some battle-scarred warriors, two pages, a chaplain, and two of her brothers who had followed her from Domremy. She acquired a standard and a pennon, bearing the lilies of France, and a representation of the King of Heaven, of whom she wanted her own king to be a vassal. She had a sword too, and learned how to use it in knightly exercises, but she vowed never to draw blood with it. Finally she sent a message to the English, calling on them to surrender and join in a crusade to the Holy Land. The rules of chivalry had been observed: the English sent back a message that they would rout the French and burn the Maid as a witch – and the battle was on.

The commander of the garrison of Orleans was Dunois the Bastard. He was a rugged, handsome character of the kind with which Hollywood has made us familiar. At first he was dubious of Joan's value. He concealed his plans from her, and consulted his peers. But Joan's instinct for taking the battle to the enemy, and her sublime confidence in what her voices told her, won him over. He may never have entirely lost his superstitious belief in her as a mascot, but on the whole he accepted her as a comrade-in-arms whose reading of a battle was as good as his own.

It took five days of storming the English strong points to justify her belief that only by attacking them where they were strong could the French defeat them. It was a battle of wills, and in that sort of encounter Joan was bound to win.

When she was wounded by an arrow during a sortie, the French morale plunged. She was woman enough to lose confidence, and the pain made her believe she was about to die. But she recovered, pulling the arrow from her breast herself, and suffered the crude dressing of the wound with bacon-fat and olive oil. She guessed the effect of her absence from the field, and insisted on returning. In the French lines her reappearance put new heart into their endeavours. The English were devastated. They were running out of supplies, and seemed halted by the sheer momentum of the French assaults. Wherever the battle was at its height, there was Joan with her banner and her encouragements. As night fell on the fifth day, the English formed into columns of march. For a little while it was thought they might be mounting a counterattack, but then they were seen marching away.

Adulation of Joan grew to fantastic heights. She got the

whole credit for the operation from the delighted townspeople, though she tried her best to persuade them that God was the author of their triumph. All along she had been insistent that every soldier should go into battle shriven and having heard mass; that swearing should cease, and camp-followers be discouraged. For her at least the battle for France was a holy crusade. She had given the dauphin the promised sign: now the second objective had to be accomplished – his anointing as King in the Cathedral at Rheims.

To do this it was necessary to mop up the remaining pockets of resistance along the Loire, and to secure Rheims from its Anglo-Burgundian sympathisers. The dauphin showed no urgency to do this, but Joan was impatient. Some members of the dauphin's court, notably his chancellor Regnault and his principal favourite La Tremouille, wanted to make for the rich pickings of Normandy; they thought Joan was an upstart and tried to oppose her at every turn. But she had a powerful ally in the Duke of Alençon, who had seen her in action at Orleans.

There was no doubt Joan had learned a great deal about the arts of war, particularly the use of artillery. The French idea of warfare had been a series of cavalry attacks; the cannon was not considered a gentlemanly weapon. Until they adopted it, they had lost the flower of the noblest families of France, charging English archers over and over again. Joan did not care tuppence whether a man was a duke or a bowman, as long as he was courageous, and would fight for her dauphin.

She preferred to gain the towns by surrender. There was no bloodlust in her undeniable joy in the fight. She was a good commander and reckoned the most successful battle to be the one where the losses were lightest. She was chivalrous towards prisoners too. Once after an engagement, when she found a Frenchman beating a prisoner to death, she cradled the man's head in her arms, and before he succumbed saw that he had the last rites.

After the Loire had been cleared of the enemy, the remaining towns before Rheims opened their gates to the victors. By the 16th of July, Rheims itself welcomed her royal master, and made hasty preparations for a coronation the next day. Out of the twelve peers who had been summoned, nine were absent and substitutes had to be found. The absentees included all the powerful dukes who had sided with the English – but it was a valid crowning and anointing. Joan, who stood near the King throughout the ceremony, knew that by her efforts France had an undisputed monarch again, and that this would have a crucial effect on her determination to sweep the English back to the Channel. Charles VII, proclaimed that day, would be a focal point of French resistance. Also present, poignantly enough, were two humble farmers from Domremy – her brothers Pierre and Jean; and her father and the faithful Laxart witnessed her triumphant reception by the people of Rheims.

Joan was all for pushing on to take Paris, the premier city, which would give immense prestige to Charles' attempts to gather his armies together and push up to Normandy where the English were entrenched. Charles, advised by his chancellor and La Tremouille, wanted to make a truce with the Duke of Burgundy first and so divide his enemies. The duke, meanwhile, went on negotiating with both the English and the French. The Maid from Domremy was not informed of these diplomatic dealings. She kept urging a march on Paris, and seemed to have convinced the king, for he agreed to an attack on the suburbs of Paris on Lady Day, 1429. Her voices had told her the day was not propitious, and she seems to have been in a bad temper, because she struck a camp-follower with the flat of her sword, and broke it.

She was in her usual position at the thick of the fight, supervising the filling of the defensive ditches with faggots, when a crossbowman struck her in the leg with a bolt. Despite this, she lay under the walls for many hours, waiting for darkness so that under its cloak the ditches could be filled, but La Tremouille gave the order to withdraw. He was greedy or frightened or both; and wanted to put all his faith in negotiation.

Joan fretted on, until Charles allowed her to recapture St-Pierre-de-Moustier in August. In a further attempt to muffle her complaints he granted letters patent of nobility to her and her family, but such honours cut no ice with Joan. She was also in receipt of considerable sums of money. She seems to

24

have been unable to resist buying armour, fine horses and clothes. She was at an age, and of an age, when such things seemed important. But her charity was equally remarked; she always had an ear for the poor in their necessity.

La Tremouille had his way, and a truce was arranged with Burgundy from Christmas to the 15th of March, and extended further until Easter. The double-dealing duke also made a pact with Bedford, the English Regent, which would give him Rheims, the whole of Champagne, and Brie. The people of Rheims sent their favourite champion a letter imploring her aid, which she promised to give. Taking only her immediate retinue, without telling the king or saying farewell to anyone, she set off – not for Rheims, which she seems to have thought safe for the moment – but for Compiegne, also under threat of Burgundian domination. A mobile force of like-minded warriors adhered to her, and she found herself close to Paris. It was torment to her to be so near and yet so far, particularly since the duke was spending the truce by raising an army to subdue Compiegne, the gateway to Paris. Joan arrived there on the night of the 22nd-23rd of May.

She made an expedition to the nearby village of Margny, which she attacked, and then was surprised by a Burgundian force, with the English not far away. Joan's party tried to return to Compiegne, whose defenders stood by and did nothing. Possibly they could not believe that their Maid would ever be defeated.

But the days of success were over. Joan continued to fight, as Burgundians appeared on every side. She was wearing a magnificent surcoat of scarlet and gold, and this innocent vanity betrayed her. It was seized by an enemy bowman who unhorsed her, and she was forced to make submission. She said that her voices had told her she would be taken, and hoped she would die quickly – but this was not granted. An appalling ordeal lay before her.

The Duke of Burgundy, jubilant when he learned who his captive was, insisted on going to see her. She was paraded before his wife, and he sent the news to his allies all over France. Needless to say, there was rejoicing too in the English camp. The French cities were devastated, and many were the prayers and penances offered for her safe-keeping. She was passed from hand to hand along the line of feudal command, and moved from castle to castle. Twice she tried to escape. Once was a spirited attempt to shut her sentries up in their guardroom, only to be foiled by the inopportune appearance of a porter at the very gate of freedom. The second time was at the castle of Beaurevoir, when she made a leap out of a seventy-foot tower, denoting a degree of desperation that suggests she may not have cared whether she lived or died. Perhaps death would have been preferable, for her captors' next move was to sell her to the English.

By Christmas she was in the castle of Rouen, safely under lock and key, and for good measure chained. Such a determined escapee had to be discouraged. There were never less than five gaolers on hand, and they were the scum of the English army. No wonder she firmly retained her male attire. The English were the occupying power, and they insisted that she should be tried by a French ecclesiastical court under Cauchon, Bishop of Beauvais, in whose diocese Joan had been captured. According to the laws of chivalry she should have been treated as a prisoner of war, and no doubt Charles VII would have been happy to pay her ransom. As it was, he talked vaguely of a rescue attempt – but, as always, did nothing.

Among the crimes against the faith of which Joan was accused were witchcraft, sorcery and heresy; in other words, there was no explanation for her success except that she was inspired by the devil. Fear and envy had brought her to trial, but her judges took care to make it a model one. It began on the 9th of January and proceeded by the prescribed stages until the 26th of May. Through it all she argued nimbly with the finest legal and ecclesiastical minds available, and she who could neither read nor write ran rings round them. Her radiant commonsense and homespun logic, her fidelity to her king and country, and the God she believed had called her to fight their enemies, shine through the accounts of the examinations that were made of her. She was alone, not allowed the adviser her youth entitled her to; but as far as posterity is concerned, she was her own best witness.

That trial came later. The one that took place in 1431 was carried out by men who saw her as a diseased person, who would cause scandal to the faith. Yet the final warning to her was couched in humane terms; they expressed themselves as being anxious to save her soul. Joan remained firm:

'As to what I have said and done, which matters I declared at my trial, I stand by them and would maintain them... And if at this moment I saw the faggots kindled, and the executioner ready to fan the flames, and were I in the fire, I could no other than say what I have said, and in this I would persist till death.'

Joan had survived the sight of a torture chamber without recanting; but in the churchyard of St Ouen, faced with an executioner, she did so. Perhaps in her weakened state, the feeling of the fresh May air on her face might have made life seem sweet after the months of captivity. There are those who maintain that the document of recantation was not read to her, or only in a garbled form, and that she did not know what it was to which she put her mark. But the next day, hearing that the only alternative was life imprisonment, she took it all back, confessing that it was fear of the fire that had made her recant. She reaffirmed her belief in her voices, and in the validity of her king's coronation, and so sealed her death warrant.

The Church could not carry out the sentence of death, so she was handed over to the secular arm, and on May 30th the whole grisly business of execution was carried out in the marketplace of Rouen. One item on the placard attached to the stake was the word 'presumptuous' – and this she certainly was. She had maintained her truth, her simple truth, against the might of the English, the University of Paris, and the combined weight of all the ecclesiastics that Cauchon could muster. Either she was divinely inspired or the most deluded victim of self-confidence that has ever walked the earth.

The feeling of the immense crowd that gathered to witness her martyrdom wavered between the expectation of a marvellous spectacle and profound grief. Even her judges wept as the flames swept toward her, and she could be heard calling on her saints and all the company of heaven. Her last cry of agony as the flames scorched her lungs was 'Jesus'. Her ashes were thrown into the river.

But it was an English soldier who gave her a scrap of comfort. She asked for a cross, and he fashioned one from the faggots surrounding her. Her enemy, from whom like everyone else she had begged forgiveness, showed compassion at the end.

It took Charles VII another twenty years to achieve the final defeat of the English and drive them back to their own country, and he only did it by means of an alliance with the Duke of Burgundy – in the end French blood proved thicker than the water of the English connection. But he never forgot the Maid who had had the vision of her country, free of foreign domination, living in peace. In 1452 he had her case re-opened by eminent lawyers who were encouraged to find anomalies in the proceedings. They found enough to justify an appeal to the pope by Joan's mother for a complete rehabilitation. Proceedings were set in motion, and the machine of ecclesiastical law moved slowly forward, until on the 7th July, 1456 the judges made the formal declaration that the verdict in the trial of 1431 was set aside, and Joan was restored to the body of the Church.

And there the matter rested for four hundred years, until in the nineteenth century there was an upsurge of interest among scholars in the doings of their mediaeval ancestors. Their books were read avidly and were unexpectedly popular. Joan's personality, which had so impressed her contemporaries, exerted its fascination once again. And France needed a heroine after the disastrous defeat of the Franco-Prussian war in 1870.

In 1894 Joan was declared Venerable; in 1909, Blessed, and finally in 1920, after a war in which French blood had been shed during yet another invasion, canonized as a Saint. She continued to inspire the French Resistance in World War II when their emblem was the Cross of Lorraine. In 1947 she was made joint patron of France.

* * *

Which brings us back to our unsung heroine on the hillside at Taizé, fingering the little badge pinned to her dress. As the mass began, and the chants of praise mounted, she heard in them the deeper notes of hope, like a weight lifted from her. She felt the war was over at last; peace had come... The peace that is not a mere absence of war, but peace with freedom. Not one or the other, but both.

28

In Taizé she forgot that so much of her country was secular and materialistic, and found in these international voices a spiritual message. Joan died for a free France, but men and women had come to realise that patriotism was not enough.

She turned to her nearest neighbour, a fresh-faced young German, and exchanged with him the kiss of peace.

St Therese of Lisieux

 young woman is going down the High Street of a small provincial town. She is wearing a plain brown pinafore dress and a short white jacket; at her neck is a cheap medal of Our Lady of Lourdes. Other people are crossing the road to escape the noise of a pneumatic drill, tearing up the tarmac; she passes near it, smiling slightly remotely, as if she were listening to a Walkman.

An old woman with a white stick peers into her face, and asks after one of the sisters at the convent up the road. The young woman answers, smiling, and enquires after her health. The old woman replies at length, indicating a degree of decrepitude that is belied by her fresh complexion and sturdy bulk. She goes on to relate a long tale of persecution by her neighbour's children. The young nun looks pale and strained, but retains her smiling interest. With an assurance that she will pray for the old woman, she passes on.

She joins the queue at the Post Office, letting a mother with a young family go ahead of her. A down-at-heel character in a greasy suit is collecting his pension. The queue tries to ignore the odour of his presence – all except the young nun, who greets him.

'Good morning, Paddy' – again the smile – 'Don't forget to buy some food,' she advises softly.

She purchases the stamps she has come for, and makes her

way across the street to the parish church, where she kneels for several minutes in front of the Blessed Sacrament, then puts a candle before the statue of St Therese of Lisieux.

Her hand shakes so violently, she can barely light the match, but that is the only indication that she suffers from agoraphobia, and every moment of the simple expedition has cost her dearly.

She has accomplished it by following the Little Way of St Therese – who would have recognised in this woman of the late twentieth century something of herself.

* * *

When France declared war on Prussia in 1870, she desperately needed a saint. Her considerable armies, hastily mobilised, were badly organised. The emperor had inherited the great name of Bonaparte, but not his uncle Napoleon's military brilliance. He did not succeed in carrying the attack into Germany, and was soon defending the soil of France itself.

Four centuries earlier, it had been saved by the efforts of a peasant girl from the north of the country, who abandoned her father's farm to rally the fading fortunes of the dauphin and his dispirited warriors, and inspired them to drive the English invaders back to their homeland. This time there was no Joan of Arc to rescue France.

In the house of Louis Martin, watchmaker and jeweller, and his wife Zelie-Marie – who ran a successful lacemaking business which she had established without capital before she was married – the national disaster was deepened by private grief.

Two of their six children – both girls; one aged six, the other a baby of three months – had died. Their two brothers had preceded them into heaven a year or two previously. There could be no doubt in their parents' minds of their destination, for they were devout people, and had considered entering the religious life before deciding that their true vocation lay in marriage. This vocation they took so seriously that they delayed the consummation of the sacrament for a year before founding their family.

The war must have touched them, for they lived in Alençon, where the Department of Orne borders that of Sarthe, and it was there that the French and Prussian armies met in their thousands at the battle of Le Mans. It was two years before Zelie embarked on childbearing again.

However, another daughter was born, on the 2nd of January 1873 (just four days before the birthday of Joan of Arc) and baptised Marie-Francoise-Therese – taking the name by which she was known, Therese, from the dead baby sister. It soon became apparent that she too was a sickly child.

This presented a dilemma to her parents, so often bereaved. Zelie was a working woman, and also managed the large household necessary to look after four other daughters. Perhaps she doubted her ability to raise yet another invalid, after losing the battle to save the lives of the previous four. It was decided to send Therese to a foster mother in the country.

Fifteen months later, as a sturdy toddler, she was gradually reintroduced to the family – though not without some tears, each time her foster mother disappeared.

But she quickly became the family's adored ornament, and her father's favourite. (When she resorted to head-banging at night, they tried to restrain her by tying her into the bed – a common practice in those days.) Despite this, there followed a time that they all remembered as idyllic.

Her mother gave Therese every moment a busy woman could spare, watching over her spiritual development with a kind of ferocious intensity, almost as if she knew that her time for it would be short. The effect was that of making the house at Alençon a sort of battery house for souls, in a way we might find rather repugnant. But infant mortality made early preparation for the hereafter seem necessary; and we must not forget the families of our own day, where immoderate pressure may be put on children to make successes in a worldly and material sense.

For Louis and Zelie Martin to have a child who was a saint would be the fulfilment of an ambition they had once had for themselves – as a G.P. might want to have a child who would be a famous consultant or as a couple in a modest way of business might hope to produce a millionaire entrepreneur.

Therese learned her lessons in spirituality so well that her mother wrote to her elder sisters, away at boarding school:

'Baby is such a queer little creature as you never saw; she comes up and puts her arms round me and wishes I were dead. "Oh, poor little mother," she says, "I do wish you'd die." Then when you scold her, she explains: "Oh, but it's only because I want you to go to heaven – you told me yourself one can't go to heaven without dying." She wants to kill off her father too, when she gets really affectionate.'

One can see the ruthless logic of childhood behind this piece of infant piety, told as an amusing anecdote, but it may have returned to haunt the little girl when her mother developed cancer and their pleasant life took on a nightmarish quality.

Therese and her sister Celine were made exiles, leaving home to play in other people's houses so that they should not disturb the dying woman, who was in considerable pain.

When the end came, they witnessed the ceremonies of extreme unction, made a last visit to their mother in her coffin and were left after the funeral to cope with their grief. Therese was four years old – dry-eyed and quite obviously suffering from shock. Celine chose her eldest sister Marie to take her mother's place, and Therese, the second sister Pauline, who was almost sixteen. She claimed later that her character changed from being lively and communicative, to one withdrawn and shy, nervous of strangers, only relaxed and at ease with her family.

The older girls shouldered their responsibilities with stoical patience and earned the love for which Therese in particular had a great capacity. She followed their commands with obedience, but the originality her mother remarked on seemed to have gone. She grew ever closer to her father, accompanying him on walks and fishing trips and visits to all the churches in Lisieux – where they had removed after her mother's death.

She did lessons, supervised by her sisters; learning to write from Marie and the other subjects with Pauline. Great emphasis was put on the learning of the catechism and Bible History – at which, with her excellent memory, she was very apt. At the end of her lessons she made a full report of her progress to her father – 'The King of France and Navarre', as she called him – and was praised all over again.

This one-to-one teaching stood her in good stead when she went to school and she was put in a class with much older girls. Their jealousy at the sight of a younger pupil surpassing their achievements gave her great pain and increased her isolation.

She often took refuge in tears, as she had done ever since her mother died. We must remember that this was her second loss; her first being the barely-remembered one of her foster mother.

Her other solace was books, though we may be sure that the selection was carefully supervised – even the newspapers were considered unedifying reading. Lives of heroic Frenchwomen were approved and she found those who fired her imagination, including the Venerable Joan of Arc, whom she regarded as a great model. Like many impractical people (she could not even brush her own hair, let alone make her bed) she was drawn to her opposite: the warrior-visionary – and there was born in her the ambition to become a great saint.

With her background, it was as natural to her as the burning desire of today's youth to become the pop stars, or TV presenters, or footballers, so adulated in the media. The people around her venerated the saints; hence her wish to be one. Her beloved father drew her attention to her patron, the great St Teresa of Avila – the gifted organiser of the Carmelite order and perfector of its Rule.

But Therese was not the only member of her family to be drawn to Carmel; Marie and Pauline were, too. Marie was still managing the lacemaking business, but when Therese was nine and at school, Pauline felt she could answer the call of her vocation and proposed to Marie that she should try it in the local Carmelite convent. Therese overheard this conversation and was devastated.

Ever since the inconsolable sisters had clung to each other after their mother's funeral, she had looked on Pauline as her substitute mother. To hear, and at second-hand, that she was to be deprived yet again, wounded her already scarred psyche as nothing else could have done.

During the weeks that followed this discovery, she never left Pauline for a moment, and plied her with childish presents of cakes and sweets, thinking that they would not be available in Pauline's new life. She said in her autobiography that at the time she had no idea what Carmel was until Pauline explained; and she must have conveyed the delights of being the bride of Christ so vividly that Therese too pronounced herself drawn to them. There is no doubt that her love and need for Pauline led her to identify with her, though she denied this. However, love begets love, and we cannot think that her new-found love for Our Lord was illusory. It may have stemmed from her love for Pauline, but one love can grow from another and be none the less real for that.

The day came when Pauline passed through the gates of Carmel, never to return to her home. She had made some attempt to soften the blow for Therese by introducing her to the mother prioress. Therese contrived to be alone with her for a few minutes and confided to her the wish to follow in Pauline's footsteps. She was informed – probably gently enough – that postulants of nine were not accepted. Pauline must have hoped that this, from an authoritarian figure like the prioress, would put Therese's ambitions into some sort of perspective.

But Therese had a full measure of that which is sometimes called obstinacy and sometimes strength of character, and is probably a blend of both. She had it in common with her heroine, Joan of Arc; and when added to this is the divine call, its tenacity is irresistible.

She returned to school, which she disliked, and the result was that she developed headaches that did not incapacitate her, but showed all was not well. These continued from the October of Pauline's entry into Carmel, until the Easter of the following year, and were probably the result of interior tension. But when her father took her sisters Marie and Leonie to Paris for the holidays, her depression took a more serious turn.

The trigger was a well-meant effort by her uncle, in whose charge she had been left, to talk about her mother. He explained that she needed distraction, and that no effort would be spared to give her a good holiday. This kindness melted all the barriers she had put up to defend herself from feeling the full measure of her grief. She was seized by a violent trembling and sensation of cold, and was soon in the grip of a total breakdown.

A doctor was called in, and such was the fear of mental illness at the time that he felt himself unable to give any name to it but 'St Vitus' dance' – which did approximately describe one of her symptoms. There were others, including a compulsion to shut her eyes when her sisters came near, and only open them again when they left. These symptoms were completely involuntary acts, though she claimed that she was quite conscious through them – an indication that there was some part of her that was detached and observed the illness. Something of the same sort is experienced by singers, musicians and actors when they perform, apparently by a spontaneous outpouring; but a segment of the mind remains outside directing the flow. Performers and neurotics share the highs and lows of extreme sensitivity; and Therese certainly seemed throughout her life to have one skin less than other people.

She did practise two arts – painting, and writing poetry – and although she derived some satisfaction from them, she was not especially talented. She uses the words of the Gospels and the psalms, or St Thomas a Kempis or St John of the Cross, to describe her love for God, in preference to her own. But she did have genius – a genius for religion.

As the illness progressed her father became convinced that she would die, or go mad. The doctor declared:

'Science is powerless before this phenomenon; there is nothing that can be done.'

He added that he had never known such an illness attack so young a child. She later thought that she might have been undergoing some sort of demoniac possession, but we have a little more (though very little more) knowledge about mental illness now, and it seems likely that most, if not all, of these terrifying fantasies came from within. There is no doubt that she was very frightened indeed.

She would barely allow Marie to leave her to take meals, but with the curious control that never quite left her, she let her sister go to Mass, or visit Pauline at Carmel, without complaint. She was comforted by visits from her immediate family, but other visitors were not welcome. She said:

'I couldn't bear seeing people sitting round my bed like strings of onions, looking at me as if I were a strange beast.'

Alongside this commonsense, human feeling, were times when she tried to throw herself out of bed, and fought against the medicine she was given, claiming that she was being poisoned. In the state of medical knowledge at the time, it is possible that she might have been.

Pauline, in Carmel, was not unmindful of her proxy daughter, and sent her a letter that she clung to, and learned by heart; an hour-glass to measure the tedious hours that invalids find pass so heavily, and a doll dressed in the beloved habit, which pleased her. We must not forget that she was still a child.

Her uncle disapproved. He attributed her illness, probably quite rightly, to Pauline's entry into Carmel, and thought she ought not to be reminded of it. We can sympathise with his kindly concern, but his was the humanitarian, worldly view. He was up against something very deep and difficult – the forging of a quite remarkable soul – and he was out of his depth.

The crisis came soon after her father, who with his intense piety sought help from the source of endless consolation, came to Marie's room, where Therese was lying, and gave her some gold coins to have a novena said in Paris, in honour of Our Lady of Victories. Therese was a child of the nineteenth century, and tokens of his love – solid gold – impressed her. She said that she wished she could have exclaimed:

'It's all right – I'm cured...!'

But her great honesty could not manufacture a miracle, even to please her father. This is important, in the light of what occurred later.

The novena began, and instead of being sustained by it, she grew worse. One Sunday morning, Marie had left her to go into the garden for a little relief from the sick-room, leaving Leonie reading by the window. Therese tried to summon her back, in deep anxiety, calling out: 'Mama!' – her cries becoming louder until she achieved the desired result. But when Marie returned, she did not immediately recognise her, and panicked, crying for her mother louder than ever. Marie and Leonie were caught up in her fear, and in despair turned to a statue of Our Lady in the room, representing the Mother of us all. Something in their intensity of concentration penetrated Therese's consciousness, and she turned to the statue, too.

It was not a piece of pious bric-a-brac, but one honoured in the family annals, as having once given an answer to their mother's prayers; so there were strong associations that may have helped to colour her impressions. We are not obliged to believe in miracles, but Therese certainly felt that one happened then. To her at least, the statue came to life, gave her a radiant smile of pity and consolation, and cured her in that moment.

Those who love Our Lady will say it was just like her; others will say that hysterics, without any faith whatever, can manufacture visions at the drop of a hat.

Therese was made of sterner stuff, and it was the first and last time that anything like it occurred in her life; she intended to keep it to herself. But she was still only a child, and when Marie, who guessed at the truth, pressed her for information, the secret came out. It was soon a one-day wonder at Carmel, where some of the sisters questioned her closely about it. Therese was never very articulate where her deepest emotions were concerned, and she became confused in trying to explain what had happened. Some of the nuns may have been sceptical. In any event, she was deprived of her original joy.

It was to be the pattern of her life.

Then came an event she was afterwards to refer to as her conversion. She had always looked forward to the ceremony, observed by French children, of leaving her slippers in the chimney-corner to be filled with Christmas presents, opened after Midnight Mass. Although the custom was generally confined to smaller children, in their depleted household, Celine and their father kept it up to please Therese until she was thirteen. As usual, she put down her slippers on the 24th of December 1886.

The little family returned from mass. Her father, tired after the long ceremony, was out of sorts, as pious people sometimes unaccountably are on their return from religious exercises. No doubt he was feeling the pull of his virtuous bed. Full

39

of childish anticipation, Therese hurried upstairs to her room, to take off her hat, but heard him saying:

'Well, thank goodness it's the last year this is going to happen!'

She was struck to the heart. It was probably the first time the 'King of Navarre' had failed his 'little princess'. Tears welled up, and Celine, knowing her sister as she did, tried to comfort her; since she lost her mother, Therese had never been able to restrain herself when thwarted. Tears were the weapon with which she had fought her loss.

But not this time. Her natural courage overcame her instinct to dissolve into the old grief, and dry-eyed she went downstairs. She deliberately acted out the delight her father was expecting at the sight of her presents, and neither by word nor sign did she betray her unhappiness. She had discovered that a greater joy could be obtained from giving pleasure than from receiving it. No one had taught her this; she had been thoroughly indulged by people who could not give her what she really wanted – the guidance of an earthly mother – yet once she had stumbled upon the truth, she never wavered from it.

She longed to try out the spiritual strength she gained from this incident, and looked for sinners to save. In her restricted life there was a dearth of them, but she had heard of a criminal called Pranzini who had been sentenced to the guillotine for murdering two women and a child during a theft. It was typical of her, that in choosing a sinner she should select a particularly hardened one. She prayed with all her might, and let Celine into the secret so that she could request a mass to be said for her intention: she was still too shy to ask for herself.

The day after Pranzini's execution the girls combed the pages of *Le Croix* for some sign of his repentance. There at the end of the column was what they were looking for. At the moment when he was being secured into the bars that were to hold his neck under the descending blade, Pranzini, who had previously refused all spiritual help, said: 'Quick – the crucifix – ' and kissed the one proffered by the attendant priest. Overjoyed, Therese regarded this as a personal favour from heaven.

But the determination to enter Carmel was stronger than ever. It was strengthened during preparation for two great events – her First Communion, and Confirmation. When Marie too joined Pauline, there was no other aim.

By the time she was fourteen it became an obsession. The ambition to be a great saint had narrowed down to that of being the youngest postulant to enter the order. She badgered everyone, going from the mother prioress to the bishop's local representative, until she had an audience with the bishop himself; quite an ordeal for a girl who had never before conducted an interview without her sister's support. They all turned down her request, telling her to wait. She decided to take advantage of a pilgrimage to Rome to approach the pope.

It was a disaster. She threw herself at his feet, crying and clinging to his knees, and was removed by force, after ignoring his wise comment that she would enter Carmel if it were God's will. The humiliation for someone as sensitive as Therese can hardly be imagined, but somehow she weathered it, and went back to pray – and to wait.

It was an enforced discipline, and she did not take kindly to it, which makes even more remarkable her behaviour when she was finally allowed to enter the convent, three months after her sixteenth birthday.

The year before, when she saw the beauties of Europe on her visit to Rome, the mountains of Switzerland and the lakes of Italy, she said that she would treasure them up when she was a 'prisoner' in Carmel. She had no illusions whatever about the religious life. She might so easily have seen it as a chance to be reunited with the family she loved, in a spiritual bond that would be a kind of heaven on earth; a liberation from the suffocation of an over-protective home. She saw it, clear-eyed, and accepted it as a way of suffering.

It is difficult for us in our day, when our ideals are life, liberty and the pursuit of happiness, to understand how she was able to give up these things, to pray for others who enjoyed them. There is no explanation except that she was possessed by an extraordinary heroism.

It took a unique form: a patient obedience to the Rule of her great predecessor, St Teresa of Avila – as perfect as she could make it. And something of her own: an attempt to recover the childlike innocence of trust in God that had been so shattered by the loss of her successive mothers.

We have seen in our own time people who have attempted to achieve this simplicity by returning to nature, and to their roots. But perhaps none of them have succeeded as she did, because she always took the nearest experience that came to hand, and offered it up to the glory of God, and to win souls for him.

In a sense she did become a warrior-saint, and Carmel was her battleground. The enemy she fought was the enemy within. She was proud, apt to make judgements on people, sensitive to the point of morbidity, constantly questioning her own motives, desperate for love in its comfortable human sense, totally unfitted for the practical tasks that were a large part of the Carmelite life; more of a mixed-up adolescent than the trusting child she tried to be... The one that is fitted for the kingdom of heaven.

To become that, she had to go back and be born again in the spirit, and birth is an often painful, dangerous and messy process. But that she did iron out her complexities must be a great encouragement to those of us who seek to do the same thing.

With patience, she offered up daily the irritations and humiliations that came from enclosed living with twenty-five assorted women who had not lost their personal foibles just because they had received a call to the religious life. She made constant acts of faith, but found little consolation in them. She suffered the complaint known as 'aridity' – a kind of spiritual depression that attacks many prayerful people at some time. She had it for most of her short life.

Yet alongside it, there was a calm centre to this gracious young nun who raised courtesy to an art, took the lowest place, the poorest food, all so unostentatiously that no one noticed she was doing it. When she became assistant to the mistress of the novices, she treated them with brisk commonsense that demanded no flattery or even respect from her charges.

She welcomed the first haemorrhage that was a sign of the tuberculosis which was to kill her. Heaven was her objective, and it seemed within sight. Yet there were many times on the long, hard way there when she doubted its existence. Dreams and fantasies that might have eased the dying were not for her. Pain-killing drugs were not considered suitable for Carmelites, and she suffered a great deal of pain. Still she remained faithful. Her last words were an affirmation of love for her bridegroom. The deprived child, the troubled adolescent, had grown to full maturity.

She died, worn out by the effort of loving, on the 30th of September 1897. She was twenty-four years old.

It was the custom in the order for a kind of holy c.v. to be circulated on the death of each of its members. A young nun was reported to have said that it would be difficult to know what to put in that of Sister Therese of the Child Jesus. Actually she wrote her own – under obedience to her sister, who was also her Superior – in the last months of her life. Somewhat touched up and prettified, it made what was considered to be good, pious reading. Two thousand copies were printed. It may have been the same young sceptic who prophesied that these would be left on their hands. But Sister Therese herself foresaw what an appeal it would make to those, like herself, aspiring to great things but forever condemned to the humdrum.

Under the title *The Story of a Soul*, it was a runaway bestseller. It poured out of Carmel to the ends of the earth, carried by missionary priests – her special care, as a Carmelite. It was read by soldiers in the trenches during the First World War, suffering privations in their anonymous millions. And the stories poured back, of the miracles performed in answer to invoking her prayers. It looked as if her proud boast of spending her heaven doing good on earth was fully justified. A successor to the pope who had advised her to go home and wait to enter Carmel, now had her statue on his desk.

In the end they had to break the rules for her, and introduce the cause of her beatification before the fifty-year wait prescribed by the Church. Amid great rejoicing, she was proclaimed a saint in 1925, just four years after her heroine, St Joan of Arc.

France got her saints at last: in 1947 they were associated as her patrons. And the young nun who had never left her convent became Patroness of the Missions – which must please her, as she had their cause especially at heart. The work of her namesake, Mother Teresa of Calcutta, may well be one of the fruits of her prayers.

The great and the learned have been puzzled by her attraction, but still they go on writing about her. For the unlettered, untelevised majority, fearful of losing their identity in this teeming world, her message that they and their deeds, however trivial, matter to a personal God, is a comfort and a reassurance.

'Little Flower', they called her.

'Little wedge of steel', someone remarked.

* * *

Our twentieth-century nun looks up at the bland plaster face above her, not seeing it at all; only feeling the delight of a sisterly presence that dispels all fear of the wide aisles and vaulted roof of the parish church. She feels courage flooding into her, and rises to her feet. Slowly she genuflects to the altar, crosses herself at the holy water stoup, and makes her way to the door, expecting at any moment the familiar panic to descend and grip her.

The outside air is mild and soft, enveloping her in a blanket of warmth. A child runs into the church porch, all but crashing into her, hiding from his mother. Even this does not displace her new-found confidence; they laugh together, and the mother reclaims her son, which reminds the young nun of the joyful mystery of the finding in the temple. She begins to believe in the possibility of a cure.

Stepping out boldly, she crosses the road, away from the protective walls of the church. Even now, with nothing to hang on to if her courage should fail, she feels light and buoyant. She walks up the hill to the convent; her feet firm on the ground, her heart free from its burden of fear.

St Therese has done it again. Even if it does not last, at least it is a respite, and she will always be grateful to her patron, by whose prayers she has received this favour. It is St Therese who has shown her the way, and she thanks her with all her heart.

44

St Monica

he sat in the great nave of the cathedral, listening to the wise cardinal archbishop's homily, and shivered a little. She was far from her native Australia, where this feast of Christmas is celebrated at the height of summer. Her face was deeply lined, and she looked old for her fifty-five years. Great glittering eyes under her black lace veil were riveted on the preacher, but every fibre of her being was concentrated on the man at her side.

He was her elder son, the most gifted of her three children. A brilliant academic, his handsome aquiline face was well-known on television, discoursing on politics and philosophy. He argued many causes, always persuasively, but in his search for truth abandoned them when he had wrung out the last ounce. Her own faith was simple, but she held it with great tenacity. She had needed to. She had married a man much older than herself; he had been hot-tempered, unfaithful to her, and of no religious belief. For many the marriage would have been impossible, but for her it was divorce that was impossible.

Wealth might have cushioned her, but they were not rich. Her husband had been the younger son of a good family who had emigrated to Australia, tried farming – for which he had no aptitude – and drifted into a small town, doing whatever poorly-paid jobs came to hand.

She went back to teaching to help pay for the private education that they believed their children should have. At Sydney University, her favourite got a doctorate, and became famous for his excellence in acting and debate. She was as much under his spell as everyone else. The two younger children were modest, likeable and pious, like herself. They were the sort of children that parents claim have caused them not a moment's anxiety. The eldest was different. He enjoyed the company of tearaways, he was a womaniser; she never knew what he would be up to next, and she adored him for it. Her husband had regarded his behaviour as proof of his masculinity, and he too centred his life on the boy.

It gave them something in common in their ill-assorted marriage, and he mellowed with the years. In his last illness (she had been widowed at thirty-nine) he had turned to her, and accepted the faith she had championed so steadfastly. Her gentleness and patience with him bore fruit, and he was received into the Church.

That done, she had been free to follow her son to London, where he had been offered a fellowship. With all the care she had devoted to her marriage, she sought to manipulate his life. She used her husband's relatives to obtain introductions that might further her son's career and marriage prospects. Above all she sought to inveigle him back into the Church. It was a success to have got him to accompany her to this Midnight Mass. She was aware of every flicker of response in her son's body, every sinew of hers willing his conversion.

* * *

Early in the fourth century, North Africa was the granary of the Roman empire, rich in corn and olive groves, and cultivated to the very edge of the Sahara. The colonists had built themselves comfortable villas, baths and amphitheatres. But by the time St Monica was born, in modest Thagaste, well inland from the prosperous port of Carthage, the boom times were over. Half-finished buildings spoke of enterprises that had been abandoned. The country was groaning under heavy taxes imposed from Rome to finance the wars that were being waged against the barbarians.

46

It was 332 A.D., and the emperor was Constantine, who had made Christianity the official religion; but he ruled over a troubled Empire. The break-up would not come for another century, but it had begun. In her son's lifetime, Rome would be sacked, and Africa invaded, and the whole mighty edifice come crashing down, all but extinguishing the culture it had built.

At the time of Monica's birth, it was still flourishing. Latin, the language of the Empire, was universal and had a great literature. The Scriptures were available to all who could read. Just seven years before, Constantine had called a council of christendom at Nicaea to settle a heresy, and the result was a hotchpotch of compromise that only incidentally hammered out the Creed. The clarity and simplicity of the message of St Peter and St Paul was being formulated into doctrine. Yet there were still eye-witnesses of the death of the martyrs, including (reportedly) Monica's own grandmother, a devout catholic christian.

For Monica was born into a catholic family. Many of the neighbours supported the Donatist heresy, believing that the validity of priestly orders depended on the personal character of the ordained. The catholic Church in her wisdom maintained the inherent nature of the sacrament, that could not be altered by weak human nature, and would protect her in the future from less than saintly priests and bishops, and even popes. This adherence to orthodoxy may have made the family rather isolated when Monica was a child, though the whole town returned to it when she was sixteen.

Legend has it that she was beautiful and pious and of noble birth, though somewhat impoverished: given to wandering off to secluded spots to pray, losing all count of time, and returning late for meals to scoldings and beatings from her nurse – who seems to have been a formidable character. Whether this was more than the wandering and day-dreaming of a small child is open to doubt. Certainly the nurse was real enough. She was of her grandmother's generation, and had been nurse to Monica's father, carrying him on her shoulders when he was a baby – and she stayed on as a family servant. The picture of a Victorian nanny rises irresistibly; fierce, dependable and omniscient. She gave the young

Monica security and certainty, and was loved by her charge. Her parents are shadowy figures. She was much in the company of servants, and another makes an appearance in her history: a pert stillroom maid, under whose supervision Monica drew off the daily allotment of wine for consumption by the household. She seems to have stood by, amused, while the little girl tentatively tried it, and over a period of time gradually acquired a taste for it. They fell out over something, as girls will; the maid, perhaps jealous of her privileged position in the family, turned on her and called her a 'wine-bibber'. Having heard St Paul's strictures, Monica's conscience smote her, and she seems to have suffered agonies, because it stuck in her mind, and years later she told her son about it as a warning against excess. Apart from this, she was intelligent, energetic and biddable. She also had a genuine love for the poor and needy, and did what she could to relieve their distress.

When she was twenty she was sought in marriage by Patricius, a pagan nearly twice her age. The wonder is that her parents promoted the match. He was notorious for his fiery temper, and wife-beating was common in African society. What is more, he was no great catch. He was a magistrate, but that was compulsory for anyone owning more than twenty-six acres of land, and carried with it the dubious privilege of collecting taxes – the uncollected ones having to be made up out of his own pocket. So imperial Rome impoverished her landowners. His son called him open-hearted, and he must have had considerable charm; perhaps the well-known charm of an older man for a younger woman. Possibly Monica, who was no heiress herself, had no other offers, and the age of twenty was not young in those days. Of course there was no other career open to her except religion, which would have meant leaving Thagaste and the company of her family. At any rate that alternative ocurred to no one.

She was denied the dignity of managing her household, which was presided over by a truly terrifying mother-in-law, from whom Patricius may have inherited his temper. This unpleasant character encouraged the servants to gossip about Monica. The feeling that everything she did was being observed and commented on critically must have been claustrophobic and unpleasant in the extreme. Added to this, she was completely subject to the whims and desires of a man whose pagan self-indulgence had never been curbed by anyone, and to whom the Christian ideals of marriage had never been presented. Yet she kept the faith, and learned to manage Patricius. Although he might bully and threaten, she kept her head and bowed it until the storm had passed. And when it had, it must be said of him that he had moments of contrition which endeared him to her. Contrary to the prevailing form in society, he never struck her.

She did her duty too, and on the 13th of November 354 presented him with a son – Augustine. The prospect of having someone of her own to love and cherish and mould must have filled her with joy. She did not despair of converting her husband eventually, but this pristine new life could be claimed immediately. She hurried to the church, and put him on the roll of catechumens; he received the mark of the cross on his forehead, and the salt on his lips, as a token that he was pledged to his mother's faith.

Monica was the sort of woman to whom childbirth brings release and fulfilment. At last she had something more to do than wait for her husband to return from the baths, or the modest entertainments Thagaste had to offer. Her passionate need to love, innate in all of us, was satisfied at last. She insisted, against custom for a mother in her circumstances, on suckling the child herself. It was a complete success. The bonding between them seems to have been complete, and it lasted for life. It must also be said that Patricius was a loving father, intensely proud of his responsive and lively son.

His advent marked the beginning of a happier phase in the marital relationship. Patricius actually began to appreciate his young wife. Her refusal to be provoked by his outbursts caused him to curb them at this time. Parenthood had given him more confidence in himself, and he opted for being a family man. There were two more children: a second son, Navigius – a gentle, retiring and rather delicate child – and a daughter, even more overshadowed by her famous brother. Often saints, with their restless energy in the pursuit of holiness, seem to owe a great deal to background characters in their lives: unsung saints whose patience with them gives them stability. Such appear to have been Navigius and his sister – who may have been called Perpetua. Navigius sustained his mother throughout her life, and Perpetua after an early widowhood became part of Augustine's household, ending her life as a nun when he dispensed with all female company.

Having grandchildren had an effect on Patricius' mother. She began to question the calumnies the slaves brought to her about Monica. Finding that there was not a word of truth in them, she ordered that the tale-bearers should be flogged, and said that any repetition would receive more of the same. She was a formidable old lady, and it was a brutal age. However, Monica's position in the household was eased, and she settled down to the education of her children. She imparted to them all the riches of her faith, especially her deep attachment to Our Lord and the Church. These lessons made such a deep impression on Augustine that when as a child his life was despaired of, he begged for baptism. In his grief Patricius assented, but broke his promise when the boy recovered.

He was a capricious character, and seems to have become bored with family life. He returned with redoubled enthusiasm to his infidelities, causing Monica – who had come to love him – great heartache. Yet upheld by faith, and the affection of her children, she radiated calm and peace. When friends came complaining about their marriages, she counselled patience and a quiet tongue. 'Least said, soonest mended' seems to have been her attitude. She was a good and loyal ally, never repeating the confidences reposed in her; her only confidant was God himself.

When it became time for the young Augustine to go to school, he was a less than exemplary pupil, and may even have been rather spoiled. He did his best to avoid learning anything that did not interest him – which included all but hunting and other outdoor sports. In spite of this, and perhaps because his mother was more aware of his promising intelligence than his masters, it was decided to move him to nearby Madaura, a university town. The education was entirely pagan, which cannot have pleased Monica, but it was the best they could afford, and both parents were ambitious for him. There it became obvious that it was the dullness of the teaching in his home town that had held him back. At Madaura he blossomed, revelling in the Latin authors; Vergil was a lifelong passion, Cicero an inspiration, though Greek was a casualty of his previous brush with education at Thagaste and he never mastered it. He became renowned for his oratory and seemed to be on the brink of a career that would gratify his proud parents.

Then he had to return home to enable Patricius to find enough money to send him for higher education at the great port of Carthage, one of the treasures of Africa. This took a year, and he did not make best use of it, running with a set of wild young companions, committing minor acts of vandalism, and generally wasting his time. But who is wise at the age of sixteen? Patricius does not seem to have worried overmuch; indeed he was delighted one day at the baths to observe that his son was now mature – but Monica became alarmed at the temptations he might meet in Carthage, and in her anxiety warned him against them.

The prospect that he might one day be a grandfather seems to have concentrated Patricius' mind. He was now approaching sixty, and the pleasures of the flesh became less important in his eyes than the prospects for his soul. By her example his wife had pointed the way for him, and in Lent of that year he took the first step toward becoming a Christian. Monica rejoiced at his conversion. Her first convert had been her mother-in-law, who would have been a Christian of the militant variety, insisting that her household should share her faith – in strong contrast to Monica's exemplary patience. There followed the happiest period of her marriage. He, the worldly-wise, sensual man, now wanted to learn what she had to teach. She, young enough to be his daughter, confounded his worldly wisdom with the sublime folly of the Christian faith. But this happiness did not last long – perhaps eighteen months at most. Soon after he had been received into the full sacramental life of the Church, Patricius died.

Augustine was settled in Carthage, where he revelled in the splendid buildings, the sight of the great fleet, the meetings and clashings of minds at the university. For Monica it was a time of great sorrow which she stifled by throwing herself into charitable work with even greater energy. She frequented the primitive hospitals of the day, not shirking the menial and sordid side of nursing. She consoled other widows, and went on counselling married women. Her spiritual life became fuller; besides being a daily attender at mass, she was to be found in church twice daily at prayer, often being moved to tears by deep meditation on the sufferings of Our Lord. She also made heroic sacrifices so that her son could continue his education. Even so there was not enough money, and she had to accept the generosity of a friend of Patricius, a wealthy businessman called Romanien, whom she repaid by becoming a second mother to his son.

But the son of her body was far from her, engaged in his own form of consolation. For he had loved his wayward father, and shared some of his qualities. The sensual nature was there, manifesting itself in the love of physical beauty, and of nature, which led him to an interest in science and mathematics and the laws of the physical world. But there went alongside all this his mother's need for a spiritual dimension. When he experienced a young man's desire to love and be loved, he was not content with transitory affairs. Beneath the deprecation of later years there is in his *Confessions* a poignant picture of the eighteen-year-old wandering about the city, seeking the romantic love his heart craved desperately.

When he found her – and he gives no details of the encounter – he suffered all the pangs of jealousy, the petty quarrels and reconciliations, and the delights of young passion. He tells us nothing about the woman who became what modern journalists call his 'live-in girlfriend'. That he loved her is certain, and she him, for she bore him a son the following year, and they named him Adeodatus ('Given by God') so she may well have been a Christian even then. She followed him in all his subsequent journeyings with admirable fidelity. Monica could not be kept in ignorance of the existence of her grandson. She seems not at this time to have received him in her house, though Augustine was a constant visitor on his vacations from Carthage. His mother's love for him never diminished, and though she disapproved of his attachment, she never failed to welcome him.

Until, that is, he took up with the Manichees. This sect

believed in a blend of Persian, Chaldean, Egyptian and Greek doctrines, with a top-dressing culled from the New Testament; and made an explanation of the physical world by philosophy, which was one of Augustine's preoccupations. It had all been set down in a series of books by an educated ex-slave called Mani. These beliefs were propounded by a select group, the electores, to mere enquirers and auditors, amongst whom Augustine enrolled himself. He was not alone. He managed to take with him many of the friends he had attracted to himself, and even his benefactor Romanien. He challenged catholics to public debate, and became known for his eloquent defence of the heresy.

This was too much for Monica. Concubines were one thing: she had borne with Patricius's affairs in silence, and she could preserve the same reticence about her son's. It was in the nature of man to give way to sensuality, and all could be wiped out with prayer and fasting on her part, and the waning of desire on theirs. But this was different. Her son had become an enemy of the Church, and was using his great gifts to damage it, and seduce others into doing the same. She was passionate in her defence of the faith, and her passion led her to do something that was uncharacteristic. The next time he came to Thagaste she threw him out of her house and said she never wanted to see him again. He took refuge with Romanien, and there must have been tears on both sides that night, for their devotion was absolute. Yet neither would give way.

Then Monica had a dream. We all have dreams, and some of them are wishes fulfilled; Monica's certainly was. She dreamt that in her great distress, a young man with a bright, eager look had come to her as she stood on a block of wood, overlooking chaos. He asked her the cause of her anxiety, and she told him that she thought her son was lost, whereupon he told her to look beside her, where her son was standing. She took this to mean that Augustine would return to the faith, and because love is not proud, she made the first move. She and Augustine examined the dream together, for all the world like Jungians, seeking the revelation of their unconscious thoughts. He interpreted it as a sign that she would join the Manichees with him. She maintained that it denoted his return to the catholics. They were still far apart, but the contact had been

53

made. All the time they remained in touch, there was hope.

This confrontation must have convinced Monica that what was happening was a battle of wills between them, and it was an unequal struggle. He was a well-educated and brilliant young man. She was a woman, and in the eyes of the Manichees, women had less of the light of truth than men. All she had was her native wit, and her certainty that God would hear her prayers for her son's conversion in the end. At that time it hardly seemed enough. She consulted a learned bishop, hoping that by his arguments he would persuade her son where she could not. He was himself a convert from Manicheism, which may have prompted her choice. We do not have his name; but his advice was just what Monica needed. He convinced her of the futility of argument, and assured her that in the course of time Augustine would discover for himself the flaws in the Manichean case. Her prayers were her best argument, and the strength of her concern for him. This was not what she wanted to hear: she wanted his active help. She resorted to her other weapon, and wept profusely. He remained firm.

'Go your way,' he said. 'It is impossible that the child of such tears should perish' – and with that she had to be content.

When Augustine had finished his studies at Carthage, he returned to Thagaste and set up a school of grammar and rhetoric. His genius in the art of rhetoric was acclaimed in his own town, and his mother had the great joy of seeing him publicly crowned in the theatre as the winner of a prize for poetry. Maternal pride is a universal emotion, and Monica was not devoid of it. Augustine continued to visit her every day, between busy preparation for classes, and his enjoyment of the company of his friends. His close companions were very dear to him. He had known many of them since boyhood, and later attracted others with his brilliant mind and loving heart. This pleasant life continued for some four years.

It was brought to an end by a personal tragedy. The oldest and best-beloved of his friends, who had been converted by Augustine to Manicheism, succumbed to fever, and when his life was despaired of, he accepted Christian baptism. Augustine seems to have blinded himself to the seriousness of his friend's illness, and teased him for submitting to the – to him – empty Christian rite. His friend became angry, and begged him in the name of their friendship never to make light of his religion again. Augustine was still convinced that his friend would recover, and left him. Before he could return, the man died.

Grief and shock plunged Augustine into a deep depression. He fled to Carthage, where he found some comfort in writing his first book, on 'The Beautiful'. The text has not survived, and we only know that he gave it, as the first-fruits of his genius, to his mother; and that as there was nothing contrary to faith in it, she found reading it a consolation for the loss of his company. Also in Carthage, he met one of the Manichean bishops, and although Augustine found him sublimely eloquent, he had begun to have doubts about Manichean philosophy.

Then, just as Monica was beginning to believe that her prayers were being answered, she had the worst blow her devotion had yet received. He wrote to her and said that he was going to Rome.

It was a logical step from the worldly point of view. Rome was the focus of African culture. For the descendant of colonists it was coming home. So might a young New Zealander or Australian, steeped in English literature, look to London. But Rome was also a place where pagan ideas still flourished, and Monica was alarmed. She decided that there was nothing for it but to make the journey to Carthage, throw herself into Augustine's arms, and beg him not to go. He must have enlarged on the glittering prizes awaiting him, for her next plea was that she should go with him.

Augustine was clearly embarrassed by the scene, which took place in the presence of his travelling companion. He was loath to shake her off too roughly, and resorted to subterfuge, pretending that he was merely seeing off his fellow-traveller at the port; while continuing his plans for departure, he endeavoured to persuade her to stay in the town. But in her state of agitation, and sensitive as mothers often are when their children try to deceive them, she followed him to the quayside where the vessel was waiting.

A contrary wind was keeping it in the harbour, and

Augustine suggested that she should take refuge for the night in a little chapel dedicated to St Cyprian. When dawn came, the vessel was gone, bearing her son far away from her. She sobbed hysterically – but she did not despair. She made an attempt to take another boat. Only when this was unsuccessful did she return to Thagaste, and even then her tenacity, and the strength of her love, would not allow her to abandon all hope of joining him.

Augustine's sojourn in Rome did not bring him the fame he hoped for. He had a severe illness, from which recovery was slow, and his previous depression returned. He, who had searched so hard for truth in so many places, grew cynically certain that it was a fruitless quest.

It was a low point for both of them. Yet by their own efforts, they both sought to change their circumstances. He gave a qualifying lecture for the chair of rhetoric in Milan, the seat of the emperors. She resolved once again to set sail for Italy. It was a perilous journey, beset by storms, but she was so convinced that God would allow her to see her son again that she stayed at the prow of the boat, looking steadfastly across the sea, the calmest person on board. When she reached Rome she was disappointed yet again. Augustine had already left for Milan.

Undaunted by the long journey, she followed him there, and they were reunited. Faced with her actual presence, her son was unable to resist her. Perhaps the fact that his mother gave such a proof of her love caused his masculine pride some satisfaction. At any event, he not only tolerated her presence, but actively sought her company. He must have conveyed to her something of the spiritual vacuum in his life, for she redoubled her efforts to fill it.

She enlisted the aid of the Bishop of Milan, known to us as St Ambrose. He was renowned for his statesmanship, as well as his clear exposition of the scriptures. Augustine had already met him when he went to pay his respects on taking up his post at the university, and was struck by his kindness. Monica tried to bring them into further contact – once pretending to need advice about the Saturday fast, with Augustine as her messenger. Her son seems to have been a little awestruck by Ambrose's air of saintly abstraction, and although he was anxious to engage him in conversation and raise his problems, he hesitated on the edge of the company that surrounded the holy man. He began, at his mother's insistence, to go and hear Ambrose's sermons regularly, and passed from admiration of his eloquence to a study of the truths about the catholic Church which he revealed. It was a slow process, and took place gradually over two years.

Once again a wise man persuaded Monica that it was futile to argue with Augustine, the master of rhetoric, and that left to himself he would argue both sides and come down upon the catholic faith – since it was the repository of truth. For Monica it was a time of self-revelation, and she schooled herself, as she had in the case of her husband, to preach by good example, and convert by earnest prayer.

It was the beginning of a long struggle for Augustine, battling within himself between passion of a physical kind and the claims of his dawning faith. In Monica the struggle was equally bitter. She desired her son's worldly success. She wanted his brilliance to bring him earthly honours, yet still longed for his conversion to the Christian ideal which is not of this world. At every point, these two were linked. And every mother who has given birth has similar hopes: the desire for her child's happiness in this world, and the next. They are not mutually contradictory, and sometimes God has ordained that both seem to be possible. It remained to be seen if it would be true in Augustine's case. She still wanted his conversion on her terms, not on God's.

There followed what would seem to us to be a thoroughly discreditable episode in both their lives. For fifteen years Augustine had lived happily and faithfully with the mother of his son Adeodatus. She had followed him to Rome and Milan. Nothing he said later can leave us in any doubt that he loved her, and she him; the child, as he grew, showed signs of his father's intelligence and was dear to both of them. He is reticent about her, but there are hints in his later writings that she was not of his class, and that this was the barrier to their marriage. He was the more sensitive to class barriers because his own family was noble but impoverished. A rich man might have ignored it; he was more troubled by the difference.

His mother, only conscious of St Paul's advice that it was

better to marry than burn, shared his awareness of his mistress's shortcomings in the worldly sense. Still ambitious for him, she obtained an introduction to a catholic girl of good family, and was instrumental in arranging an engagement to her. For some reason, Augustine went along with this. He may have felt that his career demanded it; and Adeodatus's mother took the same view, and would not stand in his way. This is love of a heroic kind, and she deserves her place in the forging of Augustine's soul. She went back to Africa, leaving her son in his father's care, and entered a convent.

Though Augustine's mind led a separate existence, he was surrounded by people who had followed him from Africa, including his patron Romanien. Ambrose's sermons had used analogies from the work of Plotinus, the disciple of Plato. This gave Augustine and his companions an interest in studying the works of the ancient Greek philosophers, now available in Latin translation. They read and discussed them, and had dreams of setting up an ideal community where everything they had would be held in common, and they would feed each other on shared ideas. This plan foundered because the wives of those who were married disapproved – as well they might, since one of the rules was chastity. Yet Augustine was still a long way from attaining that. His fiancée was not yet of marriageable age, and while the engagement was still in force – and it was to be of two years' duration – he embarked on an affair that he said was loveless, but could not drown his continued unhappiness over the breaking-off of his first liaison.

This second entanglement must have given Monica much to think about, whether she realised that it was the result of her well-meant manipulation or not. The likeness to Patricius must have struck her. He had been tempted by, and fallen into, sins of the flesh. She herself must have been tempted to despair of her son's conversion. Christian marriage might, she hoped, settle him; but she reckoned without the other side of Augustine's inheritance – her own stern piety.

Plotinus had taught him, as his mother had, to seek for the highest good that a man could reach by his own efforts. Yet he had always found the Christian Scriptures unsatisfying, lacking the eloquence and intricacy of thought to be found in ancient philosophy. The message they carried of the incarnation and redemption of the world by the Son of God had been lost on him. But now when he was most divided within himself he welcomed their simplicity. He turned to the epistles of St Paul and read them avidly. He began to believe that a very high sacrifice was being demanded of him and he was terrified, but drawn towards it as if by a magnet. He who had been schooled by his mother always to seek the highest goals, was finding them at last. But still his lower nature said: 'Not yet.'

In his perplexity he sought out a venerable priest called Simplicianus, who had baptised his other hero, Ambrose. This was a cultivated man who had lived in Rome and known many of its leading intellectuals. Among them was the orator Victorinus, the translator and commentator on many philosophical texts, including Plotinus. Simplicianus told him how Victorinus, like himself a master of rhetoric and student of Platonic writings, had said to him privately:

'I want you to know that I am now a Christian.'

And Simplicianus's reply was: 'I shall not believe it, or count you as a Christian, until I see you in the church of Christ.'

At which Victorinus had laughed and said: 'Is it then the walls of the church that make a Christian?'

It was in this year 386 that Augustine's old mentor Ambrose was refusing to allow his basilica to be used by the Arians, as he had been ordered by the Empress Justinia. He and his faithful followers, including Monica, had been besieged within the walls, Ambrose declaring that he would prefer death to surrender. To Augustine, this must have given greater weight to Simplicianus's words. Certainly Monica would reinforce them. The runner was on his mark, but the starting-gun had yet to be fired.

That happened when Augustine's little group of friends were visited by a high official from Africa who was at the Court of Treves. He noticed that Augustine was reading St Paul's epistles, and told him about the monks of Egypt, the Desert Fathers, who had given up all their riches and learning to follow in the way of the cross. The story of St Anthony, he added, had caused two of his fellow officials to renounce the world.

Augustine felt this message sink deep into his soul. It echoed the call he had experienced earlier, but declined to answer.

He retired with one of his closest friends to the garden of the house where they were lodging. He took the book of the epistles with him. There he experienced his own private Gethsemane, hammering with his fists on the forehead that held the brain which had betrayed him. He withdrew, so that his friend should not see the tears that flowed freely from his eyes, and flung himself down under a fig tree. And through the tempest of emotion a child's voice penetrated, singing a refrain:

'Take it and read... Take it and read...'

It broke his concentration, and he tried to remember which childish game it belonged to, but could not. Then he remembered the epistles, and quickly opened them, praying for a sign. He found it at the words:

'Not in revelling and drunkenness, not in lust and wantonness, not in quarrels and rivalries. Rather arm yourselves with the Lord Jesus Christ; spend no more thought on nature and nature's appetites.'

He showed his friend, and together they went in and told his mother.

She, who had lived many years for this moment, was overjoyed, and understood at last that he had settled for a life that would not bring material success, but which was built on self-denial. They retired to Cassiciacum on the shores of Lake Como, for a time of quiet preparation for the rite of baptism. Augustine wrote, and taught his band of pupils, which included his son Adeodatus, and his star pupil Licentius, the son of his benefactor Romanien. Monica was the head of the household, and the light to which they all turned when befogged by overmuch scholarship.

It was the happiest time of Monica's life.

Augustine received baptism in Milan from the hands of Ambrose, at Easter in the following year, and after that he planned to return to his home town and live in seclusion with some like-minded friends in a household presided over by his mother. But Rome, where their path homeward lay, was being blockaded by a rival emperor, and they had to stop at Ostia. It was there one evening, seated by a window, that mother and son shared a deep spiritual experience, a dual meditation on the immensity of God and the joys of heaven, of which Augustine has left a very beautiful account in his *Confessions*. It was a rare moment of perfect accord and communion which could only come to two human beings united in a pure love. Then, as if such beauty were insupportable in this life, Monica was seized by a violent illness, and within a fortnight she was dead.

She would not allow her sons – for Navigius was also of the party – to see her during her sufferings, but blessed them both, and assured them that she did not mind being buried apart from her husband, since God would know where her body was at the last resurrection. So, in perfect faith, she passed to heaven, and her grieving son closed the eyes that had so often wept for him.

He went on to become one of the greatest Doctors of the Church, and his Rule for the religious life is followed by orders of monks and nuns down to our own day. The cult of Monica was slow to take root, and was not widespread until the twelfth century; finally, in the fifteenth, Pope Martin V ordered that a search should be made at Ostia for her remains. These were brought to Rome, amid general rejoicing, and proved efficacious in the healing of sick children and the blind. In due course, and by popular acclaim, the relics were declared authentic, and her canonization was announced on the 27th of April 1430. The church where her body finally rested was dedicated not to her, but to her son, which one feels she would have wished, since she dedicated her life to him. Particularly at times of great upheaval in the Church, she has been invoked by mothers to protect their children through her prayers. Next to Our Lady, she is the patroness of mothers, and a very dear one, since she shared their hopes and aspirations in a very human way. Her feast day is the 27th of August and is immediately followed by the feast of St Augustine; so the liturgy of the Church follows the feeling of her children that they should be united for ever.

* * *

Midnight Mass had proceeded to the great thunder of the Credo; for a moment she had lost contact with her son, as the

61

organ pealed in the roof of the nave. He was elbowing his way through the crowd of worshippers. He was leaving – she must follow him to make one last plea to bring him back.

Occasionally she lost sight of him, then he would reappear; faces loomed out of the multitude, and she ignored them – the black-clad retreating back was the only thing present to her.

Then he paused at a side aisle, behind a line of penitents who had left it to the last moment to make their confessions. Wonder of wonders, he was joining them. She turned back to hear the words of the Credo:

'Et in unam sanctam catholicam et apostolicam ecclesiam' ('in one, holy, catholic and apostolic Church')... And echoed them in her heart, with tears in her eyes.

St Patrick

at was a Mayo man – was still a Mayo man, though he had not lived in Ireland for over forty years. He well remembered his first return to the family smallholding on the shores of Lough Feenagh, just after the war, when he was on leave from the United States Air Force. Their base had been in the flat Fen country of England, where they were greeted like benign invaders, which gave him a certain grim satisfaction. He had no love for the English.

The contrast between the Fens and the rocky western coast had taken his breath away. The small stone cottage that had once housed him, his three brothers and two sisters, was derelict, the slate roof scattered by the south-westerly gales, the windows gaping holes. How had they ever managed to fit into it? His comfortable house in the suburbs of Boston – he'd always wanted to live not far from the sea – had a bedroom for each of his four children. How had it all happened? Didn't they call it 'the luck of the Irish'?

In the old days, if it hadn't been for the fish they would have starved. The land produced oats and potatoes; he could still feel in his back the pain of bringing in the harvest, and of milking the cows and making cheese by the primitive methods of the thirties. There was not much profit in these activities. At the age when his own children were in grade-school, he had often been kept from his schooling by working on the land, or going out to crew one of the fishing-boats. He hadn't liked school anyway; the Christian Brothers' attempts to tame their wild pupils were drastic, based more on the principles of horse-breaking than Christian charity.

His mother spent her last breath producing her youngest child; and when his father, of whom he had been deeply afraid, died a few years later, all the tenderness he felt was directed toward the grandmother who came to look after the family. He could see her now, sitting beside the peat fire when there was a pause in the endless round of household tasks, her rosary beads slipping through her gnarled hands with their raised blue veins, praying for them all.

At his father's wake, a cousin from America had miraculously appeared. They had hung on his every word, regarding his tales of unlimited prosperity with the same awe as the legends of the old heroes, still told by aged men on winter evenings. Pat had resolved to get to this promised land by hook or by crook. His sisters had escaped by way of entering religious orders, but he had no vocation, and no taste for the book-learning which the religious life would have demanded. An offer from a neighbour to add their land to his provided a small sum to start the nest-egg he needed for his passage money. He added to it by working all the hours God sent – protected from squandering it on the local poteen, no doubt, by his grandmother's prayers.

Of course America was not quite the country that his cousin's vivid words had painted. Even the traditional immigrant work in the construction and service industries was thin on the ground when he arrived. But his hard childhood had given him an ox-like stamina, and when the cousin disappeared to try his fortune on the West Coast, he contacted the local Catholic church, more for the company of his own kind than piety, and the priest put him in the way of work he heard about on the grapevine.

The war gave him a new horizon. The Air Force became his father and mother, fed and clothed him and educated him to drop bombs on military targets – and on helpless civilians when he missed. By his second tour of missions, this began to worry him, and he consulted the chaplain, who took his problem of conscience seriously. He began to practise his religion with fervour, even at the risk of ridicule from his fellow-aviators – less courageous than himself in acknowledging their deeper feelings.

He married an English girl of farming stock, who was willing to convert out of love for him; and back home again at the end of hostilities he set up a construction business of his own. He more than repaid the help that the Church had given him in his hour of need, and was active in charity. He paid his workers a fair wage; the apartment blocks he was eventually contracted to build were well-constructed, of good materials. He had every hope that his only son would take over the business, so that he could found a dynasty in his new country; and that when the boy married, his eldest son would be called Patrick too. Hadn't the sight of the great saint's own mountain, Croagh Patrick, loomed over the other side of the bay in his childhood? And hadn't the holy man herded cattle and pigs, like himself? If only young Pat would show some sign of settling down...

* * *

At the dawn of history, Ireland was green with forests, out of which mountains raised their rocky summits, reflected in lakes that teemed with fish. The original inhabitants were an ancient people; long-headed and dark, similar to the Welsh, the Bretons, and the Basques, they worshipped the spirits of the dead, together with an assortment of nature-gods, and were certainly in residence in the Bronze Age, leaving burial mounds to prove it. In time they were joined by their neighbours – Picts from Scotland, less than twenty miles away, across the North Channel.

By about 300 BC came the Celtic invasions, pushing the vulnerable residents to the far west and south, and bringing with them a more sophisticated culture and social organisation, which flourished in Ireland.

The Celts organised themselves into five kingdoms covering the whole island; their kings were in uneasy alliance, often at war amongst themselves. Eventually they took out their abundant aggression on raiding Roman Britain, imitating in their own land the earthworks that the Romans used for defence, and instituting a professional soldier-class.

The kings ruled over lesser chieftains, the heads of clans who were free-men with a common great-grandfather. They owned slaves that they captured on their raids, and there was a more indeterminate class bound by temporary agreements to provide meat, (cattle was their main currency), vegetables and malt, in exchange for land-leases and protection during troubled times.

But by far the most influential class were the Druids. They combined the offices of priests, clerks, court poets, lawyers, philosophers, historians and scientists. They took over the primitive religion of the people which they found on their arrival and added to it the worship of their own high gods and dead kings. The numbers of the latter were constantly rising, as it was believed that the sacred powers they held could be transferred to anyone brave enough to kill them. The tales of these gods and royal forebears were relayed throughout the tribes by the priests who met in annual conventions on a nationwide basis. The tales certainly lost nothing in the telling – a fate that was to overcome Patrick himself.

Trees had a special significance in this well-forested land; most of the solemn rituals took place in groves believed to be sacred. Among these were the ceremonial burning of sacrifices – sometimes human, more often animal. The Druids used to interpret signs from the remains, so influencing the royal courses of action; we may be sure they took full advantage of the opportunity to manipulate matters and increase their own power. They also divined the significance of any unusual phenomenon in nature – cloud formations, an eclipse, or the movement of birds. Animals, wild or domesticated, had their own special properties, and descent from beasts of particular cunning or ferocity was often claimed. Some animals were so highly regarded that they were forbidden as food, and used only in rituals.

All the elements – the celestial bodies – and every part of the landscape, from the mountains to the humblest stream or well, was associated with some branch of worship, if only of lesser immortals like leprechauns and fairies. So it was that the land was steeped in paganism, engrained into the people over many centuries.

Ireland never suffered the challenge of a Roman invasion.

When Agricola planned one from northern Britain it was vetoed by his Roman superiors, who considered they had their hands full with the troublesome Picts who still held Scotland, and Agricola was displaced in favour of a less ambitious governor, content to leave Hadrian's Wall as the limit of the Empire in the north-west.

So it was difficult territory for evangelisation. Yet there were Christians scattered about, mostly in the south – settled travellers who came in through the trade routes. Irish gold was found as far away as the Baltic, and Irish wolf-hounds were in demand all over Europe as hunting dogs. There were also captured slaves, who brought their religion with them.

Patrick himself was one of these. He was born into a Christian family and baptised 'Magonus Sucatus Patricius'. His grandfather Potitus was an ordained priest – celibacy among the clergy was not insisted upon in those early times. His father, Calpurnius, was a deacon; his mother is a shadowy figure who may have been called Conchessa, and may or may not have been a niece of St Martin of Tours. The family were of Romano-British stock from a place called Bannavem Tabernius – a location Patrick failed to identify in the fragment of his autobiography that has come down to us. It has been variously described as being at Dumbarton on the Clyde – on the Cumbrian coast – on the banks of the Severn – or even more remotely, in Gaul, around Boulogne. This is unlikely, for although in later life he had a love for Gaul, Patrick spoke of Britain as a man speaks of his homeland.

In his youth he was something of a tearaway, like his great contemporary from the far south of the Roman empire, St Augustine of Hippo. Whatever pains his pious father and grandfather took to persuade him to acquire proficiency in Latin, the language of the priestly and professional classes, must have been lost on him. It was a deficiency that would continue to dog him in the future. He evidently preferred to be off on his father's country estate, enjoying the freedom of an outdoor life. And it was there, when he was a teenager, that he committed a moral fault that haunted him into old age. It was the culmination of a generally relaxed attitude to religion – possibly the rebellion often felt by the children of married clergy against the laws of the church, applied by over-anxious, over-pious parents. At the time, the sin – whatever it was – caused him no great feeling of guilt. At sixteen, well-born and privileged, his aim in life was to enjoy himself as much as possible; and it was then, out of a clear sky, that disaster overtook him and changed him irrevocably.

Across the Irish Sea, Neill of the Nine Hostages, a great Celtic hero who made raids into Britain from Scotland to Devon with his fleet of wooden ships powered by oar and sail, was on the warpath. He – or another man like him – invaded Calpurnius's estate and carried off the entire household, adding them to the thousands who were already slaves in Ireland.

Patrick seems to have been put ashore in the north-east, possibly at Larne, to the north of what is now Belfast. Whatever his port of entry, it could not have taken long for a purchaser to be found for a strong, well-nourished youth in his mid-teens. Tradition has it that his master was a chieftain called Miliucc – probably a Druid – who had lands on the mountain of Slemish. Torn from his life of privilege, Patrick found himself on the lowest rung of the ladder, only just above the animals he was required to tend.

To be a slave in those days was the lot of many, and hard for them all. But for a Roman citizen like Patrick it was to drink the cup of humiliation to the dregs. Rome conferred pride on her citizens; even a Christian full of humility like St Paul was proud to claim his right to appeal to the highest court in the empire; and Patrick had not as yet learned humility.

He worked as a shepherd and herdsman, like many of the characters in the Bible – that Bible which Patrick had scarcely taken the trouble to read. In all weathers, he spent long nights in the woods and on the mountainside; he was in the power of a master who no doubt regarded him as an investment, and considered overfeeding him would be uneconomic.

Whatever feelings of rage and despair Patrick must have had, he did not allow them to consume him utterly. He came to accept his privations as a just reminder that he had forgotten God in his days of luxury. With penitence came the grace of God and a true faith. The separation from family and friends, and the cessation of his pleasant life were enforced, but his acceptance of his fate as part of the divine will was truly heroic, especially as it was far from a passive reaction. He flung himself into a relationship with God with all the fervour of youth – later he would say that he was never to match it again. Untaught, he stumbled on a regime that the hermits of the desert in far-away Africa would have found familiar. He began to pray, cramming a hundred of the prayers he must have learned as a child into each day. But that was not enough; he had to rise before dawn and watch into the night, to add more to his total. Like many young athletes – and he became a spiritual athlete of great stamina – he was obsessed with times and records: this all added to what was to prove to be iron self-discipline.

Surrounded as he was by God's creation, the most beautiful landscapes, and on intimate terms with nature in all its manifestations, he was receiving a unique training for his future work – though he did not feel this at the time, and indeed always deplored his lack of formal scholarship.

Captives often develop a relationship with their oppressors, and Patrick was no exception. He seems to have had a regard for his master; there is no triumphant note in his account of leaving Miliucc after six years – his tone is almost regretful.

When freedom finally beckoned, it was in a dream. He was out in the open and had eaten nothing, which often results in broken sleep. It seemed to Patrick that a voice spoke to him, and assured him that he would see his native land again – that a ship was ready for the voyages, but it was at present in a far away port. The message was so powerful and urgent that although he had no knowledge of the location, nor anyone who lived there, he set out at once into the unknown.

He walked for nearly two hundred miles, upheld by his faith in God, and found that indeed there was a ship just about to sail. He spent the night in a hut, recovering from the effects of his forced march, and in the morning presented himself to the captain as able to pay for his passage – presumably by working, as it is difficult to see what other means he could have had. The captain rejected his offer bluntly; Patrick's faith was shaken, and he started to return to the hut. But he appealed in his disappointment to the God who had called him, and before he had finished the prayer, the crew of the

69

vessel shouted to him that he could join them. Perhaps they saw in the young man's expression something that impressed them, and led them to make the captain change his mind. In any event, they greeted him kindly and allowed him to join them on his own terms.

The ship's cargo included a pack of Irish wolf-hounds, and conditions on board must have been squalid and noisy. It took three days for them to reach land again. They were probably making for Nantes or Bordeaux, because those were the best markets for the dogs, but at the mercy of wind and weather they landed in a place that was desolate and uninhabited. There was no choice but to trudge on foot until they reached some more civilised spot. Unsure of their direction, they wandered for twenty-eight days, men and dogs growing lame and weak from lack of food. But Patrick must have kept up his devotions even on the march, because the pagan captain discovered he was a Christian. It may even be that he made the crew his first apostolate, and tried to convert them, for the captain, when they reached the point of despair, called on him to pray the Christian God for help. Patrick responded to his half-ironic request, and his faith was rewarded. Soon after this, a herd of pigs crossed their path, and using their last reserves of strength, they fell upon them.

For two days they paused in their journey and fed the dogs and gorged themselves. Patrick described what sounds like a bad attack of indigestion – a weight like a stone pressing down on him, preventing him from moving. He ascribed this to the devil, and from some half-forgotten lesson of child-hood, it came into his mind to shout the word: *'Helias!'* While he was doing so, the sun rose in splendour – bad weather had been one of the crosses they had to bear – and as it fell upon him and warmed him, he forgot all his miseries in shouting: *'Helias, helias!'* in praise and thanks. The sailors too gave thanks in their own way, by eating wild honey they had found, as a thank-offering to their gods. But for Patrick, this kind of ritual meal would have been a betrayal of his faith, and he would have none of it.

Restored by food and fire, they journeyed on in dry weather at last. By the tenth day the food was gone and once more they faced starvation, but before they were reduced to this extremity, they reached some kind of native settlement. There is a gap in Patrick's narrative at this point that tradition has filled with wanderings through Gaul and Italy. He never explains why he did not immediately go back to Britain. It is just possible that he might have felt the first stirrings of a vocation, and wanted to explore them in the company of the groups of holy men and women who were setting themselves up in a primitive version of monasticism.

One such was on the island of Lerins, in the Mediterranean, near Cannes, which has a strong tradition that it housed Patrick at this time, though there is no written record to substantiate it. (Of course there would not be, if his position in the community were that of a lowly enquirer.) The head of the Christian centre was a man called Honoratus, famed for his holiness. Whatever happened in these lost years, we know Patrick returned to Britain, where his family, who must have given him up for lost, welcomed him with joy – though they could hardly have recognised the boy who had left, in the man who came back in his mid-twenties. Britain had changed too: the Romans had departed in 409, leaving a void of uncertainty behind them.

Patrick was not able to enjoy the company of his family for long. Again he began to have vivid, revelatory dreams. One was of a young man who gave his name as Victoricus, coming with letters from Ireland. Patrick took one and read it, and found that it spoke with the voice of the Irish, calling him back to them. Returning to Ireland was the last thing he wanted to do, and he attempted to ignore it – only to find like others before and since that the pleading of the innocent cannot easily be set aside. Some response – even a negative one – had to be made.

Then he had another dream, as vivid as the first, but the call was deeper, and came from Christ himself. The words Patrick chose to describe it are an echo of St Paul – and indeed the whole of his testament is Pauline in character. He and the earlier great missionary apostle have much in common: they both journeyed often, suffering physically and mentally from imprisonment and rough treatment in the course of their missions. They both dealt with their converts in much the same way, a mixture of encouragement, scolding and exhor-

71

tation; sometimes treating them as saints in the making, at others like unruly children with everything to learn. They both scorned human philosophy, and had a close personal relationship with Christ, whose message they preached simply and purely, inspired by the Holy Spirit.

It was characteristic that once he had committed himself, Patrick was spurred to action. His problem was what to do next. Britain had lost the protection of the Christian emperors: it was to be another century before St Gregory would send St Augustine of Canterbury out on his great mission. There existed no one in his native country who could give Patrick authority to preach. And he was a layman – not even a deacon like his father. He could not go to Ireland without the priestly power to bring its people the sacraments. There was one place where he could gain the proper authority – he set out for Rome.

He does not appear ever to have reached it. According to tradition, he broke his journey at Auxerre, attracted by the personality of its bishop, St Amator. Patrick seems to have put forward his preposterous notion of evangelising the Irish on their wild island at the westernmost point of the known world – and St Amator listened to him, then set Patrick to acquiring the learning that his ill-spent youth had denied him. Under the guidance of St Germanus he studied the texts of the Old and New Testaments, and certainly took them to his heart, though he was never to be happy when expressing himself in Latin. The years went by, and in 417 St Germanus succeeded St Amator, but Patrick was still only a deacon. The waiting must have been almost intolerable to a man of his ardent temperament, but he never lost sight of his mission – in spite of the discouragement of his peers and superiors who thought his persistence smacked of presumption. He seems to have fared better with converts of barbarian origin, who were later to accompany him on his mission. He must have welcomed them: their background would recommend them above the scholarly priests who despised him.

It may have been one of these priests who became a close friend and mentor: his name was Deisignatus, and to him Patrick confided the sin of his youth, particularly the moral fault that had haunted him all through his trials, and for which he could not forgive himself. Even the unburdening of it to his friend before becoming a deacon did not quite do that. It remained to keep him humble, and to remind him of his kinship with all sinful men.

In 430, Deisignatus was chosen to accompany St Germanus and St Lupus of Troyes to Britain, where the Pelagian heresy was gaining a hold. This heresy was damaging the Church by denying the doctrine of original sin and leaving the way open for all kinds of deviations from the body of doctrine so painfully built up over the centuries. In the convention that discussed ways of dealing with the situation, the question of the scattered Christians in Ireland came up. It was proposed that someone, elevated to the office of bishop, should give his authority to the prevention of the spread of Pelagianism, and to support the Christians by converting the pagans who surrounded them.

Deisignatus was present when this proposal was made, and advanced Patrick's name as a suitable candidate for the post. On the face of it, he was an unlikely choice, as his detractors were swift to point out; they considered him too lacking in learning and sophistication, and ignored his wide practical experience of Ireland, his knowledge of its people, and the pagan religion they practised.

Deisignatus then did something quite extraordinary, as if he had himself lost faith in Patrick's suitability. He made public the sin committed thirty years earlier, which Patrick had confessed to him – and so lost Patrick any chance he might have had of evangelising his captors, and giving them in return for their harsh treatment of him the greatest gift he could offer: the Good News of the Gospel.

The night that the news of Deisignatus's betrayal of his trust arrived from Britain, sleep must have been slow to come to Patrick. But when it came at last, it brought a healing vision of God himself, assuring him of his displeasure at Deisignatus's perfidy, his special care of Patrick, and his love for him.

This gave him the strength to bear his disappointment when another candidate was accepted by Pope Celestine, and sent to Ireland a year later. But Patrick possessed the divine obstinacy that gives the great saints their power, and he never lost sight of his mission. Within a year, the preferred candidate died in the mission field, and Patrick's faith was justified at last. He was the second choice – perhaps the only one – and Pope Celestine authorised him to be ordained bishop.

He could now plan his campaign to convert the Irish. It was the voice of the people that had called him, but he knew he must first convert their kings and chieftains if they were to be allowed to worship in peace. He decided to travel in some state, so that he could impress them by showing a spiritual power that could match their temporal one. He knew he was going into hostile territory, and could count on no hospitality there; the existing Christians were poor, and he would not ask them for the little they had.

Tradition has it that he landed at Invadea, at the mouth of the Vautry, and made his way north into Ulster. His caravan, though rather differently composed, resembled the organisation of a modern papal visit, with its collection of secretaries, communicators with the media, security men and specially-constructed vehicles. It might suit the personality of the principal visitor to travel lightly, but then as now, these trappings were necessary. Patrick knew that he faced many dangers, including the possibility of assassination. Not only had he to be wary of the military might of the kings; the Druid priests were even more to be feared, since he was seeking to deprive them of the reason for their existence.

There is a record of his retinue. This record, although of a later date, is so specific in naming names, from his assistant bishop to his cook, that it rings true. It shows that there were three women in the party, who acted as embroideresses. The names are all Irish, and must have been recruited locally; included among the artisans was one called Tassach, who remained faithful to him throughout his mission. It is said that no man is a hero to his servant, but Patrick was a hero to the charioteers who shared his journeyings in the unsprung vehicles, over roads that were very rough where they existed at all. One of the drivers, Odrahan, had a premonition of a special danger awaiting his master, and persuaded him to take the reins himself, intercepting a fatal spear-thrust meant for the saint.

It is said that on his way north, Patrick passed near the lands of his old slave-master, Miliucc, and paused on the brow of a hill overlooking the place of his servitude. There he saw a great fire burning, and received word that Miliucc had shut himself up in his house, surrounded by his treasures, and set it alight, so he might perish in the flames. This news silenced Patrick. For two or three hours he brooded upon it, then broke into a tremendous cursing of the dead chieftain and all his descendants. Irish tales are rich in curses, and the story of Patrick is no exception: they roll off the tongue of the teller with particular resonance, and can be used to enhance the dramatic effect. Whether Patrick was really as fiery-tempered as the legends would have us believe, or whether he was reacting to great emotion, as inarticulate people often do, this rejection by the proud old pagan who would rather die than listen to his message must have hurt Patrick very deeply.

He had better fortune in Down, with a chieftain called Dichu, whom he converted, and who gave him a plot of land on which to build a church. He insisted that the pattern of this wooden structure should be used in other places, by other converts. These were now coming in greater and greater numbers as he won the ear of their overlords. If persuasion failed, he was not above buying their favour, boasting that he could obtain it for the price of fifteen slaves – a good strong slave could be exchanged for a cow.

The Druids were a different matter; more subtle, better educated, and with more to lose, yet the nature of the Celtic religion worked in favour of the Good News brought by Patrick. Their belief in the indestructibility of the souls of the dead helped them to understand the resurrection of Christ; their sacrifices were a distorting mirror of his one perfect sacrifice for the sins of the whole world. Their ritual meals were a mirror of the eucharist, and Patrick saw to it that it should be celebrated with fitting solemnity, in well-appointed buildings. He soon began to count his converts in hundreds.

He did not discourage convert Druids from retaining their positions as lawyers, doctors, poets and musicians, as long as their powers were circumscribed. It helped that they had a self-destructing prophecy of a man who was to come, with a wedge-shaped head and a shepherd's crook, his altar in the east of his house, who would encourage the people to cry 'Amen' to his call to worship. Patrick, with his mitre and crozier, fitted this description exactly. Many Druids became Christian priests – especially the poets, who had a sensitivity to Patrick's message. He also numbered many influential women among his converts: queens and chieftains' wives, who were equal in Irish law to their husbands. There were slave-girls too, prepared to suffer for their faith at the hands of their pagan relatives, for whom they represented negotiable currency, and their masters who demanded sexual favours as part of their duties. Many of these women took vows of chastity, and performed the work of deacons, or banded together in convents.

When Patrick felt that he was secure enough in the north and west, he set forth on the greatest adventure of his adventurous career – the march on the High King Laoghaire, in his great stronghold on the Hill of Tara in Meath.

He seems to have chosen Easter as the time for this momentous meeting. Laoghaire was in his great hall, which could seat up to a thousand guests at banquets. It was the time for the national convention of all the lesser kings and chieftains, to review laws and settle disputes. Each man was independent in his own territory, but the same laws applied to them all. Laoghaire – the son of the same Neill of the Nine Hostages, who had pillaged the west of England when Patrick himself was a victim of the raids – kept his authority by sheer force of character and military supremacy. Patrick could have been in no doubt that he presented a very formidable challenge.

Apparently he had the right to keep everyone in darkness until his own fire was lit; and Patrick threw down the gauntlet by lighting the paschal fire. There followed a direct trial of strength between him and the Druids at the court. The legends echo the majesty of the Old Testament, when Elijah battled for the supremacy of Yahweh over the priests of Baal; and they end with Laoghaire converted out of fear, and the unbelievers perished. Stripped of its exciting embellishments – in which Patrick demonstrates magical powers superior to the best that Laoghaire's wizards could perform – the historical result was that the high king gave Patrick full permission to preach in the area of his jurisdiction, and a gratifying number of his relations and officers became Christians. But when it was Laoghaire's time to die, he was buried according to the old pagan ritual.

Though so much had been won, Laoghaire's protection was not absolute; dangers remained, and there was much for Patrick still to do. On one occasion he and his caravan were ambushed and put in irons by a resolute chieftain. His companions feared for their lives, but Patrick was reassured by one of the dreams that came to him when things were at their worst, and he placed himself in the hands of God. The dream promised him that they would all be released in sixty days – and the chieftain released them in sixty days exactly; Patrick went on his way, with his faith reinforced.

His converts could now be reckoned in thousands, and their organisation and education became an ever-present problem. Like many people who feel the want of education, he had a healthy respect for it, and was always on the look-out for likely lads he might recruit to the priesthood; each of them received a grounding in the faith, and a copy of the Latin alphabet. He made Latin the language of the Church throughout Ireland – where once the Druids had the only key to learning, he threw it open to all who had the capacity to study.

During his lifetime, he ordained some three hundred and fifty bishops, each one living in a complex containing a church, a clergy house and a kitchen. He was sometimes hard put to it to find suitable candidates. He sent a despairing appeal to a friend, requesting him to recommend someone – preferably a celibate, but at least having only one wife and one child, and of sufficient wealth not to be tempted to line his pockets with bribes. The friend confessed himself able to think of only one person who fitted these modest conditions.

Patrick never lost his fighting spirit. When a chieftain called Coroticus, a Pict from Scotland, made a raid on the Irish coast and desecrated a church where the newly-baptised were still in their white robes, killing some and dragging others to captivity, he was consumed with righteous anger. A letter to Coroticus, who seems to have been at least nominally a Christian, requesting him to return the unfortunate prisoners, met with no response. He appealed to the chieftain's soldiers to turn against him and refuse to eat or drink with him. The tone of the letter, which has come down to us, proves that when the spirit moved him to compassion for his converts, and hatred of a sin against them, he could express himself very well indeed – even in Latin.

Later in his life, he felt the need to recharge his fervour and in imitation of Christ he spent forty days and forty nights fasting on a bare mountain in Mayo, now called Croagh Patrick. To this day, the descendants of the people who first heard the faith from Patrick's own lips, and held to it despite many invasions and persecutions, still make their pilgrimage to the chapel and oratory at its summit.

Then Patrick went back to his pastoral work: the care of the churches and monasteries he had founded, and the constant exhortation to the newly-converted so they should not fall back into paganism. He seems to have been tireless, striding and driving across the country like a prophet from the Old Testament; he is even spoken of as physically throwing down idols with his own hands. But as the years advanced, he slowed down sufficiently to set up his See in Armagh. He spent a long time training his successor – Benignus, who had shared his journeys, man and boy. Finally, we are told, when the shadow of death came near, Patrick went back to the first church he had built, at Saul in Down, on the land that he had been given by Dichu in the early days of his mission.

His faithful artisan Tassach brought the Holy Viaticum to the dying saint: he was in his middle seventies when his great heart ceased to beat.

Immediately, there was a quarrel about who should possess the body of the saint – often a problem in the turbulent childhood of the Church. Claims and counterclaims have left his burial place uncertain: the grave he is said to share with St Bridget – the Mary of Ireland, who died in Kildare in 523 – brings many pilgrims to its site in Downpatrick. His feast on the 17th of March is celebrated worldwide, among the people he once despised as barbarians, but came to associate himself with as 'We, the Irish…'

As workers, writers, musicians, scholars and missionary religious, they have taken their faith with them throughout the world, giving it as generously as their patron himself. And they have made known everywhere the 'Lorica', to which he is said to have contributed several stanzas – the 'Breastplate of St Patrick', that begins and ends:

78

I arise today
Through a mighty strength, the invocation of the Trinity,
Through a belief in the threeness,
Through a confession of the oneness,
Of the Creator of creation.

* * *

Pat woke up with a start. Was he getting to be an old man, dropping off while mulling over his thoughts? Then he became aware that it was the ringing of the telephone that had broken in upon him. He picked it up, and was greeted by his son's voice. Pat had believed him to be on a salmon-fishing trip in the west, and thought it might be bad news which had caused him to interrupt it. The war had left him prone to anticipate bad news in unguarded moments.

Pat's voice went on, spilling over with an enthusiasm that his father had missed in him since he was a boy. He could hardly take in the meaning of the words, but managed to reply:

'You must do what you think best, son.'

Slowly, he replaced the receiver. It was a shock – no doubt about that. What would happen to the business now? The girls' husbands had careers of their own. He abandoned his plan of retiring to Florida. How would he tell his wife when she came in from the meeting of Catholic Mothers? She would calm him and reassure him, with her English knack of defusing explosive situations. She would be proud of a son who would take his skills to work for the deprived people of the Third World.

And if he did become a missionary priest, that was an honour.

His grandmother would have said it was a risk you took when you called a boy 'Patrick' – that he would have no son to carry on the name.

79

St Bernadette Soubirous

ou would not have thought that she was the happiest girl in the world. She was undersized for her ten years, pale and thin; her clothes ill-assorted purchases from jumble sales. The time when her father had a job, and her family had lived in reasonable comfort, was the vaguest of memories. More vivid was their time in bed-and-breakfast accommodation, when they had tramped the streets in all weathers; that was when the bronchitis had begun. Between the bronchitis, and looking after her younger brothers and sister when her mother was at work, her attendance at school had been intermittent and she could not read or write.

But she was an expert shopper, getting full value out of every penny, and had friends as well as enemies among the stall-holders in the market, where she picked up bargains in the way of spoiled vegetables. Controlling her siblings was no trouble either, though they were healthier and stronger than she was, having been raised in the comparative affluence of a council flat in a high-rise block. They went in awe of her sharp tongue, and were entertained by her gift for impersonating the characters she met on the street.

She saw to it that they got to the park at every opportunity and that they worked off their high spirits at the playground there, rather than in the vandalism current among the juvenile population of the block. Her father had suffered from chronic depression since redundancy, and took to his bed as much from that as to save heat and light. Her mother was a fighter like herself, and with the obstinacy of her Irish peasant forbears, refused to submit to poverty. She was pious too, and though she could not get to mass very often, had enrolled her family in the parish school, and saw to it that they knew who was who in the religious pictures she had brought from home.

Her elder daughter loved the one of Our Lady of Lourdes. It was her comfort when she woke wheezing at night and could not sleep. Propped up with pillows, her mother making the black tea with honey in it which she thought so superior to the doctor's prescriptions, she would gaze at the picture, and dream of going one day to drink of the miraculous spring, never to be ill again.

And wasn't it a miracle in itself that she should actually be going this summer? A nun at school had told her that the rich parents of a child who had leukemia wanted a companion for their daughter, and she had been chosen to fill the place. Too modest to believe that the sharp-eyed nun had noticed her qualities, she thought it was sheer luck. And she was the happiest girl in the world.

* * *

In France, the reign of Louis Philippe had drawn to a close. With rapid expansion in industry and communications – notably the growth of the railways – it had been a prosperous time for the middle classes. They were solidly conservative, church-going, but smugly contemptuous of the poor. The working masses became disaffected, and in 1848 exploded – with memories of the great Revolution only a generation away. But even the volatile French were sick of revolutions, and the bourgeois element polarised quickly round the figure of Louis Napoleon, nephew of the great Bonaparte, accepting him first as president, then as emperor.

All this barely affected the small country town of Lourdes, far away from Paris, in the Pyrenees. Although it had a population of only four thousand, it boasted Law Courts, and these brought visitors. In the high season, fairs were held there, and it was a regular stop for the stage-coaches and carriages of the rich on their way to popular spas nearby. There were slate and marble quarries on the mountainside, and mills on the banks of the river Gave, which ran to the east of the town.

It was in a mill on one of its tributaries, the Lapaca, in the shadows of the chateau-fort that dominated the little town, that François and Louise Soubirous had set up home on their marriage in 1843. They shared the mill with Louise's widowed mother and sisters, François having married into the family to work the mill. It made a modest living for all of them – which was just as well, because a year later there was another mouth to feed. A daughter, baptised Marie-Bernarde after her aunt, was born on the 7th of January 1844. She was always known by the diminutive: Bernadette.

When she was ten months old, her mother, pregnant with another child, was working by the light of a resin candle when it spluttered and set fire to her bodice. It was the end of nursing Bernadette, and Louise had to look for a foster-mother for her. She was found in Bartres, in a valley some three miles to the north: she and her husband were customers of the mill and had lost their first child. Louise and her sister Bernarde carried the little girl to Bartres in her cradle, and left her there; Bernarde staying for a few days to settle her into her foster family. The bonding was successful, and the young couple – Marie and Basile Lagues – became very fond of Bernadette, who consoled them for the loss of their baby son. After she returned to Lourdes when she was nearly two, they became constant visitors to the mill. But in her absence, tragedy also struck the Soubirous family; the baby Louise had expected – a son called Jean – had died aged only two months. So before her second birthday, Bernadette had been the consolation to two bereaved households.

That she was a consolation is a tribute to her sunny nature. She prattled away in the Bigorre dialect spoken by her parents, and charmed everyone. Until she was six, by which time she had a sister, Toinette, aged three and a half, she was happy and healthy; but then she developed the asthma that was to undermine her constitution for the rest of her life. Things were not going well with François's business either. The mill became less prosperous when his mother-in-law moved into another house with her daughters, and was no longer able to keep the accounts. François and Louise were open-hearted people, given to offering their customers snacks while the grain was being ground, and waiving payment until better times came. The whisper went round that they were an improvident couple; the truth was that they were too generous to be businesslike. They were also proud, and willing to work. But the mill was not making money, and by the time Bernadette was ten and a half, they could no longer pay the rent. They were forced to take on the tenancy of an even less profitable mill, and eke out a living by doing odd jobs on the land, and for other millers.

At this unpropitious moment, Louise gave birth to a son, Justin. There had also been another boy, Jean-Marie, who was now four. They did not succumb to the cholera epidemic that swept the district six months later, but Bernadette did. Her mother attributed her recovery to the prayers that were offered up to Our Lady, to whom the people of the region had an especial devotion. Despite her illness, Bernadette was her mother's right hand, taking care of the younger children when her parents were working, preparing simple meals, and running errands. Her attendance at school was interrupted both by her ill health and her duties to the family. She could write a few capital letters, but apart from that she was illiterate, could speak no French, and knew only a few basic prayers.

By the time she was twelve, they were destitute, living from hand to mouth. François Soubirous was no longer a miller; Louise worked in the fields, and sold the wood that she gathered to buy bread. The children went scavenging in the streets for bones and scrap-iron and rags. They were forced to find a lodging in a gaol, considered too damp and dark to house criminals. There was practically no light, the smoke from the fire filled the room, the door was heavy and reminded them of its previous existence as the 'Cachot' – a prison. It was an appalling atmosphere for an asthmatic. The whole family lived, ate and slept in this one room.

At their lowest ebb, disaster struck again. By this time Bernadette was thirteen, but looked younger than her eleven-year-old sister, who had attended school more regularly and could read; there was talk of preparing Toinette for her first holy communion. The same privilege had not been thought of for Bernadette, whose attendance at the odd catechism class had revealed that she could not master it. But the new blow – François' arrest for the theft of a billet of wood which he had found and taken home, believing that it belonged to no one – fell when they were least equipped to bear it. He was imprisoned for only nine days, but the disgrace to the once proud family was devastating. They would in future be looked on with pity or contempt.

But the Lagues stood by them. They now had a healthy family of five, and a flourishing farm. They could use an extra pair of hands, especially hands as willing and capable as Bernadette's. She went to them as an unpaid servant. But the white bread which her mother insisted on for her, because she could not stomach the normal peasant diet of coarse milloc, was freely available; butter too, and sometimes meat. At first she even went to school, though she was so backward that she was put with much younger children. But she proved too useful when it was time to put out the sheep to the upper pastures, and she was sent with them as a shepherdess. This work was considered much more important than going to school or to catechism classes, though Bernadette longed to learn to read and make her first holy communion. Marie Lagues had a pang of conscience about the way they were exploiting her, and tried to teach her in the evenings, but after a day's work in the heady mountain air, they were both tired, and the girl found it impossible to retain any of her instruction. The lessons ended with impatience on Marie's part, and tears of remorse on Bernadette's. She looked upon herself as slow and stupid.

Even her father, on a visit to Bartres, took advantage of her ignorance to tease her. She had noticed one morning that her lambs had green marks on their backs. Her father assured her that it was because they had been eating too much grass.

'Will they die?' she asked anxiously.

'Probably,' was the off-hand reply.

Their shepherdess burst into tears. Then he told her that it was only the dealer's mark which had been put on them, unknown to her. She shamed him by explaining that, since she had never told a lie, she could not believe he would deceive her. But this trivial incident was revealing of her absolute honesty and childlike trust, and leads us to think that she was unusually innocent for a girl of fourteen.

At last, in the January of 1858, her parents yielded to her entreaties to let her go back to Lourdes to commence her preparation to receive the eucharist. Despite the poverty of the life in the Cachot, her family was there, and she was devoted to them. And so she went back happily to keep a rendezvous with the Queen of Heaven. Like her she was poor, and like her was to be highly favoured. But at the time she would have laughed at the idea of any such similarity.

Thursday, the 11th of February, a cold damp day, was a school holiday. Because the firewood was getting low, Bernadette and her younger sister decided to go and gather some. Before they went out, Jeanne Abadie, a classmate of Toinette's, dropped in and decided to join them. Louise Soubirous was dubious, because Bernadette had a cold, but gave her consent when she promised to wear the one white cape that the family possessed. Like everything they had, it was second-hand, but it was warm. Louise also insisted she should wear stockings with her sabots. Bernadette took a basket, in case they found any bones.

They were going down a track to the forest when an old woman advised them that a neighbour had been cutting trees on his land, which lay between the Gave and a small canal that drove his saw and flour-mill. Bernadette – with the memory of her father's arrest in mind – advised against going there, but the woman assured them that there were dead branches and bones in the area, so she agreed. The mill was not working and the water of the canal was only knee-deep. Toinette and Jeanne raced ahead, having seen a bone and some branches on the other side of the Gave, where it was overlooked by a rocky promontory, the Massabielle.

There was a grotto in the rock, and inside it was a hollow alcove, fringed with brambles and bushes.

Toinette and Jeanne threw their sabots over the canal and waded across. Bernadette, conscious of her frail health, and judging by their shouts that the water was icy cold, hesitated, calling on them to help her over by putting down stepping-stones, or carrying her across. Toinette paid no attention and

Jeanne answered roughly that she must do as they did, or stay where she was. Then they went out of sight.

Bernadette did not want her sister to be alone with Jeanne Abadie, who was notoriously wild, and she felt lonely in these unfamiliar surroundings. She decided, whatever the cost, that she would follow their example, and started to remove her stockings. She was then arrested by the sound of a strong wind stirring the bushes round the alcove in the grotto. Everything else was still. And then came a soft light... And then the lady...

She was to describe her in minute detail over and over again in the years that followed. She never found the words to convey that attraction that sent her into ecstasy. The vision did not speak, but she held a rosary on her right arm. This gave Bernadette the idea of taking out her own tuppenny rosary. She tried to make the sign of the cross, but her arm fell back. The lady turned toward her with her own rosary in her hand and crossed herself. Bernadette followed her action, and lost the fear that had troubled her at first. The lady slipped her beads as Bernadette prayed, but her lips did not move, except to accompany the 'Glory be...' When it was finished she bowed and smiled, retreated into the niche and disappeared – leaving the young visionary awestruck.

She was still a little out of this world when Toinette and Jeanne returned on the other bank. She was so pale, Toinette thought she was dead, but the sturdy Jeanne Abadie pooh-poohed the idea. Toinette threw some small pebbles at her sister without being able to break her concentration. Then suddenly she came to herself, and crossed the canal to them, remarking that the water seemed quite warm. She seemed to have acquired superhuman strength from somewhere, and carried her own bundle of wood, bounding up the hill, and even helping her sister who was normally stronger. It was then, still vibrant with joy, that she told Toinette about the lady whose beauty had moved her so much. After this she became silent and preoccupied.

Later, Toinette told their mother, who became angry and attacked them with the stick she used to spread blankets. Nothing would make Bernadette budge from her story – not even her father's conviction that it was some sort of manifestation of evil she had seen… She knew better. When evening came, tired out after the events of the day, she became tearful at family prayers. Her mother was alarmed, fearing for her daughter's health as she always did, and extracted a promise that she would never visit the grotto again.

The news of the lady's appearance might have remained with the family, but next day Jeanne Abadie spread it amongst the girls at school. When the teachers got to hear of it, they advised Bernadette to keep silent or risk being laughed at. Bernadette herself would have been quite happy to comply; at this time she wanted to keep the lady to herself. She was prevailed on to mention it to her confessor on the Saturday, and he advised her to tell the parish priest, but Bernadette was afraid of the Abbé Peyramale, who had a reputation for being formidable, and begged her confessor to tell him. So the parochial clergy were informed; and they dismissed it as childish nonsense.

Sunday was the beginning of the Shrovetide festivities, and many people had planned an expedition to Lourdes from the surrounding villages. None of them paid much attention to a gaggle of schoolgirls crowding round one of their number, after high mass. Bernadette wanted to go back to the grotto, but dared not ask her mother. The girls, scenting that something might happen to add excitement to their dull lives, prevailed on her to seek the necessary permission. Louise fell back on every mother's last resort:

'You must ask your father.'

The chattering group passed on to the stables where François Soubirous was grooming relay horses in the presence of his employer.

His answer was a flat: 'No.'

But his employer pointed out that if the lady carried a rosary, she could not be evil. François was silenced, and the excited children took this for consent. Fetching some holy water from the church, they hurried to the Massabielle.

They went in two groups, one led by the eager Bernadette; Jeanne Abadie was in the other. Bernadette instructed them to start saying the rosary. Already she was learning the best way to please her lady. After a few 'Hail Marys', she remarked that there was a bright light – and then the lady appeared.

Bernadette found it hard to believe that the others could not see her, and described her to them. Then she remembered her father's fear that the vision might be evil, and walking as near her as she dared, sprinkled the rock with holy water, and said:

'If you be from God, stay.'

This rather discourteous remark appeared to amuse the lady, because she smiled. Bernadette rejoined her companions and knelt down amongst them, becoming lost in concentration.

The sudden crash of a stone against the boulder she leaned on – hurled by Jeanne Abadie in revenge for being left behind – made her start for a moment, but she was soon lost in contemplation again. The effect on the girls was shattering; they accused Jeanne Abadie of killing Bernadette, mistaking her ecstasy for death. Jeanne was not intimidated, and pointed out that she was still kneeling. But the girls were very frightened, and leaving Toinette beside her sister, they went to the nearby mill for help. It belonged to a family called Nicolau, and the miller's wife ordered her son Antoine to go with her to the grotto, in case a man was needed.

The sight of the little girl, her face pale but smiling, though tears welled from her eyes, moved him profoundly. Nevertheless, he carried her back to the mill. He remarked afterwards that though she was small for her age, her struggles to stay there were so intense that he was worn out by his efforts. They made her comfortable by the fire, and after a few minutes she returned to this world. Her mother was sent for, and as mothers will when they discover that their children are not after all in danger, she became very angry. The miller's wife reproved her and said the child was an angel. Louise collapsed in tears, and slowly they returned to the Cachot.

Visitors from the surrounding villages had seen the little procession going to the mill, and there was talk in the crowded inns that night of the goings-on at the Massabielle. The gossip reached the ears of a Madame Millet, a prosperous neighbour for whom Louise sometimes worked. She interrogated Bernadette, and decided that the vision might be the late president of the Children of Mary, come to beg prayers for her soul. Bernadette was sceptical about this, but consented to go to the grotto with Madame Millet and her maid: she would

89

have gone with anyone who could wrest permission from her mother. This was granted, and Thursday the 18th of February was the day chosen.

When the lady appeared on this occasion Bernadette was more like her normal self. She placed the paper, pen and ink which Madame Millet had provided on a flat stone, and passed on her request that the lady should write down her name.

The lady found this amusing, and bestowed a kindly glance on the two strangers, saying there was no need to write anything down. She had, however, two messages for Bernadette: one that she should do her the favour of coming to the grotto every day for a fortnight; and the other a warning that she would not be happy in this world – only in the next. It was the first time she had spoken. The communication between them was progressing.

When Bernadette tried to explain how she heard her voice, she touched her breast and said: 'It reaches me *here*.'

True to her promise, she went the following day after the first mass. This time she was accompanied not only by Madame Millet but by her mother, her aunt Bernarde and some other women from the poor quarters of Lourdes. They were all overcome by the change in Bernadette's appearance when she saw the lady, but were still anxious about her. When giving the account of what had happened this time, the visionary mentioned the noise of a turbulent crowd seeming to swell up from the Gave, with one voice dominating the rest, shouting: 'Get out of here!'

Bernadette explained that the lady had silenced these evil sounds with a single glance.

The Saturday vision was a peaceful encounter in which the lady patiently taught her, word by word, a prayer that was especially her own, and that she was to say every day for the rest of her life. So was forged the bond of devotion between them. Bernadette learned quickly, as she had not been able to learn in school; she was the clear, empty vessel that was being filled to the brim with love.

Sunday, 21st of February, marked a change. Bernadette was surrounded by a great crowd who had taken advantage of their day off work to observe the goings-on in the grotto. The crowd was large enough, and included enough of the rough quarry-workers and labourers of the region, to cause the gendarmerie to send a token force of three policemen to keep order. However, the crowd remained calm, and there were no disputes or untoward incidents. Bernadette was oblivious of all this, and also of one of the local doctors who stood nearby to test his theory that she was mentally unbalanced. He could find no irregularity in her pulse or breathing, when she was in ecstasy; though he did notice that at one point she had been in tears. Bernadette said afterwards that this was when the lady had looked over her head to the world beyond, and asked her to pray for sinners – and she realised that the vision was not only for her but for all the world.

But this was not the end of the events of that Sunday in Lourdes. The crowd from the Massabielle had been joined by others who had not been there. They gossiped in the town square, taking sides, because by no means everyone was convinced that Bernadette was telling the truth. The police were called out again in larger numbers, and the mayor himself held a meeting to discuss the situation. It was decided that the Public Prosecutor should interrogate Bernadette. She acquitted herself well: her sincerity was obvious, and she seemed to be guiltless of fraud or deception. He put no obstacle in the way of her going to the grotto.

It was far otherwise when M. Jacomet, the police commissioner, looked into the case during the afternoon. Bernadette had been at vespers when she was called into his presence. He bullied and threatened, and twisted her account of the apparitions to trap her. As always, she remained calm and unruffled, which angered him more. If her father had not come in to share his daughter's shame (as he thought) and gone to pieces in the presence of the man who had put him in custody once before, Bernadette's triumph over M. Jacomet would have been complete. As it was, François Soubirous assured him that he was upset by his daughter's antics, and the number of visitors now thronging the Cachot, and that he would put a stop to the whole business.

On Monday she set out for school as usual, but on the way felt a compulsion to return to the grotto. To do so she had to pass the police station, and when she was seen, two gendarmes were told to accompany her wherever she went. This time she knelt down and told her beads as usual, but the lady did not appear. Bernadette was distraught. She had kept her side of the bargain, at great cost: why had the lady abandoned her? Seeing her distress, her parents relented. She should be allowed to go the next day, though she must go at dawn when no one was about.

But they reckoned without the interest that had been aroused. The police escort had called further attention to the procession. About a hundred people gathered in the darkness, including, for the first time, some middle-class sceptics who came out of curiosity. One of them, Jean-Baptiste Estrade – who occasionally wrote for the newspapers, and admitted that he had come to scoff at the enthusiasm of the unlettered mob – left a moving account of the beauty and grace of Bernadette's actions during her sublime experience of conversation with the lady; as well as the fact that when the ecstasy was over, her face became that of a peasant girl again, and she melted into the crowd with her mother. There was no doubt in his mind that he had been in the presence of the Queen of Heaven, though Bernadette had never claimed that honour. The local paper, in view of the public interest, was forced to take notice of the proceedings, but gave a garbled account culled from the unsympathetic police reports.

Wednesday, the 24th, the eighth apparition, marked yet more progress in Bernadette's mission. She called the crowd, which now numbered four or five hundred, for demonstrations of penance on behalf of her lady, who now showed that she had a more austere side. She had led her young messenger through contemplation of her beauty, to an acceptance that the vision would have to be paid for.

The next day, Thursday, mingled pleasure with pain. The people, again some four hundred, had gathered before dawn: Bernadette had difficulty in making her way through them. What they saw in the flickering light seemed ridiculous and disgusting. They watched her pass on her knees deep into the grotto, then come out again towards the river, still moving on her knees over the rough, broken stones. Then with great purpose she returned to the grotto and scrabbled in the dirt with her hands. When she turned round, her face was muddy, and her aunt hastily wiped it.

The crowd turned on her in surprise and shock; here surely was the evidence that she was mad. Worse was to follow. Apparently on orders from the lady, she started to chew some weeds that grew among the rocks. The people who had watched in prayerful silence on preceding days experienced a revulsion of feeling. Great disillusionment spread amongst them. For the first time, scornful laughter was heard in the grotto as the crowd dispersed.

Bernadette bore it all with equanimity. The lady had directed her to bathe at the spring in the grotto. After a moment of misunderstanding, when she had turned toward the river, she had done her best to obey. What did it matter that there was no spring, only a patch of mud? The lady had commanded, and Bernadette was too much in love to question that command. Chewing the bitter herbs evokes echoes of the Old Testament, and were no doubt part of the call to penance of the previous day. And the fact that Our Lord cured a blind man by anointing his eyes with dirt and spittle is an indication of the way divine symbolism works.

Yet the grotto had not lost its attraction for the fickle crowd. Word had spread as far as Tarbes, the regional capital. Still the clergy made no move; only the police recorded the movement of events. Bernadette returned to the grotto on Friday, to find that the lady was absent. This caused her great distress, as the humiliation by the crowd on Thursday had not. She was ruled entirely by her absorption in the beloved, and not by human considerations.

The next day, Saturday the 27th, the lady exacted an act of penance from her young devotee, who kissed the ground frequently in token of her humility. The muddy patch had become a spring, which was flowing freely, and she drank from it, then ate some blades of grass. It is interesting to note that each day's vision was establishing a ritual to be followed, deepening the bond between them. The lady had also given Bernadette a commission which she confided to her aunt Bernarde on the way home:

'Go and tell the priests to have a chapel built here.'

They both took this to mean the local priests who, without going to the grotto, had sent reports to the Bishop of Tarbes. The clerics were anxious not to get mixed up with what they regarded as the antics of a hysteric, nor with the uninformed credulity of those who followed her.

On her aunt's advice, Bernadette went to her confessor, the only priest she really knew. He would do nothing without the permission of his superior: the parish priest, Abbé Peyramale. Even Aunt Bernarde, normally strong-minded, was afraid of this character, who was built on the heroic scale, both physically and temperamentally. So Bernadette went to his house alone, and found him in the garden reading his breviary. He took her indoors and asked what she wanted of him. Bernadette gave the lady's message, and would no doubt have been happy to leave his terrifying presence, but he questioned her brusquely, making her understand that he had no patience with her or with the nameless lady who appeared on a rock in the middle of nowhere. He demanded that the lady should make herself known, and threw in a request for a miracle – that she should make the rose-bush at the grotto bloom in the middle of winter. Bernadette departed meekly to inform the lady.

She performed her acts of penance again, joined by a crowd of some two thousand, for it was a Sunday. It was a police sergeant, no less, who in a burst of enthusiasm ordered them all to kiss the ground, as Bernadette conveyed the curé's flippant response to the lady's request.

Afterwards, she dared his presence once again to report that the lady had merely smiled – then probably escaped with relief. But the manner of the faithful child, carrying the message with resolution no matter what he said to alarm her, had moved him more than he would admit at the time.

However, the civic authorities rushed in where he feared to tread, and Bernadette was taken from the high mass she attended, to be examined by the magistrates. It was not so much an examination, as a bullying session. Like the wicked uncles in the fairy tales, they threatened her with imprisonment if she went to the grotto again. They had got as far as magnifying this into a threat of death, when the sister superior of her school came in and heard them. She was far more upset than Bernadette – who remained calm and cool – and burst into tears, begging for the custody of the child. This was granted, and Bernadette's powerful opponents were forced to pass the buck by making a report to the attorney-general at Pau. Unwittingly, these determined men acted as the lady's emissaries in spreading the news of her appearance wider still.

The fortnight of visits which the lady had asked Bernadette to make was drawing to a close, and on the Monday she gave her a proof of her love. Bernadette had taken an elaborate rosary to the grotto to oblige an invalid lady too ill to go there, who begged her to use her beads. After she had begun to tell them, the lady asked where her own were. Bernadette took them from her pocket and the lady indicated that she would prefer her to use those. So it seemed she had singled her out, after the public pronouncements, for a private intimacy.

At some time during the fortnight – quite when, she would never divulge – the lady entrusted her with three secrets for herself alone. This was a bond between them that she clung to all her life.

Tuesday, 2nd of March, brought another public message, necessitating another visit to the terrifying Abbé Peyramale. This time she was accompanied by her aunts and mother. The request was that people should come to the grotto in procession. This brought an outburst from the curé, directed against Bernadette, accusing her of setting the whole town in ferment.

Bernadette pointed out that she had never asked anyone to follow her, but the abbé insisted that if the lady would not give her name, he could do nothing. This was uttered in a fit of rage, which appalled Bernadette into forgetting the rest of the message. She was hurried away by her relatives, but later her love recalled her, and accompanied by an older friend, she returned to the parish priest once more, and stammered out that the lady wanted a chapel, too –

'A little one', she added, in apology for the enormity of the demand.

The abbé's reaction was to issue a counter-demand that the lady must give her name. If she did so, the chapel would not be a small one; it would be a big one. With that Bernadette had to be content, though pressing the lady for her name yet again was a mission that lay heavy on her heart.

Worse still, the lady did not appear on Wednesday at dawn. She left the grotto in tears but, about nine o'clock, felt the interior attraction drawing her back, and was rewarded by the lady's return. She sent Bernadette to the curé once again with the request for a chapel. This time he was kindly, but adamant that the next move was up to the lady.

When the last day of the fortnight came – Thursday, 4th of March – the excitement was at its peak. It was market day, and people from the surrounding countryside were on their way to Lourdes before dawn, sure that something stupendous would happen. Some had waited there all night. Perhaps the lady would be visible to them, or show some extraordinary sign of her favour to Bernadette. The police and the military were out in force to control the expected throng. The grotto and the bank on the far side of the Gave were a seething mass of humanity. The crowd was estimated variously from eight to twenty thousand; there were certainly too many to count heads. Bernadette's ecstasy lasted longer than usual, but nothing remarkable happened. She bowed and smiled often, said her beads three times, made the wonderful sign of the cross that seemed to reflect the action of the lady when she made hers, and which would be remarked on for the rest of her life. Beyond that – nothing.

Yet people felt they had been in the presence of something unworldly, and for two hours Bernadette was besieged in her home, where an upper room had been made available to her, by people who wanted to touch or embrace her. Then she dared to go back to Abbé Peyramale, to remind him – as if he could have forgotten – of the lady's request. His answer was the same:

'Get the lady to tell you her name.'

But the lady had made no promise to return. No wonder that, tired out and unhappy, the little girl ended the day in tears.

And there, thought the mayor and the public prosecutor, and the police commissioner, and all the unconverted intelligentsia, the phenomena would cease. There had been no terrible accident on the slippery slopes of the Massabielle – no untoward dispute among the crowd – no evidence of Bernadette's family exploiting the situation for gain... Nothing more would be heard of the matter.

Bernadette went back to school, and by all accounts was

the life and soul of the playground, when her health permitted. But candles began to be lighted at the grotto. A statue of the Blessed Virgin appeared, despite the lady's refusal to meet Abbé Peyramale's challenge and identify herself. Rumours began to circulate about the spring: cures were attributed to the water. Bernadette kept away from the grotto, but the people of Lourdes did not. A stern note was received by the prefect of the Hautes-Pyrenees from the minister of education and public worship, demanding information about the incidents at Lourdes. News of the lady had reached the seat of government in Paris.

On the 25th of March, the feast of the Annunciation, Bernadette felt the call of her beloved again. When she arrived at the grotto at five o'clock in the morning, the lady was already there. For Bernadette the reunion was rapturous. She was emboldened to ask the lady's name again – not once, but three times. Twice came the usual bow and smile. Then, opening her arms and lowering them in a gesture that embraced all present, she said:

'I am the Immaculate Conception.'

Bernadette heard the words in her native *patois*, but did not understand them. She had to repeat them all the way to the curé's house in order not to forget, like a child repeating a shopping list with unfamiliar items. She could not greet the curé, but blurted out the stupendous title – then had to explain it was not herself she meant, but that this was what the lady had said to her. Abbé Peyramale was, of course, perfectly aware that three years earlier Pope Pius IX had formalised the doctrine that the Mother of God was conceived without sin. Seeing that Bernardette had no understanding of what she had said, he dismissed her without any explanation. No doubt he needed time to think.

The result of his deliberations was a qualified retraction of his previous position. He did not oppose the setting up of an altar in the grotto, and agreed to receive for the poor any money deposited at it. Bernadette had to submit to an examination by three doctors, who decided that although they discovered no physical or mental abnormalities, she had probably been the victim of hallucinations.

Easter came and went, marked by great devotion on the

part of the townsfolk. They included visits to the grotto in their pious fervour, as did several thousand strangers. But it was not until the 7th of April that Bernadette felt her own mysterious inner call. It was marked by the curious incident of the candle she carried, which slipped down and flickered against her wrist. The local doctor, who was standing by her, could find no mark of burning, and she herself was quite oblivious to the occurrence. Yet when the vision had left her, the medical man tried the experiment of putting the candle-flame near her left hand, and she drew back, exclaiming:

'You are burning me!'

While she went on trying to learn the catechism with painful slowness, the authorities had been busy, emptying the grotto of its improvised altar and bric-a-brac of pious devotees. After an attempt to find out if the miraculous spring had any mineral qualities that might establish the town as a spa – which was scotched by the investigating chemist – the mayor forbade access to it, and had barricades erected. He found this necessary because the cult had been latched on to by fraudulent 'visionaries' who had brought the place into disrepute. There was some talk of removing Bernadette to a hospital, but she found a champion in (of all people) the Curé of Lourdes, whose reputation prevented any action on the part of the civic authorities.

On Friday, the 16th of July, Bernadette had one more brief visit from Our Lady – as she could now call her. The planks of the municipal barrier were high, and she had to view their meeting place from afar, but she was unconscious of this. By now she had made her first holy communion, and when asked what gave her greater pleasure – receiving Our Lord or seeing his mother – she replied wisely:

'I don't know: the two things go together, and can't be compared. All I know is that I was intensely happy in both cases.'

This answer, like all the others in the interrogations that followed, bears the mark of simple truth.

One of these interrogations was conducted by no less a person than the governess to the prince imperial. Bernadette had to have an interpreter, as she could still not speak French, but Madame Bruat was impressed with her, and carried back a favourable report to the empress. Louis Napoleon himself intervened in the matter of access to the grotto; there was great rejoicing amongst the people of Lourdes as the barriers were taken down.

The Bishop of Tarbes had set up an episcopal commission to enquire into the events at the Massabielle. Bernadette was the principal witness, and everyone wanted to hear from her own lips the story of the apparitions. She told it again and again, always with a simple dignity, as if it had all happened to someone else. Her health began to give rise to anxiety, and as winter drew on she was sent away to a spa. She returned much recovered and was confirmed in the February of the following year. There remained the problem of what to do with her. The visitors to her home tired her with their questions. even the birth of a new brother, Bernard-Pierre, to whom she was godmother, could not outweigh the disadvantages of being at everyone's beck and call. Eventually, in 1860, Peyramale arranged with the nuns who had taught her that she should be taken into the hospice as a boarder. She was sixteen and a half years old.

At the hospice she learned arithmetic and sewing, and how to read and write in French. She did not lose her high spirits, and was still capable of the small irreverences to her teachers that were common to her age. Popular with everyone, she chose to be indistinguishable from her companions. Only her devotion remained remarkable, and the graciousness of her signs of the cross learned from the vision and never forgotten. She did not escape visitors, but these were monitored by the nuns. They also saw to it that she was able to visit her beloved grotto, and light a candle, and relive the great days.

Two years later, in 1862, the episcopal commission published its findings. The full weight of the Church came down on the side of the lady. It was declared that the Blessed Virgin Mary had appeared to Bernadette Soubirous, and that the cures at the spring were incapable of natural explanation: that visits to the grotto were efficacious to faith, and that devotion to Our Lady of the Grotto of Lourdes was permissible. And Our Lady was to have her chapel, with the active cooperation of the Bishop of Tarbes. All Bernadette's commissions from the lady were to be accomplished.

But what was to become of the messenger, now that the message had been delivered? Though she must have felt vindicated for her faithfulness to the lady, she had not been promised happiness in this life, and she did not achieve it.

For Bernadette, the coming of spring did not bring relief. She suffered from rheumatism, bronchitis and violent attacks of asthma. At one point, when pneumonia was diagnosed, her life seemed to be in danger, but after a few sips of water from the grotto she made a full recovery. For four years more she was to be with the sisters in Lourdes, moving up to the top class with the daughters of the wealthiest families, yet quite capable of turning to and helping in the kitchen when her health permitted.

There were still visitors. One was the sculptor commissioned to carve a fine statue of Our Lady in Carrara marble, to occupy the niche in the grotto where the lady's delicate feet had rested. As always, Bernadette cooperated with his enquiries, and astounded him with the radiance with which she reproduced the attitude of the vision, when she announced her name. Ever truthful, she gave her verdict on the finished statue:

'Ah, it's beautiful,' she said. 'But it isn't her...'

For many reasons, it was decided that it would be a good thing if she had a vocation to become a nun, but the sisters did not press her. She had been asked if any of the three secrets with which she had been entrusted by her heavenly visitor concerned this subject, but her silence was complete. If her own guardians were reticent, the same cannot be said of other orders, who were anxious to have her in their congregations, and were not above attempts at recruitment. She rejected their well-meant efforts to attract her by trying their habits on her; she poked mild fun at them, and sent them away. When the Bishop of Nevers called to sound her out about her possible vocation, she pleaded poverty and her chronic illness as barriers to her joining any order. The sisters of Nevers – the order that maintained the hospice – were reluctant to accept her, but when the bishop pointed out the propriety of the step, they said they would entertain a request if she made it to them. Still Bernadette awaited the direction of Our Lady herself.

She took a further two years to deliberate, and finally, in

1866, two momentous events took place. The consecration of the completed crypt of the chapel in the grotto took place on the eve of Whitsun, and on Whit Monday a great mass was attended by thousands of worshippers, many of whom had travelled by the newly-opened railway from Bordeaux. Lourdes was en fete, with triumphal arches over the streets, and Bernadette was in the procession, walking with the Children of Mary. In spite of her attempts to hide herself amongst her companions, she was mobbed; in an excess of religious fervour, admirers even tried to snip off pieces of her veil. Bernadette was scathing about this pop-star treatment, and described it as idiotic. She must however have relished the silence and reverence at the elevation, when it was reported that there was no sound but the ripple of the river. Great changes had been made to accommodate the crowds, levelling and paving the ground, and she was hard put to it to recognise the spot where she had seen the first apparition.

But it was still the place where she had experienced some of the bliss of heaven, and when – having been accepted for the novitiate of the congregation of Nevers – she visited it for the last time on the 3rd of July, she shed tears of grief, and could hardly bear to leave. Her family were sad to part with her, especially since they had been bereaved of all the children who had been born while Bernadette was boarding at the hospice. She comforted them, and reminded them that she could not stay in Lourdes for ever. While she was there, she had become a kind of pious peep-show. She once complained jokingly that she was paraded like a strange animal. She hoped to find in the mother house at Nevers a peaceful anonymity.

To understand the attitude of her superiors, especially the mistress of novices, Mother Marie-Thérèse Vauzou, it is necessary to mention that they had before them the awful warning of the case of Melanie Calvet, the visionary of La Salette, who had also been entrusted with a message from Our Lady. She had become a member of a community in Grenoble in 1853, just five years before Bernadette's great days. Melanie, like Bernadette, had become the object of near-veneration by very distinguished people. Unlike Bernadette, this adulation had made her act in a prima-donna fashion on occasion: so much so, that the Bishop of Grenoble had refused to allow her to take her annual vows when the time came. Too proud to stay in the novitiate, she had left the convent. There was a mutual agreement that this failure must not be allowed to occur in the case of Bernadette.

To satisfy the curiosity of the community once and for all, she was summoned to give an account of the apparitions. Thereafter, the subject was forbidden. After being a postulant for three months, during which time she was treated exactly like the rest, she was clothed, and received in religion her baptismal name of Marie-Bernarde. Her novitiate was interrupted by a bad bout of bronchitis, and she spent months in the infirmary. Repeated coughing brought on a haemorrhage, and once again her life was despaired of. When the doctor said she would not last through the night, her request to take her vows was allowed. The Bishop of Nevers presided at the bedside ceremony. The experience was a physical as well as a spiritual tonic, and she made a recovery.

From then on, her relationship with the novice mistress deteriorated. Mother Marie-Thérèse Vauzou was from a professional family, and seems not to have understood the girl, born of poor parents, and academically backward. She regarded her as good for nothing, and told her so; but in fact she became acting infirmarian and pharmacist, and showed real aptitude for the work. According to Mother Marie-Thérèse, she could do nothing right. There seemed to be a real incompatibility of temperament. Mother Marie-Thérèse liked her charges to be confiding; many discovered that beneath her cool exterior was a heart of gold. Sister Marie-Bernarde had great reserve, and the secrets Our Lady had entrusted to her were scrupulously guarded. She had not feared the policemen and lawyers in Lourdes, but she was in awe of the Mother Superior of the convent, and Mother Marie-Thérèse Vauzou who succeeded her, regarding them as instruments of God. At their hands, she suffered much.

With her contemporaries in the religious life, she was a much-loved companion, mimicking the foibles of the visiting doctor with accuracy and wit, and making them laugh until they cried at recreation. At the stroke of the bell heralding the great silence, she became the sober, recollected nun again.

She sang songs in her native *patois* to amuse her patients. Yet deep within her she carried a cross. Our Lady did not spare her a dark night of the soul, when she felt unsure that she could ever love her bridegroom enough. She once described herself as the broom that Our Lady had used and then put back behind the door.

After a spell as assistant sacristan, in which she was able to demonstrate her skill as a needlewoman, even these lighter duties proved impossible, and she became a permanent patient in the infirmary.

To a nun who rallied her with: 'What are you doing there, you lazy little thing?' she replied: 'Doing my job.'

Asked what this was, she answered: 'Being ill.'

She offered up all her pain, her attacks of breathlessness and vomiting, for sinners – a spirit of penance that led back to the time when Our Lady had called for it in the Massabielle. She had a card, with the times of masses being offered in all parts of the world, pinned to the curtains of her bed, so that during sleepless nights she could be joined with them. At the last, she suffered great agony in every part of her body, yet she insisted that Lourdes was not for her. She died on the 16th of April 1879, in the thirty-sixth year of her age. In the final months of her illness, she had affirmed – in almost the same words as in her youth – the apparitions made to her twenty years before. This was at the request of the Bishop of Tarbes, and with the authorisation of the Pope.

Thirty years later, her cause was initiated, and there was no lack of miracles attributed to her intercession, or testimony to the sanctity of her life, for she had impressed everyone with her honesty, simplicity and devotion.

Even Mother Marie-Thérèse Vauzou, who ended her days in Bernadette's hometown, came on her death-bed to have a devotion to Our Lady of Lourdes, though the memory of Bernadette continued to plague her. But there was no dissentient voice when, on the feast of the Immaculate Conception in 1933, Bernadette was canonized by Pope Pius XI. In addition to the customary *Te Deum*, the *Ave Maria* was sung, just as in Lourdes. Her feast is celebrated on the anniversary of her death, 16th April.

* * *

The little pilgrim had pushed the wheelchair of her benefactress all over the town. She was very tired, and her chest
felt tight, but she would not hand over the task to anyone else.
It was her payment for the bliss of these days in Lourdes, the
first holiday of her life.

As the torches flared, lighting up the niche where the statue
of Our Lady stood, she joined in the singing with her breathy
little voice. Like Bernadette before her, she felt rich and highly
favoured.

Of such is the kingdom of heaven.

St Catherine of Siena

he had pulled all the strings she knew to get on the committee examining the new Abortion Bill. She felt she owed it to the handicapped child who had brightened her existence during his brief life. In spite of the grief his birth had caused her, she remembered it all these years later as a happy experience.

Her marriage had not been an easy one. Her husband was in the Navy, and away a great deal. She had been warned that it would be difficult for her to conceive, and this had aroused an obstinate determination in her to try, and go on trying, and this in turn had put a great strain on the relationship. When their prayers were answered, she entered on her pregnancy full of joy.

Then the scan had revealed abnormality, and she had been offered an abortion. They talked it over and came to the same conclusion. Their baby had a right to life. She had never regretted the decision, even though it meant staying at home full time, and having to be always within easy reach of doctors and hospitals. She had cherished every limited movement her son had been able to make, and the radiant smiles which had transformed the little face that had never been ugly to her. When well-meaning friends had hinted that, as he would probably die young, it might have been better for him not to be born, she had felt first anger and then pity.

It was in her initial grief after his death that her public life had begun. She formed a self-help group for other couples who had lost children. She had found a voice, and learned to use it persuasively. Almost as a test of herself, she stood for the local council, acquiring a taste for politics. Her husband had encouraged her, knowing she was unlikely to have another child. She saw that by going further and becoming a parliamentary candidate she could serve the cause of needy and disabled children in a larger sphere.

Her first opportunity had come in a by-election. The media, lacking news-fodder at the time, had looked for an angle and found it in her story. From being a no-hope chance, she had become a favourite, though some groups hearing her views gave her a hard time – even her Irish ancestry became an issue. She had to make alliances with people she disliked and disapproved of, but she never hid her faith, or her intention to put it at the forefront of her thinking. By polling day her name was known to people she could never have reached by vigorous campaigning. When the result was declared, and she had won by a slim majority, she pledged herself to serve the constituency, particularly the children.

The place on the committee was her next big objective. To those who accused her of emotional bias she adopted a tone of reasoned argument. When she needed to appeal to the heart, she would do that too. She was amazed to discover, in the letters of St Catherine of Siena, that the great doctor of the Church had adopted similar tactics. She found in Catherine's intense political preoccupation a chord that struck her, and she appealed to her:

'St Catherine – stand by me.'

* * *

Several elements conspired to overthrow the faith of the Middle Ages in the mid-fourteenth century. One was the war between England and France which dragged on for most of that time and ensured that they could never combine to defeat the ravaging Turks, firmly entrenched in the Holy Land and on the edges of Europe. Secondly, the popes had left their natural habitat in Rome, and were resident in Avignon under the influence of various French monarchs, thus leaving the warring Italian states with no unifying centre. The third, and perhaps the most devastating and insidious in its effects, was the Great Plague carried by infected rats on ships from the East. It arrived in Italy through the great ports of Venice and Genoa, and in France through Marseilles. The contagion spread quickly to every part of the continent, leaping the seas in trading vessels. No respecter of persons, it decimated rich and poor alike, causing the break-up of the feudal system in which every man knew the responsibilities of his station, and the monastic system which had maintained the authority of the Church. This devastation occurred in a single year – 1348 – when Catherine Benincasa was a year old.

She was one of the youngest of twenty-five children born in the city-state of Siena to Jacopo Benincasa and his wife, Monna Lappa. The cruel statistics of infant mortality at the time were borne out by the fact that barely half the family survived. Nevertheless it was by any standards a large and busy household. Jacopo plied his trade as a dyer in workshops attached to their living quarters. He presided over an assortment of apprentices and journeymen, and owned a farm and a vineyard in the country, so there was no shortage of food and wine. As a burgher of Siena, which was ruled by a committee of the people – the noble families were excluded unless expressly granted bourgeois status – he had a voice in the government of his city. As if his own family were not large enough, he adopted an orphan boy, Thomas Della Fonte, nine years older than Catherine, who had lost his relatives in the plague. It was not his only work of charity; he also had a forgiving spirit. When he was unjustly accused of not paying a debt, to avoid trouble he paid it over again. In an age when almost anything could be turned into a family feud, this was considered remarkable.

Monna Lappa's father had some pretensions to being a poet; she, however, had more of Martha than Mary in her character, and devoted all her energies to providing for her family, which she dominated with a sharp tongue. Firmness and practicality were the qualities that led to her success in her role.

Catherine gained the nickname of Euphrosyne, a tribute to

her merry spirit as a child. Her adopted brother – who had more patience with her than her natural siblings – was her favourite. When she was six he found he had a vocation to the priesthood, and the Benincasa, grudging no help they could give him, helped him to enter a Dominican novitiate. This seems to have had a profound effect on the little girl. From the kind of piety that is half play – saying one 'Hail Mary' for each step in the flight that led down from the street into the house – she became altogether more thoughtful. Spiritual experience amongst young children is probably less rare than is usually imagined: they are naturally secretive and occasionally inarticulate. It was not until much later that Catherine managed to explain what happened to her on the way back from visiting her married sister, Bonaventura. She was with her brother Stefano, and they were looking out for the familiar landmark, St Dominic's church, which was near their home. When it came into view, Catherine saw above it some kind of heavenly vision. She stood transfixed while her brother, seeing nothing, urged her on. Whether or not it was a childish wonder at her first conscious view of sunset clouds, she became convinced that she had seen the figure of Our Lord, greeting her with a priestly blessing. She certainly burst into tears when the vision left her, and her behaviour underwent a marked change.

She became quieter, seeking the solitude so difficult to find in the busy house. This had the effect of infuriating her mother, robbed of a potential pair of hands to help ease her own burden. Monna Lappa began to make demands on her small daughter, keeping her occupied with tasks suitable to her age. Outwardly conforming, Catherine was inwardly rebellious, once running away to 'become a hermit' in a cave; and on another occasion contemplating cutting off her one claim to beauty, the gold-brown hair that was the fashionable colour, in order to follow her beloved Thomas into a monastery, disguised as a boy. Her fantasies never took the form of simply becoming a nun.

This tolerable life of childhood vanished when she reached puberty. Like all the girls in Siena of a similar age, she could not set foot outside the house alone. Worse still – there was talk of marriage, which Monna Lappa considered the real vocation of her daughters. Such discussion filled Catherine with horror; it was not in the least what she had in mind for the future. Then when she was fifteen her favourite sister and confidante Bonaventura died suddenly. Too late in the family to have known death amongst her siblings, Catherine was devastated by her grief. And Bonaventura was not there to add her softer counsels when a definite suitor for her hand appeared. She was vehement in her absolute refusal to marry him, or anyone else.

The family turned to their priest son, Thomas Della Fonte, and asked him to use his office, and her affection for him, to impose their will. He seems to have thought of Catherine as the child he had left behind, not the obstinate adolescent she had become. Yet the passion in her resolution touched him. He agreed that she should not marry unless she wished to, but when he expressed what seemed to him the only alternative, she surprised him by refusing to become a nun either. She protested that she wanted to remain at home and make her own rules for serving God. How should she impress this on the family? Father Della Fonte caught sight of her golden hair – the dressing of which had become a bone of contention between Monna Lappa and her daughter – and jokingly suggested she should cut it off, to convince them that she meant business.

She did so instantly, hacking away at it inexpertly. Then, overcome by her own temerity, she covered her head with a veil, fearing the consequences of what she had done. These were not long in coming. Monna Lappa excelled herself in her choice of curses. Her brothers and sisters teased her as cruelly as only members of the same family can. Her father was deeply disappointed to see a beloved child's disfigurement. It was decided that she would lose the last stronghold of her privacy – her single room – and share with Stefano, so that he could keep an eye on her. Then her mother dismissed the servant who waited on the family at meal times, and gave Catherine her work. The other children sent her to Coventry except when issuing orders. Meanwhile Monna Lappa reminded her constantly that when her hair grew again, she should marry, whether she liked it or not.

Only Catherine appreciated the situation. She was following a Master who was the servant of all, and here she was, doing a servant's work, despised and rejected as he had been. The Benincasa were not the first to discover that it is impossible to humiliate those who choose to follow Our Lord as closely as that.

Deliverance came when her father entered the shared room while she was praying. Something in her attitude moved him; he beat a hasty retreat, and rescinded his previous orders. Catherine was restored to the bosom of her family, and the little room she cherished so dearly. It was not much larger than a prison cell, but to her it spelled freedom.

Her mother became increasingly solicitous, fearing that she was depriving herself of food and sleep – as indeed she was. She feared that her child was sickening for something – the worst fear of every mother – and after a fruitless visit to some thermal baths, her fears were confirmed: Catherine was suffering from smallpox. Monna Lappa nursed her devotedly, and was willing to accede to her desire to become a Dominican Tertiary if she would only get well.

Most of the other members of the Third Order were elderly or widowed, pledged to daily recitation of the Divine Office, rules of fasting and abstinence, the observance of rising for matins at 3 a.m, and praying twice in the night during Lent and Advent. This was no more than Catherine had already imposed on herself. The chief advantage from her point of view was the freedom conferred by the religious habit she would wear. She overcame the reluctance of the Prioress to consider her on account of her youth: her pock-marked face was enough to ensure that she was unlikely to be offered the temptation of a light and worldly life. When she recovered, she made her submission, and obtained her heart's desire. Her reception of the habit was a symbol of a status that owed nothing to family, or husband, but was peculiarly her own. The next step was to find God's will for her, and this she set out to do.

No mistress of novices in the order would have suggested the regime she marked out – would indeed have discouraged it. She made no concessions to human frailty, as the founders of monastic orders had always done. What she did, she did alone, and we must admit that she made mistakes; but these were more than rectified by her sincerity of purpose, and it must be believed that God turned them to his glory in the end.

We have to remember that she was sixteen – an age when extravagances of emotion are common. And she was in love with religion, and prepared to give up everything that did not feed that love. She became to all intents and purposes a hermit, never leaving her room except to go to church. The room was shuttered against the distractions of the street outside. Her food was restricted to bread and water and bitter herbs – and not always the bread and water. So she laid down the foundation of the anorexia that was to be with her for life. Sleep was confined to a bare half-hour every other day, lying fully clothed on a plank bed. She never spoke except to make her confession.

In vain Father Della Fonte pleaded with her to restrain her austerities. He was a good priest, but neither experienced nor especially gifted in argument, and Catherine's will to suffer was in a class of its own. She experienced the rewards of her devotion – heady visions and ecstasies. It was also her lot to be tempted by unholy desire natural to her youth. Her answer to that was to redouble her penances. It was when her ecstasies became public after receiving communion at St Dominic's that the friars and other tertiaries began to be disturbed. She would lie rigid and unresponsive for hours afterwards, and became a spectacle for the small boys of Siena, who would kick her inert body. When her communions were stopped because she was giving scandal, she prayed to be delivered from the ecstasies, except those experienced in private. And her prayers to be allowed communion sometimes were not granted. The young recluse was talked about, and the possibility of fraud suspected. The Middle Ages were not more credulous than our own, and the sceptics of the day were united against Catherine.

If her ardent spirit experienced the heights of religious experience, she also knew the depths. There were times when she doubted herself and her beliefs; when prayer seemed empty and God far away.

She longed to be able to read the Scriptures to give her strength. She broke her vow of silence in order to ask to be taught to read. Even that was criticised; it was not considered

111

proper for a woman to learn Latin. She laboured away, at first without success, then one day she was studying a manuscript, and suddenly the words made sense to her – though she never mastered writing and spelling. The psalms struck an instant chord with her, and in St Paul's epistles she found a great friend and companion.

The novitiate lasted some three years, coming to a climax when the rest of Siena was celebrating Shrove Tuesday. Her family had joined the noisy merry-making in the streets, and she was alone. It seemed to her that her room was filled with a vision of all the company of heaven. In a mystical ceremony, she was betrothed as a bride of Christ, who promised her that she would never lose her faith again. The joy she experienced was short-lived. A few days later she was given a divine call to go out into the world. She who had willed herself to retreat from it was now commanded to surrender herself and serve the will of God through her neighbour. She felt great reluctance to leave her solitary life, but she obeyed the call – instantly, as was her custom.

Her family were sharing a meal when she came quietly to join them. It had changed in composition during her absence. Married sisters had left, and her brothers' wives had joined the household. In one of these – Lisa, the wife of her half-brother Bartolomeo – she found a sympathetic ally. She needed one, because the others found her uneasy company. What were they to make of someone who would fall into ecstasy in the middle of a domestic chore? Lisa, who came of a family of good standing in Siena, would pick up the cleaning or cooking or laundry-work where Catherine had left off.

Not that Catherine was a passenger. Because she did not now spend much time in sleep, she worked through the night at the never-ending task of keeping the house tidy. She had a feeling for order and cleanliness, and her willingness and rapidity made her worth a host of paid servants. Her father put almsgiving into her hands, and she dispensed it so liberally that her mother complained the larder was always empty. She was even more generous with her own few possessions, giving away her cloak to a beggar. This was hastily retrieved, since going without a cloak was the mark of a prostitute. When this was pointed out to her – 'I would rather go without

112

a cloak than without charity,' was her serene reply. This flouting of convention was typical of her.

Dominican tertiaries had a special devotion to visiting the sick, and Catherine took to nursing with her usual energy. She worked in all the hospitals of Siena, gaining respect for the quality of her skill. Against her mother's wishes, she even nursed lepers, in their secluded house outside the city, choosing a patient notable for her cantankerousness, who abused her while accepting her services. Her mother, like most of the Sienese, feared the infection and forbade her to go, but she persisted until her patient died, repentant at last. She performed the grisly business of burying the corpse, whereupon an eruption on her hands, which had confirmed Monna Lappa's worst fears, cleared up as if by a miracle.

Inevitably, with the return to the world, came an exposure to local politics. In 1367 her brother Bartolomeo became a member of The Twelve – the rulers of the city. According to custom his period of office was only two months, but the standing of the Benincasa rose, and we may be sure that Catherine, with her quick mind, absorbed many of the conversations that took place around her, and formed her own conclusions on political questions. Talk was also rife in this year about the return of Pope Urban V from Avignon to his see in Rome. Catherine, like everyone in Italy who supported the move, must have hoped that this might bring a peaceful influence to bear on the warring Italian states.

The following year her father died, and she nursed him in his last illness. She had always found him more sympathetic than her mother, and the bond was strengthened by her vision of his soul entering heaven. Any sadness she could have felt at the loss of an understanding parent was made up for by new friends she acquired. Some of these had been critical of her independence, and had accused her of hypocrisy, but criticism did not long survive a first meeting with her. These friends included prominent theologians as well as humble priests, and women from the most notable families. To each of them she made a direct personal approach, persuading them to reform their lives. The proud became humble, and the poor in spirit gained confidence in her company.

The hope that Urban V might bring peace was short lived.

The emperor Charles IV, King of Bohemia, passed through Siena on his way to meet Urban in Rome. This was a signal for the aristocratic families to gather their forces and attack the government of the people. Both sides appealed to the emperor who came down on the side of the people, but left hastily for Rome, leaving chaos behind him. The government split into factions that skirmished with one another. When Charles returned he made things no better, despite gaining authority by having been crowned in Rome. The whole city turned against him and he was easily bribed into removing his troops. Left to themselves, the warring factions carried on their futile tactics. The streets ran with the blood of armed men, and the hospitals filled with the wounded. This went on for over a year. At one point Catherine had to lead her brothers to a place of safety in one of the hospitals, and put them in the charge of the rector who was a friend of hers.

Urban became sickened with turbulent, hostile Italy, and longed for France, where he eventually returned; in spite of many embassies to persuade him to stay, including the intercessions of Princess Bridget of Sweden (later St Bridget) and the poet Petrarch. He did not survive more than a few months in Avignon and was succeeded by Gregory XI, who was a firmer character; and hope rose again among Catherine's friends in Siena. It was reported to them that the new pope had approached the King of England, the Duke of Flanders and the Doge of Venice to join in a crusade against the Turks. This was preached and promoted throughout Europe, and Catherine saw it as the one hope of uniting Christendom.

Just before this, her friends had been thrown into a state of shock by reports of her death. When they reached her house, she certainly seemed to be lifeless, and they began to mourn. Four hours later she assumed her normal appearance, but was overcome by grief at having to return to the body after an existence outside it in which she experienced what she described as 'the hidden things of God'.

But now all her thoughts were on the crusade. She began a flood of letters to her increasingly influential acquaintances, backing it to the hilt. It must be remembered that to fight in a crusade brought spiritual benefits. Catherine was severely practical in her care for souls. She knew that some of the

114

people she approached were incurably bellicose. Her object was that they should fight – if fight they must – for a good cause. One of them at least sent to her door no less than an emissary from Bernabo Visconti, Lord of Milan – a man famous for his opposition to the papacy. He had once forced the late Urban V, when an abbot, to eat a bull of excommunication he was about to serve on him, seals and all. Yet this obdurate character sent to Catherine for her advice. She treated him to it, as she did everyone else, without fear or favour. She urged on him the duty of respecting priests because they alone had power to administer the sacraments, and reminded him that the source of the pope's power derived from the inspiration of the Holy Spirit. Then, and only then, did she introduce the subject of the crusade as a means of atoning for the sins of his past life.

Her fame grew, and could not help but bring her to the notice of the Master General of the Dominican order. Here she was, a mere tertiary, the daughter of a dyer, being consulted by the highest in the land. Even in Siena she had been reviled; her fasting gave scandal, though she protested it was involuntary and that food made her ill. Enemies insisted it was no business of hers to preach the crusade. Even her ecstasies were suspect: the Church does not like presumption, even in its saints. So she was summoned to a general chapter of the order in Florence, in May 1374. The result of the examination of her case was that no restrictions were placed upon her, but a reliable member of the order, Raimondo Delle Vigne of Capua, was appointed as her confessor and director.

He was an aristocrat, deeply learned and pious. Furthermore, he was cautious where she was impetuous; he weighed his words, while hers flowed freely. At first their relationship had its teething-troubles. He reserved his judgement about the value of her mission. The very energy of her conversation sent him to sleep whereupon she woke him, asking:

'Am I talking to the walls or to you?'

The force of her personality wore him down, and he endeared himself to her by allowing her to receive communion whenever she wished. Soon he was preaching the crusade with almost her own enthusiasm. It seemed that no one could resist her for long.

When they returned to Siena, the plague had broken out. Even Catherine's preoccupation with the crusade was forgotten as the pestilence spread. She sought out the sick and nursed them. These included her half-brother Bartolomeo, and six nephews and nieces, all of whom succumbed to the disease. Delle Vigne looked as if he would become another victim, but Catherine prayed over him, and his life was spared.

When autumn came and the plague abated, Catherine's letters about the crusade began again. She dictated them to a young poet, Neri Di Landoccio, who had been of her inner circle for some three years, and had been converted by her from a frivolous and dissolute life. She wrote to anyone she thought would be useful – the English mercenary Hawkswood, who was a feared and noted participant in the inter-city wars of Italy; the notorious Queen Joanna of Naples, popularly supposed to have murdered her first husband, and who, by the age of fifty, had acquired three more. Catherine had been attracted to her because one of her titles was 'Queen of Jerusalem', and to her she sent the usual summons to a holy war. Intrigued by the directness of her approach, they all composed gracious replies.

In January 1375 she was invited to Pisa, where the streets filled to welcome her, and the common people flocked to kiss her hand. When Delle Vigne accused her of enjoying this form of adulation, she protested:

'But I didn't even see how they saluted me; I was so interested in them.'

This interest was repaid by a host of conversions, and Father Delle Vigne and her adopted brother Father Della Fonte were kept busy hearing confessions all day, as the priests of Pisa were overwhelmed. In spite of the sceptics, the body of the faithful behaved as if she were already canonised. She was overjoyed when Father Delle Vigne received a bull from Pope Gregory with instructions to begin organising the crusade. At last things were moving on to the practical plane where she felt at home.

Not that her spiritual life was neglected in all this planning. She prayed as fervently as she had done in the old days, alone in her room in Siena. One morning in April 1375, after making her communion at a mass celebrated by Delle Vigne, she seemed to be longer than usual in her thanksgiving. Father Delle Vigne noticed that she was gazing with great intensity at a crucifix painted on the wall. Then she fell inert into the arms of two of her female followers. When she came to herself, in excruciating pain, she whispered to Father Delle Vigne that she had received the stigmata. She felt near to death. Against her will, this was reported round the city. She had received the wounds as she meditated on the passion; they were invisible, but caused her pain – sometimes acutely – to the end of her life. Like St Francis, who received the same privilege, she seems to have been very reticent about it.

Gregory XI was a more decisive pope than his predecessor, but was no more happy in his choice of papal legates to the Italian cities. They were mostly French and out of sympathy with the aspirations of the city states, which began to band together against the papacy in a loose confederation that became known as the Tuscan League. Gregory decided to call Florence, the ringleader, to answer for its apostasy in Avignon. Catherine, as a committed Italian, knew that the behaviour of the papal legates had been provocative, though she held no brief for abandoning allegiance to the Holy See. She adopted her usual method of approach, by correspondence, pleading with Gregory to give the Italians worthy and acceptable prelates, and going on to press him to return to Rome and preach the crusade that would unite divided Christendom. At the same time she wrote to an influential friend in Florence, calling on him to make plain to the Florentines the dangers of putting themselves at odds with the vicar of Christ. She herself went to Lucca and Pisa to encourage them not to join the Tuscan League. She was welcomed in both cities, but was unable to achieve her objective, and they joined in March 1376.

Catherine marshalled her forces, and Delle Vigne was asked by the Florentines to intercede on their behalf with the pope. Their embassy had been ordered to appear before him at the end of the month, and Delle Vigne, bearing a letter from Catherine calling passionately for peace and reconciliation, arrived about the same time. On the 31st of March, a solemn assembly heard the Florentines' defence for their conduct. It was an arrogant and unrepentant catalogue of the crimes of

117

the papal legates. Gregory was stung to fury and issued a decree announcing the excommunication of the leaders of the war, the end of civil and religious rights for all Florentines throughout the world, and the forbidding of anyone, high or low, to have dealings with them. For a trading city, it was a death blow.

In Siena, Catherine was seething with impatience. She offered herself to Florence as a negotiator. With individuals she was patient, but officials drove her to tears of frustration. She sent the poet Neri to Avignon with yet another missive to 'the sweet Babbo' (as she called Gregory) begging for peace. It had no effect, and the edict against the Florentines began to be imposed.

In April she again offered herself personally to the Lords of Florence as a peacemaker. So often face-to-face contact with her had disarmed the most obdurate hearts, that she felt confident of success. With a papal army ready to invade them the Florentines were inclined to clutch at straws. They invited her to their city, which she found united politically, but the populace were mourning the loss of the sacraments, and were in the grip of a religious revival. Eventually the leaders acceded to her request to represent them – although unofficially – in Avignon. She set out with twenty-three of her followers and arrived at the papal court in June. The pope made her his guest in the city, and granted her an audience two days after her arrival.

It was a momentous meeting between the Dominican tertiary and the supreme pontiff. In a sense they knew each other through letters; hers, so certain of what he should do that she sounded almost arrogant – his, gentle and tender, asking for her opinion. He had lived always in the magnificence of the papal court, being the favourite nephew of Pope Clement VI. He had been made a cardinal at eighteen. He vacillated between extreme timidity and an obstinacy that made him impervious to reason. He was also of good personal character, and renowned for his learning. Catherine could barely read, and could not write, and spoke only in the Tuscan dialect. Delle Vigne took on the task of interpreting her words into Latin. Yet a direct dialogue did take place. The young woman (she was still only twenty-nine) had an eloquent face, and with her gift of intuition, seemed to understand the man at whose feet she knelt. He accepted that she should negotiate for peace with Florence, as long as she did not unduly compromise the honour of the Church.

As for returning to Rome, he had taken the decision to do it, and although his ardour for the crusade had cooled somewhat, it was still very much in his mind, depending on Catherine's success in making peace in Italy when the Florentine ambassadors arrived. They were expected within days. With this Catherine had to be content for the moment, though she did press her view that the crusade would help to unite the papacy and the Tuscan League. Then rumours began to circulate that Florence was levying heavy taxes on the clergy, and she wrote off in haste to the council of war in the city, telling them in no uncertain terms that they were being provocative in their turn, and the only hope of peace was to come in a penitential spirit to Avignon, and that their intransigence was spoiling her work on their behalf.

Six weeks went by with no sign of the Florentine ambassadors. Catherine became the latest novelty for the ladies of Avignon; they were frivolous and worldly, and flocked around her – and she hated every moment of it. It must have been a huge relief when the ambassadors arrived, but her hopes of peace were dashed as they utterly repudiated her. The pope, who was prepared to listen to her, would not interview them, and his attitude was summed up in his own words:

'Either I shall destroy Florence, or Florence will destroy Holy Church.'

It was Catherine's first outright rebuff, and she took it well, not berating anyone, and confining herself to a letter reproaching the city for ignoring her counsel – not because she was hurt, but because an opportunity for peace had been missed.

Gregory XI at last made some positive moves toward his journey to Rome. This frightened the French cardinals a good deal, and Louis of Anjou, the brother of the French king, came to Avignon to add his voice to those who counselled delay. But he met Catherine, and was speedily given something else to think about. She saw him as a potential leader of the crusade, and fired him with her enthusiasm. For his part, he

119

credited her with the ability to settle the war between England and France, which she brushed aside as a mere local dispute, only needing the announcement of the crusade to settle itself.

(It needed another heroic woman to take the major part in ending the English occupation – St Joan of Arc. However Catherine did send one of her letters to the King of France, urging him briskly to end the quarrel with England and get on with the real business of the crusade.)

Catherine's brusqueness with the ladies of Avignon had made her enemies. Some of them were related to men of influence in the Curia. Three of these arrived one day to examine her in doctrine. Despite their efforts they could find no fault in her interpretation. But Catherine was conscious that the papal army was ravaging the Italian cities, and that Gregory must lose no time in returning to Rome. It was a battle of wills between her and the cardinals, and her will was the stronger. She bombarded the wavering pope with letters, dismissing plots to kill him if he left Avignon as not worth considering. She made a concession to his timidity and advised what she called 'a holy deceit', telling him to depart without prior warning.

This he did, but his father gave the game away by throwing himself at his feet and imploring him not to go, having heard the popular rumour that he would be poisoned as soon as he got to Italy. Gregory, no doubt more afraid of Catherine's reproaches than his father's, stepped over his prostrate body.

Her mission accomplished, she and her companions set off for Siena, the pope and Louis of Anjou both contributing to their expenses. Other privileges accorded her were a portable altar-stone so that she could hear mass wherever she was; permission to work for the crusade, and to open a new convent – St Mary of the Angels, near Siena, in a dilapidated castle given her by an admirer. On the way home they were delayed by storms and illness. Catherine nursed the sick as she had always done, adding her prayers to her practical skills – though a long debate took place about the case of Neri, the poet, who was in such pain that he was forced to crawl on hands and knees. Asked by a friend to cure his distress, Catherine hesitated, on the grounds that if she died before him, the sensitive Neri would go to pieces, and she thought he would be better off in heaven now. The friend pleaded; she acceded to the request against her own judgement, and Neri recovered. But Catherine was not infallible; after her death he did have a bad breakdown, but again survived, living a holy life as a hermit. The incident shows Catherine at her toughest, and we do not wonder that she had enemies.

The pope fared no better on his journey, and must have looked back on the pleasant days in Avignon with regret. When he finally reached Corneto in the papal states, there was a Christmas letter from Catherine to greet him and urge him onward. It was not until January 1377 that he eventually received the rapturous welcome of the eternal city. A thousand musicians serenaded him, and the streets were carpeted with flowers. He was too tired to savour his triumph, and too apprehensive of what might happen when the fickle Romans came down to earth.

In understanding Catherine's attitude to war, we must remember that she experienced it at first hand, much as civilians in Africa and India and the Middle East do now – wars between tribes sharing the same faith. These were what saddened her, not the crusade against Islam, in which warriors fought each other, where the Christian dead earned salvation, and Moslems were offered a chance of conversion. It was not long before she was once again in demand as a peacemaker in a feud between two branches of a local family, the Salimbeni. This involved travelling to their castles deep in the country, and staying there for many months. While she was away the party in Siena that had always been suspicious of her influence prevailed upon the governors of the city to order her return home. This she flatly refused to do until her work was finished. The war between Tuscany and the papal army was still going on. She sent Delle Vigne with a letter to Gregory, imploring him to make peace, and again calling for the crusade. But without the magic of her presence, her appeals fell on deaf ears, and she was not given the courtesy of a reply. But when the peace with the Salimbeni was concluded, and she returned to Siena, she received an unexpected order to go to Florence, as Gregory's representative.

Unfortunately, when she arrived there, she got embroiled in the particularly dirty business of getting rid of local rulers –

who were prolonging the war – by 'admonishments'. These were denunciations of one official by another, for error or incompetence, and as in the McCarthy 'witch hunts' in America the system was open to all kinds of exploitation, including personal revenge. As soon as Catherine realised this, she spoke out against the practice, but her name had become associated with it, and the damage done. The members of the artisan class rose against the abusers of privilege, and rioting began throughout the city. A mob broke into the garden of the house where Catherine was staying, threatening to burn her as a witch.

She welcomed this chance for martyrdom passionately, running toward her persecutors and crying:

'Here I am!'

The weapons dropped from their nerveless hands, and they retreated; leaving her in tears, as being unworthy to die for peace.

But she had lost her friend, Pope Gregory XI, and his successor, Urban VI – an Italian, but a resident when the court was in Avignon – was an unknown quantity. Delle Vigne gave him one of Catherine's letters, couched in the same loving terms that she had used to Gregory, and urging the same objectives – peace, and the crusade. This time her prayers were answered; a courier was sent from Rome, and on the 18th of July 1378 rode into Florence bearing an olive branch. There was just one more insurrection by the populace, and then Florence entered into a more tranquil phase. Catherine was free to leave, but there was still a cloud over her name, and she was not bidden to the general rejoicings or given any official recognition of her work for peace.

Urban VI made himself thoroughly unpopular with the French cardinals, introducing reforms instantly and without tact. Catherine, when she heard of this, cautioned him to proceed slowly, without antagonizing anyone, and as a prudent measure to surround himself with men of good character whom he could trust, by creating enough new cardinals to outvote the French. All of this advice he ignored, with the result that the entire college of cardinals deserted him, proposing to hold a conclave to elect a new pope.

Catherine was devastated, and appealed to the secular

powers who were supporting the cardinals to desist. She also wrote scathingly to the cardinals themselves, declaring that they were corrupting the whole world. She pledged her support to the rightful pope, and said she would take her stand by his side in Rome. In preparation for this, she made arrangements for the organisation of her convent, St Mary of the Angels. She had no other legacy to make, but she then proceeded to produce a treasure that became, with her letters, the document on which was founded her reputation as a Doctor of the Church, and which has enriched the faith through succeeding centuries.

It is a dialogue between God and the human soul – and she dictated it to three of her followers, taking turns, in the course of four days. Into it she poured all her hard-won experience of God and his divine Son, the bridge between earth and heaven. There are several treatises, dealing with discernment, prayer, tears, divine providence and obedience. She who had striven for perfect love of God pointed out the impossibility of loving him enough, and the duty to love one's fellows in recompense. The men who wrote at her dictation were almost overwhelmed by her spate of words, sometimes spoken in a state of ecstasy. She described it afterwards as 'the book in which I found some recreation'; which sounds as if she counted it less than her efforts in the political sphere – a mere way of passing the time as she waited to hear from Rome. But it is an enduring memorial, as her political work was not, and has been the inspiration of souls ever since

The schism in the Church was complete, and the religious orders began to go over to the rival pope, Clement VII. It was said by her enemies that Catherine was contributing to the division by her championship of the unpopular Urban. It was even said that having one pope in Avignon was better than having two claimants to Peter's chair, and that Catherine's insistence on the return to Rome had resulted in the last state of the Church being worse than the first. That this would not have been so, if all her advice had been followed, weighed only with her closest friends, and they were dispirited. Yet they all wanted to go to Rome with her, and the choice of the party was difficult. Catherine looked forward to being united with her dear Father Delle Vigne, but their meeting was brief.

He was sent by Urban on an embassy to the King of France in an attempt to get him to take Urban's side. Catherine wept bitterly when she saw him off on his mission, for they had gone through a great deal together.

Her own mission was to rally everyone she knew to Urban's side. There was some talk of sending her to plead with Queen Joanna of Naples, who had declared for Clement, but although Catherine relished the thought of reclaiming such a notorious and influential sinner, it was judged that the route south was too dangerous. Delle Vigne found the way to France barred, and was the recipient of a stinging letter from Catherine, who did not shirk martyrdom for herself, and expected the same spirit in others. It was a time in which even her best friends seemed to have failed her. She spent a whole year, learning of their refusals for one reason or another to join her. For a woman of her strong loyalties and desire for action, it was deeply frustrating.

To this mental anguish were added physical infirmities. Yet still she managed her daily walks to worship in St Peter's; her letters rained continually on the commanders of the Urbanite armies, pleading with them to fight like Christian soldiers and not spare themselves. Her little community was composed of eight women, including her mother and sister-in-law, and sixteen men. The women looked to the housekeeping, undertaking their tasks on a weekly rota, so that the rest should be free for prayer or writing. Their needs were simple, as they ate only one frugal meal a day. They lived on alms contributed by well-wishers, and if these were not forthcoming, they begged in the streets. Catherine herself did not consider it beneath her.

She continued to advise Urban on every detail of his papacy, trying to persuade him to curb his hasty temper, or to go barefoot to St Peter's to celebrate one of his few victories. She sent her beloved poet Neri to the court of Naples in an attempt to pin down the vacillating queen to support the rightful pope. He at least, though reluctant, was faithful. Still the letters poured out to all the crowned heads of Europe, reminding them of their duty to the lawfully-elected Vicar of Christ. Round Urban spies multiplied, and Catherine heard of a plot to kill him. She was overwhelmed with horror, but when she wrote to him, it was to urge him not to provoke the Roman government by an angry denunciation. She always did her best to make a diplomat out of him. She was about to dictate another letter, this time to the cardinals, when her strength, which had been failing, finally gave out, and she fell to the floor unconscious, having suffered a stroke. It was the 30th of January 1380.

She wrote about the experience to Father Delle Vigne, who had been received back into her favour, comparing it with her previous experience of being out of the body; but while that had been blissful, this was terrifying. She had come through it by meditating on the Blessed Trinity. Her sufferings, she told him, she offered up for the good of the Church, and commanded the little fellowship – all of whom, from the oldest to the youngest, called her 'Mama' – to Delle Vigne's direction. She made particular mention of her writings, and left it to him to dispose of them as he thought fit, for the honour of God.

Somehow she managed to survive, hearing mass in the chapel of her house daily, and receiving communion, which was her only food. Nothing else passed her lips; not even water. Then she would make the mile-long walk to St Peter's, and stay there from tierce until vespers. She had particular devotion to a mosaic of Giotto and Cavallini in which St Peter was depicted being uplifted by Our Lord after his attempt to walk on the water. To her, this symbolized the frail figure of the successor of Peter, and the hope she had that Our Lord would uphold him. She was gazing at it one day when she had a second stroke and was paralysed from the waist down.

The little fellowship realised at last that the end was near. She was skin and bone, and racked with fever. They never left watching beside her plank bed which had boards put round it so it was very like a coffin. For a few days around Easter, her thirty-third birthday, she rallied a little, but it was a false hope. At dawn on Sunday, the 29th of April, her last agony began. Supported in the arms of one of her most faithful women friends, she received the plenary indulgence which was the gift of the pope she had served so faithfully. When she was anointed, she began to struggle, throwing up her arm as if to shield her face, and calling out:

'*Peccavi, Domine, miserere mei*' (I am a sinner, Lord, have mercy on me') – again and again.

After this she became calm and serene, sending messages to absent friends, including the faithful Neri. Then gradually her voice died away. Once she roused, repeating the word 'Blood' three times, then her head fell forward, and the heart that had bled indeed for the peace of the Church ceased to beat.

She had prevailed on two popes to reform the Church, and if they had been half the man she was, they would have done it. She had a dream of uniting Europe in a holy war that would have changed the face of the Middle East. She blazed a trail for women politicians like Indira Gandhi, Golda Meir and Margaret Thatcher, in an age when women who did not marry into the monarchy or become great abbesses were of no account. They share her strength of purpose and subtlety, if not her sanctity. That remains shining in the pages of her *Dialogues*, and in her letters; the documents of a fearless soul, who was no harder on anyone than she was on herself. These are her true and lasting monuments.

The pope himself planned her requiem mass, and she was buried in the church of Santa Maria sopra Minerva. Three years later Delle Vigne had the coffin opened. The head was reverently removed, carried in a casket to Siena, and placed in the church of St Dominic's where she had so devoutly worshipped. Her mother, who lived to a great age, was present. In 1461 Catherine was canonized by Pius II, her cause having been held up because of the schism. She was declared the patron of the Dominican order; her feast is on the 29th of April.

* * *

Was that the telephone — ?

She found herself straining to hear it all the time, though she tried very hard not to let it rule her life. Even the ordinary tasks – cooking and cleaning – could not take her mind off that important call. It was ridiculous to have made one thing so important. She could work for the Abortion Bill in so many ways. With sudden resolution she sat down at her word-processor and started to tap out her message. She would do what St Catherine had done, and send a letter to every influential person she could think of. Her whole attention was riveted on its composition, as she marshalled the arguments once again. It was a plea from the heart, and had the intensity of a prayer.

Dusk was falling when she finished, and she hurriedly snatched the print-outs from the machine and looked for her car-keys. There would not be much time to get to the Post Office. She wanted to send them off before the last post went. The stack of envelopes was ready. She realised she had worked for hours without thinking of so much as a cup of coffee.

As she went out of the door she heard the telephone. She felt almost impatient, so absorbed was she in the new enthusiasm. And then she thought:

'It might be...'

It was. The chief whip asked her if she would serve on the committee. She stammered her acceptance, trying to control her emotion. Her prayer of thanks was to the Saint who had inspired her.

St Thomas More

he summer storm was over. The rain had ceased to lash the windscreen, and the lightning flashes had retreated to the far horizon in the South African sky.

He would never get over the contrast between the bleakness of the township, and his own leafy suburb of Johannesburg. He travelled between them as little as he could; he was not a brave man. He wasn't even sure how he had become known as a lawyer who was prepared to defend black activists. His father had followed his grandfather into the legal profession, and he had never doubted that he would take the same route: it was in the blood. But while they had delighted in untangling the intricacies of land rights and gold concessions he had sunk deeper and deeper into the hot swamp of politics.

It had begun when an old girl-friend had sat on a 'Blacks only' bench in a park. It was so unheard-of in those days, she had trouble getting herself arrested. But it was while he was preparing her case for the magistrates' court that he'd started to go into the apartheid laws, and what he read of them appalled him. It had snowballed from there. A certain obstinacy, inherited from his dour Dutch ancestors, had led him on. Once he accepted that blacks had a human right to be treated as equals, there was no going back – even when the death threats began to arrive from both sides.

He had been as cautious as possible. He had a duty to Kate and the children. Now the storm was over they would be in the pool under the jacaranda trees, ducking each other and shouting. He couldn't wait to get out of his clothes, stiff with mud churned up by army trucks going in to disperse yet another mob rioting in the township. They were so desperate that, even though apartheid was being slowly dismantled, like the cement blocks in that faraway Berlin Wall, the scent of freedom had gone to their heads, and they wanted it now – now... They had been educated to trust no one, not even each other. Only the thin, strong line of the law, stretched between them and civil war, held any hope of peace

As he drove up, Kate was waiting for him at the gate in the tall wire fence. She unlocked it, and hugged him as soon as he entered the garden.

'I've had a call from mum and dad,' she burst out. 'They want us to visit this summer.'

'But we'd planned to visit for Christmas. What's all the excitement?'

'This time they want us to think about staying for good.'

She searched his face: he was silent. It wasn't the first time his Australian in-laws had suggested emigration. Kate was thinking of the children – everyone was thinking of the children. It was tempting to remove them from this country which sometimes seemed like an explosives dump with a flaming torch poised over it. There in Australia was a big Catholic family of cousins for them to play with; and they were bilingual, Kate had seen to that. It was tempting, he couldn't deny it.

'Well, we don't have to decide now,' he said, as lightly as possible.

'Of course not,' she agreed.

It was later, when the children had gone to bed, that they had a chance to re-open the subject.

'I'd have to start again from the beginning,' he said.

'But I can work while you're studying,' she countered. 'With the families so close, I'll have lots of help with the children. And you don't have to be a lawyer – you often complain about it.'

'I have to be a lawyer,' he said flatly, but with conviction.

She paused; she knew that tone when he had finally shut the door on argument.

'Do you know who the patron of lawyers is?' she said finally.

'No.' He gave in, unable to follow her line of thought. 'Who is it?'

'St Thomas More. He was a lot like you. So obstinate, he stuck his neck out once too often, and got his head chopped off.'

She turned on the television. It was an Australian sit-com, one of her favourites. She relaxed and laughed as the action speeded up. Her laughter moved him more than tears could have done. She deserved a break – more than a break – a peaceful life without stress. The room was dark except for the flickering picture, as he struggled with his problem...

* * *

England in the latter part of the fifteenth century was still suffering from the effects of the Wars of the Roses. The dukes and earls, who took sides in the great battles over the succession to the throne between rival claimants from the Yorkist and Lancastrian sides, hoped to gain favour if their men won. They did not care about the people whose corn they trampled and houses they burned. Eventually, sick of civil war, they would have welcomed almost anyone who might unite their country and restore peace. So when young Edward IV rode into London in 1461 at the head of his army, he was acclaimed by the people of the city.

And Thomas More was born a Londoner, in Milk Street – one of the maze of streets named for the trades plied in them, off Cheapside. His father was butler and steward at Lincolns Inn, a post that often led to a career in the law, and did so in his case. His mother was a member of a respected city family – her father was later elected sheriff. There were six children of the marriage, two of whom left only their names in the family records and probably died soon after their births. Thomas was the second child and elder son; born on the 6th of February 1478. His sisters and brothers all figure in his story; they were a devoted and united family, in spite of losing their

131

mother early. Thomas was on excellent terms with his father's choice of three successive wives; no traumas haunted his later life on that account, as he was to show in his loving relationships with all his own children.

Thomas was three years old when Edward IV died. He had a vivid memory of hearing the news the same night from a neighbour; one of Richard of Gloucester's serving-men was listening, and exclaimed that now his master would be king. News travelled fast in the narrow streets – even without the benefit of television journalists. Only two years later, Richard's crown was seized at Bosworth by Henry Tudor, a Lancastrian. He married Elizabeth of York and united the warring factions, by his prudence and good management steering the ship of state on an even keel at last.

The young Thomas More received his first education at St Antony's School in Threadneedle Street: most of it consisted of learning by heart, for there were few books – the first printed book was produced in the year of his birth, and they were still rare. Whatever may be thought of the methods of education, the boys of St Antony's were able to think in Latin, and debated in that language with the boys of other schools. They were proud of winning – rather as a school today might pride itself on its success in sporting fixtures.

When his father considered that he had reached an age to leave school, he was lucky enough to find him a place in the household of Cardinal Morton, Archbishop of Canterbury and Chancellor of England. The placing of young boys from the age of eight or so in great houses was a relic of the age of chivalry, when they became pages in order to progress to becoming knights. Foreign observers were rather shocked at its survival in England, and accused their parents of wanting to be rid of them; similar arguments are heard now about the merits of education in boarding-schools.

In Thomas More's case the results were happy. Morton was sociable, and known for his learning, good humour, and good table. He entertained all the most famous people of his day; his chaplain was something of a playwright, and private theatricals figured amongst the pastimes offered at the great festivals. An account exists of young Thomas, caught up in the excitement surrounding the Christmas season, stepping out of his place as he served at table, to join the players. He appears to have improvised a part for himself.

Whatever the other performers may have thought, it pleased the cardinal, who predicted a great future for him when he grew up. No doubt it was in the cardinal's household that he learned the careful balance between obsequiousness and over-familiarity with great men that would stand him in good stead in his later career.

Morton considered that the young More would benefit from some time at Oxford, and his father consented. He spent two years there, perfecting his Latin and making his first acquaintance with Greek, which was receiving attention from some of the famous scholars. He never forgot the poor diet and penury of his time at university: his father kept him very short of money, and the hours of study were long and hard, but Thomas bore him no ill-will and claimed it was good for him because he could not afford any distraction from his work. His temperament was exceptionally sunny, and free from resentment.

Oxford was the place for ambitious clerics, but the Inns of Court in London led to a career in Law, the key to secular preferment, and when he was sixteen Thomas More entered the Inn of Chancery. From there, having acquired sufficient knowledge of the family profession, he joined his father at Lincolns Inn. The gentlemen lived well, and it must have seemed luxurious after Oxford. Admitted at the same time was the young man who married his elder sister Joan; Thomas became a life-long friend of his brother-in-law. Whether he accepted and made the best of his relatives or was merely very lucky in them, we cannot tell at this distance; the fact remains that the feuds plaguing many close-knit families never seem to have spoiled the relationships of the Mores.

In London he worked hard at the Law, but his exception-ally swift and active mind had room in it for other things. He developed friendships with scholars, all in holy orders: Colet, who founded St Paul's School, Linacre and Grocyn. They had met at Oxford and discovered in one another an enthusiasm for the Greek language, their taste for it whetted by those fortunate enough to encounter it during their travels abroad. All brilliant men, they were to inspire a poor Dutch monk with

133

enthusiasm for the new learning. He was the illegitimate son of a priest, and had subsidised his studies at the University of Paris by tutoring. His name, later to be well-remembered, was Erasmus.

Erasmus arrived in England in 1499 at the invitation of the English Lord Mountjoy, who had been one of his pupils in Paris. Mountjoy's wife's father was a family friend of the Mores, and was probably the link in a chain of friendship that was to last all their lives. But there is a good story that they met at a Lord Mayor's banquet, and according to the account of a mutual friend, they exclaimed to one another:

'You must be More or no one – !'

'You must be Erasmus or the devil!'

Erasmus, the impoverished scholar, was not an easy friend, but like everyone else he put his prickliness and over-sensitivity aside when he was with Thomas More. While they were both visiting Mountjoy at Greenwich, More led him in the direction of Eltham, where Henry VII's children were living. Erasmus, not used to great men's houses, must have been taken aback at the collection of young royalty on view, surrounded by retainers and tutors. The socially adroit More was prepared with a poem for the young Henry, the senior prince present, but Erasmus had nothing, and felt put out that his friends had given him no warning of the honour in store for him. He was on the look-out for patrons who would back him while he perfected his Greek studies.

At dinner, he was further humiliated by a message from the young prince that he would welcome a sample of his writing. When he returned to Mountjoy's house he sat down and with difficulty – for it was some time since he had attempted verse – he repaired the omission. It took him three anxiety-ridden days to compose his adulation of the king, his children, and his country.

But his enthusiasm was genuine. He loved everything about England, from the standard of its scholarship to the custom of kissing in greeting the slightest of acquaintances – something their more reserved continental neighbours wondered at. He was also encouraged by the conviction of More, Colet and the others that he could help them to restore theology to its former esteem in the eyes of scholars, but as yet

134

he lacked confidence in his own powers. It was typical of him that he should blame them for expecting too much of him.

But the rootless academic had discovered an object in life – no less than to unlock the riches of the Bible by translating the original Greek text into more accessible Latin. The key was to be found in further Greek studies, and he returned to Paris with renewed heart for the task.

Thomas More was also seeking a direction for his life. His father urged the claims of the Law; Thomas was a good, loving and dutiful son, and he bowed to his wishes in continuing his work at Lincolns Inn, combining it with the post of reader-in-law at Furnivalls Inn. But deep within him was a call to explore the spiritual life; a cry from a soul that was not satisfied by the prospect of the rich pickings to be gained from high office in Henry VII's England. He was not attracted to the path followed by his contemporary at Oxford – another Thomas, later to become Cardinal Wolsey.

There were rumblings about the need for reform of the clergy, and Wolsey's career – with his acquisition of multiple livings, his currying favour for his illegitimate son, his luxurious life-style and appetite for flattery – was to be an extreme example. The reformers now in London, amongst whom More would count himself, were agitating for a return to the simplicity of the early disciples. They hoped to rescue the biblical texts from the top-heavy weight of mediaeval symbolism. What had been meaningful and poetic for the people of the Middle Ages was of little use in this age of expanding commerce, increased exploration and colonisation. Along with these came a new interest in science, and natural explanations of phenomena that had puzzled and frightened their forbears. The air was thick with new ideas, and Thomas More was in the vanguard of those ready to accept them.

But he had another, secret life. He spent all the time he could with the Carthusian monks of Charterhouse, sharing as far as a busy layman could do their austere life of worship, intercession and penance. It was probably at this period in his life that he made his first purchase of a hair-shirt, commonly believed to tame the appetites and discipline the senses: More felt he had need of both. No one who has known the discomfort of coarse wool next to the skin can withhold admiration for his unfailing good humour while wearing this instrument of torture. He was also attracted to the life of a Franciscan friar, and was associated with the Observant Franciscans at Greenwich.

He found time to contribute a preface and epilogue to a grammar published by a friend – his first appearance in print. It was to this friend that he wrote an account of Catherine of Aragon's arrival in London to marry the eldest of Henry VII's children, Prince Arthur. He must have been no stranger to great royal events, and on this occasion, joining the crowds who downed tools to welcome the Spanish princess, he was captivated by her youth and beauty. He never wavered in his devotion to that first vision of her.

He also lectured on St Augustine's great masterpiece, *The City of God*, at the invitation of his friend Grocyn, and drew all the most learned men in London to hear him; earning their admiration was a remarkable achievement for someone so young. About this time too, he wrote a light-hearted play in verse which appears to have been designed as a diversion at a feast given by the serjeants-at-law. He is spoken of as writing and acting in several plays, as well as producing able, if not outstandingly good, verse. In 1504, he was elected to Parliament, which had been called to vote Henry VII some money in order to provide a dowry for his daughter Margaret's marriage to the Scottish king. Henry had asked for a very large sum which was cut to just under half, largely through the efforts of Thomas More. The king may have marked him out as a trouble-maker, but it did him no harm with the tax-payers who were footing the bill.

Hair-shirted or not, More did not succeed in subduing his sexual desires, and for such a devout young man, marriage was the only honourable course. His search for a wife ended at the home of John Colt, near Roydon in Essex. Colt had three beautiful daughters amongst a large family of eighteen, and More was attracted to the middle one – but the eldest must have been in love with him, for when she showed her distress at her sister being preferred, More pitied her situation and decided to marry her instead. We know very little about his choice, except that her name was Jane, and she was ten years younger than her brilliant husband. They had a house in

Bucklersbury, off Cheapside, and it must have been a great shock for a girl brought up in the country to be introduced to the smells and noises of London, where neighbours lived in a proximity that was claustrophobic to anyone not used to it.

More succumbed to the temptation of many intelligent young men, thinking that because his bride was young, she could be moulded to the image of an ideal wife. He tried to interest her in books and music, and questioned her about sermons she had heard. Worse still, one of their first visitors was Erasmus, and the poor young woman probably had to sit through dinners while the two great scholars exchanged Latin epigrams above her head. But her attention was soon taken up by another wifely duty; she became a mother, four times in as many years. The names of the children chime like a ring of bells – Margaret, Elizabeth, Cecily and John.

More and Erasmus were now collaborating, translating some of the works of Lucian. Diplomatically, More dedicated his part of the joint work to one of Henry VII's secretaries, but this did not mollify the monarch, in spite of a reference to him as 'most prudent of princes'. He was not pleased by the compliment, seeing in it a reminder that More had dared to interfere with the royal revenues.

The rumours that reached More of the king's possible vengeance were enough to make him consider moving his growing family abroad, but the year of his son John's birth – 1509 – saw Henry VII's demise. His son, another Henry, had succeeded his brother Arthur, both as heir-presumptive and as husband to Catherine of Aragon.

The reign of Henry VIII began with high hopes, not least amongst the scholars who had embraced the new learning. More hurried to pen verses of congratulation, praising Henry's looks, his athletic prowess, his appreciation of good scholarship – and wished him and his wife the grace of founding a dynasty that would rule England for many generations. Adulation was heaped on the young king from all sides. Thanks to his father, his treasury was full, and foreign travellers reported the richness of the houses of his great men and merchants, the skill of his craftsmen and architects. The shrines of St Edward the Confessor at Westminster and St Thomas a Becket at Canterbury drew gasps of astonishment from these observers for their magnificence. The monastic churches were scarcely less well endowed.

Erasmus, now a man of wide renown, was encouraged to come back to England, and while visiting More and his family at Bucklersbury he wrote his first best-seller: *The Praise of Folly*, which he dedicated to his host. More himself became under-sheriff to the City, and in that office instructed the mayor and sheriffs on the legal side of their judicial functions. During his tenure he abolished the fees that had been due from litigants, and enjoyed even greater popularity with the citizens of London on that account.

But tragedy was to strike the pleasant household in Bucklersbury. When the youngest child John was only two, the family were left motherless. In haste, More looked about for a substitute. Within a month he had procured a dispensation from the banns being heard, to marry Mistress Alice Middleton, widow of a worthy London merchant. She was past her first youth, the mother of children that More must have approved of, because he took one daughter into his house. Alice spoke her mind bluntly, uttering the first thought that came into her head, and was a good manager of household affairs. She was something of a shrew, and knew it, and repented of it, and learned to play the lute and the virginals to please her husband. One is reminded of that other disparate marriage, between Shakespeare and his Anne. Both he and Thomas More seem to have derived a certain amount of quiet amusement from their voluble wives, satisfying their need for intellectual female company in their daughters, and in spite of appearances, they loved their wives heartily.

But there were clouds on the horizon. Unlike his father, Henry had his eye on the old English territories in France which had been lost when St Joan of Arc took a hand in the fortunes of her country, during the reign of Henry VI. He responded to an appeal by Pope Julius to make war on the French king, Francis I, seeing himself as the true knight of the Church − a vision that had attracted young men since the crusades. Wolsey had the king's ear, and Wolsey's ambitions extended to occupying the Holy See himself one day. Most of More's circle were pacifists and tried to discourage Henry's commitment to the war, though as courtiers they were shrewd enough not to try the king's patience too far. The war ended on Pope Julius's death; England gained some towns in France, and peace returned.

From his earliest years, More had been an author, though he was so busy that most of his writing had to be done between 2 a.m. and breakfast, when the busy household began clamouring about him. He had trained himself to function at full power on only four or five hours' sleep. It may have been anxiety about Henry's real aims as king that caused him to begin his historical study of tyranny: *The History of Richard III.* Despite a favourable account of Henry's grandfather, Edward IV – the darling of the city, for More was a Londoner – the subject was dangerously controversial. He seems to have realised this, and left unfinished a larger plan to extend it to his own time. Even so, Shakespeare mined it extensively as a source for his play on the same subject. Between them they painted a picture of a power-hungry villain so vivid, it remained unchallenged for four centuries.

In 1515 there was an interruption to More's busy practice as a barrister. He was sent to Flanders as an ambassador, to represent the king in a dispute between the London merchants and foreigners trading in the capital. This dragged on for six months, and he became bored with the negotiations: he missed his family, and he missed the fees he could have earned at home, to feed and clothe them. He was offered a pension from the king for work well done, but turned it down, thinking he would forfeit the trust of the City if he became so obviously a king's man. But he made some congenial friends in Europe, and it was to amuse them that he started writing the book that gave him fame in his own time, and added a new word to the language – *Utopia*.

It was a traveller's tale. Men were looking to the West, eager to hear of the rediscovery of America which had taken place some twenty years earlier. More's brother-in-law John Rastell was planning a voyage there, which must have been discussed by the family in the house at Bucklersbury, and the author took great pleasure in describing the island minutely, its cities and its churches. Of course it was fiction; but despite the tall stories told within its pages, even a cleric like the Vicar of Croydon seems to have given credence to Utopia's existence, for he professed himself anxious to be a missionary there. This must have pleased More, whose humour was of the dead-pan variety; his own family were often uncertain whether he was joking or not.

The good vicar would have found it a pleasant mission. Although Utopia was not a Christian state, it was tolerant of all religions, provided that they did not cause dissension by power-zealous proselytism. Primarily, it was a vision of an ideal state governed by reason for reasonable men, and owed a great deal to More's studies of the Greek philosophers.

It is easy to call it an up-date of Plato's *Republic*, but there is implied criticism of the Europe of More's own day – the intolerance in religious matters, the unequal distribution of wealth, the devastation caused by war. Along with compassion for human frailty was a stern judicial system. No man in Utopia was born to slavery, but hardened criminals could become slaves, and be bound to a life of community service.

There was an ingenious plan to broaden the outlook of both town and country dwellers by swapping jobs in two-yearly cycles, but the scheme was voluntary, and the Utopians would not have sanctioned the cultural revolution. More had the townsman's love of the country; his father had an estate in South Mimms, and he could not conceive that anyone would object to dividing his time between the two cultures. Although Chairman Mao, Karl Marx, or the abbot of a mediaeval monastery would have found much to please them in Utopia, it was calculated to enrage the nobles and rich merchants of the time, as well as ultra-orthodox Catholics, who had never liked More's humanist friends, nor their championing of pagan Greece.

But long study of the Greeks had gained More's respect, and he sought to show how far men could realise an ideal state by using reason and imagination, as they did, and how superior it could be to the nominally Christian states of war-torn Europe. But we can have no doubt that the author who described the lofty churches in Utopia, with their priests in magnificent vestments, lit by a myriad flickering candles, in a dim twilight conducive to prayer, would have found something missing – for the Utopian altars were empty. More would have found life without the sacraments difficult. He heard mass every day of his life; perhaps he did not think the Vicar of Croydon very foolish after all.

While More was completing the manuscript at home, his friend Erasmus published his finest work, the New Testament he had been working on ever since his first visit to England. In the preface he expressed his hope that it would be accessible to all; to women, and to working men of all trades, the Scots and the Irish in the West, and even the Turks and Saracens who were threatening the East. He could hope to be acknowledged as the first scholar in Europe. When he came to stay with More, he took the manuscript of *Utopia* back with him to Antwerp, and saw it through its first printing.

In November 1517, the German priest and academic Martin Luther, only five years older than More, incensed by the Holy See's attempt to raise money for its secular state by the sale of indulgences, struck the first blow for Protestant reform by nailing his ninety-five theses to the door of Wittenburg Cathedral. This set the theologians of Europe talking and writing furiously in Latin, their common language. The murmurs of controversy grew to a roar, which was to touch the lives of all, from the highest to the lowest – but in England the repercussions would take a while to make themselves felt.

In 1517, what concerned London was a riot that took place on the eve of May Day. For some time there had been jostling and molesting of foreigners, for the city had its share of insular feeling even then. And there were always malcontents – discharged soldiers from foreign wars, and dispossessed country men whose lands had been given over to sheep – whom London drew like a magnet. The authorities were worried, and as under-sheriff More went to see Wolsey, now Henry's chancellor, to discuss what should be done before the situation got out of hand.

Wolsey's answer was to order a curfew to cover the early hours of May Day itself. This inflamed the apprentices, gathering in the streets to celebrate the festival; May Day was traditionally theirs, and they refused to leave. Angry words were spoken, and one of the rioters arrested. Bystanders joined in the argument, and more people came to see what was happening, rousing their neighbours, until about a thousand people were packed into the streets round Cheapside. They were More's neighbours too, and he had a great deal of sympathy with them. He addressed them to such effect that they seemed ready to disperse. Unfortunately, some stones were thrown, setting off a wave of violence, and looting and prison-breaking began. This continued for several hours, but the very force of the attacks scared the law-abiding back into their houses and shops, and the aldermen and officers were able to stem the tide of disorder. But when some armed nobles arrived to join them, the lieutenant of the Tower discharged his cannon into the streets, causing further damage, and hundreds of arrests were made.

In these circumstances, justice was impossible. At a later enquiry More tracked down the instigators to two disaffected apprentices, who got off scot-free. Others were less fortunate, and there were many hangings, the bodies being left at the scene of the riot as a grim reminder. Together with some of the aldermen, More pleaded with the king and Wolsey for clemency toward the rioters, and a mass pardon was given at Westminster Hall; this enhanced his reputation with the city folk. The incident is used in the opening scene of an Elizabethan play: *Sir Thomas More* – Shakespeare's hand has been detected among its writers – and More's personal courage, impartiality and compassion would be remembered in his own city long after his ignominious death.

It was probably his ability to sway the volatile citizens of London, and his appearance on behalf of the pope in a shipping dispute heard before Wolsey, which led to his entering the king's service. He travelled abroad again as a negotiator with some French traders at Calais. Henry and Wolsey liked More and respected him, and he became a member of the king's council, though at first the only post open to him was the fairly minor one of 'master of requests'. This meant presiding over poor men's complaints against the actions of the rich, a cause near to his heart, and to Wolsey's. They were united in wishing to make the laws of England fair and impartial. When Wolsey went head-hunting foreign scholars, giving them large sums of money to attract them to the court, and selecting young men as readers for the six places he had endowed at Oxford, More must have approved – particularly since four of the places went to his young friends.

Better still, in the early years of More's appointment, Henry and Wolsey appeared to have a genuine wish for peace with their European neighbours. More went with them when they met Francis I of France at the Field of the Cloth of Gold, and helped to cement the alliance of common interest between Henry and his wife's nephew, Charles V of Spain. More's promotion in the service of the king was rapid. In 1521 he was made under-treasurer, a post similar to chancellor of the exchequer, and received a knighthood.

Henry's favour was a mixed blessing. He demanded attention morning, noon and night, and not always on state business. Sometimes he merely wanted a witty and learned companion, and he had decided that More fitted these requirements exactly. On one occasion he sent for Sir Thomas while he was praying before the Blessed Sacrament, and on being told that the king required him, he replied:

'I *am* with the King.'

Henry, at that time a pious man, took this answer in good part.

But what pleased him more than his preferment was the marriage of his eldest daughter Margaret to William Roper, a young lawyer who had been in More's house for three years. More loved all his children, and strove to keep his love impartial. His son John, the youngest, might have been described as a 'good average scholar'. His sisters however were brilliant; More believed that girls should be given the same education as their brothers, and they were tutored by able teachers at home. Yet when they all wrote to him – in Latin – he took care that John received special praise for his efforts. He even tried to educate his wife, and succeeded in making a musician of her; but when it came to a demonstration of the globe, she remained a staunch flat-earther.

Margaret, however, was the member of the family to whom Thomas remained closest. Apart from her brilliance and her ready response to his love, he had nearly lost her in an epidemic of 'sweating sickness'; an illness that may have been similar to influenza. The rest of the household believed that she owed her life to her father's agonised prayers. He said afterwards that if she had died, he would have withdrawn from the world altogether.

It must have been wonderful to visit him in his house in Bucklersbury, and later, when he moved to the village of Chelsea, where his garden sloped down to the river. There, with more space than in the City, he was surrounded by his relatives and friends, and a collection of animals, including a monkey that amused them all with its lively curiosity. A jester, Henry Patterson, who must have been a remarkable character to get laughs from such an intellectual audience, remained with the family for years. Nor was charity neglected, for More founded an alms-house in the neighbourhood, administered by Margaret Roper.

Holbein, while still struggling for commissions, was encouraged by the More family to produce a group portrait. He made many studies that survive today, but the canvas was finished by a less gifted hand. The artist's portrait of More has made him live for succeeding generations, fleshed out by the descriptions of his friends. There are constant references to his wit, gentleness, modesty and generosity: that he loved music – he could not sing, though that did not stop him doing it – that constant writing caused one shoulder to stoop, and that young men rearranged their gowns in imitation of his.

But Margaret's husband rebelled against the Catholic tradition and was converted by the doctrines of Luther, which had percolated into England about this time. For a high court official, it must have been rather like having a Moslem fundamentalist marry into the family of an Anglican bishop. Roper did not keep his beliefs to himself, but tub-thumped at Paul's Cross, the Hyde Park Corner of its day. When he was arrested for heresy and brought before Wolsey, he was not deterred; More's intervention saved him from public disgrace, but Wolsey's reprimand had no effect, and he seemed determined to ignore his father-in-law's arguments too, and those of his friends. More gave up, and placed the problem in the hands of God. His prayer was answered; Roper returned to the Catholic faith and lived in it, becoming More's constant friend and biographer.

Henry VIII took the opposite side in the battle of words unleashed by Luther. In reply to Luther's *Babylonish Captivity of the Church* the king wrote *The Assertion of the Seven Sacraments*. More read the book when it was finished, and tidied up some of the loose ends.

He counselled Henry to differentiate between the Pope's spiritual power and his position as a secular ruler, but the king ignored his advice and continued to be an ally of the pope, who had conferred on him the title of 'Defender of the Faith'. Within two years he was committed, far from reluctantly, to entering a war with France on the pope's side.

He called the Parliament to vote him funds for a continental invasion, and More was elected Speaker. Anticipating trouble, he made a petition in his opening speech that the members should have the right to speak freely, without any penalties if what they said in the heat of the moment should incur His Majesty's displeasure. This was granted, and Wolsey came to the House, demanding a subsidy that would amount to a tax of four shillings in the pound on every man's lands and goods. He attempted to debate with individual members, but they hid behind More's position as Speaker, asking him to sum up their opinions and make their reply. More turned away from a direct answer, saying that the House was divided, but his tact did not mollify Wolsey, who left in disgust. After seventeen weeks the Commons voted for the tax and Parliament was dissolved. Wolsey made a half-hearted attempt to get More out of the spotlight by sending him as ambassador to Spain, but More pleaded ill-health, and he did not persist.

The wealth of England flowed into the bottomless pit of the French war for the next two years, and Henry seemed no nearer his goal of recovering the old territories. By 1525 he was in need of more money, but the war was so unpopular, and the animosity of the people so strong, Wolsey did not dare to call Parliament again. More's star was still in the ascendant. The king visited him at Chelsea, and walked in the garden with his arm round More's shoulders. Roper was delighted by this mark of favour, but More knew his monarch too well, saying that he took no pride in it; if his head could win the sovereign a castle in France, he knew he would lose it.

Meanwhile the forces of his ally and nephew Charles V – now emperor – had gained an unexpected victory over the French, which altered the delicate balance of Europe. To redress it, Henry proposed allying himself with his former enemy, and declaring war on Charles. Their relationship made this difficult, and Henry cast about for some means of annulling it, claiming that his marriage to his late brother's wife had been incestuous. He also wanted a male heir and Catherine of Aragon had failed to produce one. Henry consulted More, now elevated to the Duchy of Lancaster, and they consulted the Bible and the books of the Doctors of the Church, but came to no definite conclusions, so Henry arranged to have himself tried for incest by a papal court.

Meanwhile Charles, flushed with victory over the French, turned to and sacked Rome, capturing the pope. Even Henry could not take on such a formidable opponent, and More was sent to Cambrai in France to represent England at the peace talks between Francis and Charles. He had always considered war to be the principal enemy of good government, and wanted a strong, united Europe that would stand firm, discouraging further encroachment from the Turks and Saracens. The Peace of Cambrai seemed to promise this; it was to hold for fifteen years, and he regarded it as one of his greatest contributions to the health of his country.

Wolsey, who might have been entrusted with such important negotiations, was absent. Henry blamed him for the failure of his continental adventures, and thought that his policies had left England isolated from her neighbours. Most important to him at that moment, Wolsey had not succeeded in freeing him from his marriage. More had judged Henry's temperament rightly when he said that he would trade his head for a castle in France; but it was Wolsey's head that Henry wanted now, and he had a warrant issued for his commitment to the Tower. Wolsey knew this was a death sentence, and little in his life had prepared him for it. He died on his way there – of terror, some said.

Believing that More's tact and loyalty would serve his turn, the king now offered him the chancellorship; sensing his disapproval of the annulment of his marriage, he assured him that his duties would not include this particular problem.

During his time as chancellor, More was to walk a tightrope. He knew the fickleness of royal favour, the king's ability to charm, and his inflexible anger. Why did he – a man uniquely impervious to flattery, ever ready to turn from public affairs to look to the welfare of his immortal soul – accept a post so fraught with danger? Perhaps the answer is that he hoped to defend his luckless queen, and steer England away from the perilous rocks that loomed ahead.

For Henry's part, he was well-satisfied to have appointed a layman in place of a cleric. He thought his new chancellor would be more malleable in the matters he wished to raise with the Church in England. He intended to fine the clergy a large sum for not speaking out against Wolsey, and to force them to acknowledge his right to be called 'Supreme Head of the Church and Clergy of England'. He did not realise that the chancellor had a more sensitive conscience than most of his clerics. With a slightly changed form of words – putting in 'As far as the law of Christ allows', at the insistence of Bishop Fisher of Rochester – the motion was passed. It was easier to obtain their consent because the Parliament over which More presided was fiercely anti-clerical, as was the mood of the country.

Despite his promise to More that he would not be pressed on 'The king's great matter' (as the euphemism for the royal divorce went), Henry required him to make a statement to Parliament. More trod warily, saying that the king thought himself guilty of incest in his marriage to Catherine, and that no other woman was involved; he made it clear that he was only reporting his royal master's words. This appeared to satisfy Henry, and the Parliament was dismissed.

When it next met, pressure had built up against the bishops, from the Commons below and the king above. For His Majesty, the divorce had become a necessity, since he was in love with Anne Boleyn and convinced that she would give him the son he wanted so passionately. The Commons had been persuaded that the dissipation of Henry VII's wealth, and the ills that afflicted the kingdom, were due to the corruption of the clergy, and held the bishops responsible; they passed an act to withhold all moneys normally paid to Rome.

Then Henry played his trump card. He claimed that the bishops' oath of loyalty to the pope, made at their consecration, was not compatible with their oath to him. The implication was that in any quarrel Henry had with the pope, if they took the pope's side they would be guilty of treason. The bishops, as fearful of the king's anger as Wolsey had been, hastened to comply with his demands. More alone held firm, and resigned the chancellorship, on grounds of ill-health.

At a stroke of his pen he became a poor man. He gathered his extended family around him and explained with a great deal of humour that they would embrace poverty by degrees. First he suggested that in order to cut their budget they should eat as they did when he was a barrister at Lincolns Inn. Following his career backwards to his days at Oxford, he pointed out that, meagre though the meals there had been, many great scholars survived on them. Finally, if they were reduced below that level, they should go busking round rich men's houses, regaling them with the *'Salve Regina'* (Hail, holy Queen). He found places for the servants he no longer needed, and having battened down the hatches, he waited for the storm to break.

More welcomed his self-imposed unemployment as a chance to attack the Lutheran reformers. He had contributed to the debate before, having received permission to read their books in order to answer their arguments. He took on Luther himself, and Tyndale, the translator of the Bible into English. His objection was not that Tyndale wished to make the Bible accessible – More would have welcomed that. After all, he defended his friend Erasmus' Greco-Latin version, which had made the New Testament available to scholars, against the orthodox Catholics who wanted the interpretation of Scripture to be restricted to churchmen. What his scholarly mind could not tolerate was its bias, and its inaccuracies. Years of living close to the unlettered had made him wary of the Bible becoming a fashionable talking-point in alehouses. He was fond of the common people who made up the bulk of the population, and defended their rights, but he also knew their limitations. The May Day riot had left him in no doubt that even a street-argument could spark off a conflagration, and having lived through one, he dreaded another civil war.

In his retirement he defended the sacraments; the right of the Church to own property, and the use of the crucifix, relics, and prayers to the saints as aids to devotion. He also penned a reply to charges that he had persecuted heretics with undue severity: in fact, while he was chancellor there were no heretics burned in London. Over-zealous heretics did make him angry, and he caused two such to be flogged in his own garden – one for trying to corrupt the faith of the children in his care, and the other for horseplay during mass. That was the sum total of his vengeance, and even his worst enemies could not make out a case for cruelty against him. He scotched an accusation of enriching himself while in office by his reputation as the most incorruptible administer of justice; his relations considered him almost too scrupulous, and complained of his refusal to favour his own family in any way – he had refused a small fortune from the bishops for his service to them.

But he was a marked man, and some charge had to be found to bring him to trial. It came about through the revelations of Elizabeth Barton, a serving-maid turned nun, whose visions had a political slant. It was not even a new story; More had examined her when he was chancellor, and reported back to Henry that the visions revealed nothing that an untutored girl might not have deduced for herself, and that he would not venture to judge the matter of her sanctity. Encouraged by getting a hearing from some distinguished clerics, Elizabeth prophesied that if the king married Anne Boleyn, he would cease to be king very shortly afterwards. On the 28th of May 1533, Henry's secret marriage to Anne Boleyn was pronounced valid, and two days later Anne was crowned queen in Westminster Abbey. More was invited to the coronation by some good friends, still in favour, who thought his presence might do him some good in high places – but he did not attend. Later that summer, the pope pronounced the marriage invalid, and excommunicated Henry. The king refuted the maid's prophecy by remaining on the throne, and accused several carefully-chosen men of condoning her treason by listening to it without denouncing her.

When the Bill of Attainder was introduced into the Lords, More's name was on the list. He would have been happy to defend himself on the matter; he had written to the maid, warning her of the dangers of dabbling in politics, and urging her to apply herself to spiritual matters, which should have been evidence enough of his innocence. Henry could not risk a public enquiry, so More faced a committee of four, including Cromwell, his master secretary (later to be called 'The Hammer of the Monks') – Lord Audley, his successor in the chancellorship – the Duke of Norfolk, who had regretted his resignation, and Cranmer, the new Archbishop of Canterbury. Knowing More's dexterity in defence, they moved the goalposts and brought up Henry's book in favour of the papal supremacy, trying to make More admit that Henry had written it at his instigation: but More brushed this accusation aside with contempt. The committee, finding that he was not to be moved by threats, or by promises of regaining the king's favour, dismissed him.

Going home with Roper, he was in a particularly good humour, and Roper, a serious man who never understood More's moods of elation, asked if he were happy because things had gone well. His father-in-law replied that he could not remember. He had just won a bout with the devil, and committed himself so far with their lordships that he could not turn back without being very ashamed of himself – and so he was happy. Not surprisingly, the answer did nothing to comfort William Roper.

The following month, after attending a Sunday sermon at St Paul's, More dropped in at his old house in Bucklersbury to visit friends now living in it. There he received notice that he was to appear before the commissioners who were administering an oath, further to an Act of Parliament requiring all citizens to affirm that the offspring of Henry and Anne should succeed to the throne. The amended oath included a declaration of the validity of their marriage, the invalidity of Henry's union with Catherine of Aragon, and a repudiation of any oaths 'to any foreign authority, prince or potentate' – in other words, the pope.

That night must have been sad for the family at Chelsea, as Thomas made his farewells. They knew it was possible that they would not see him again. He had admitted to his closest confidante, Margaret, that he had tossed and turned in the marital bed while Dame Alice slept, debating what he should do when the anticipated blow fell.

Next morning he rose early, and went to Chelsea Church. It was here, on the death of his father, Judge More, that he had built a tomb to serve as the family vault, and it contained the remains of his first wife. This was More's daily reminder of the inescapable end of human life, and today, as on all great occasions, he followed his custom of receiving the sacraments of penance and communion.

He would not allow his wife and children to see him into the boat to Lambeth, shutting the gate firmly on them. Roper, who shared the river journey, reported that his face showed 'a heavy heart.' Suddenly More exclaimed:

'Son Roper, I thank Our Lord the field is won.'

As usual, Roper did not understand him, but not wanting to seem ignorant, he replied:

'Sir, I am thereof very glad.'

At Lambeth he was shown the oath, and said that he would take the part relating to the succession, but not the rest. He was ordered to wait in the garden, but spent some time watching from a room above, the weather being very sultry. Below him the Archbishop of Canterbury's men, who had taken the oath, were laughing and hugging each other, no doubt with relief. The king's confessor had refused to sign, and More was also concerned about his friend, Cardinal Fisher, Bishop of Rochester, but could not find out any news of him. A further interview with the Commissioners followed, and he again refused the oath, but with saintly forbearance said that he did not blame those who accepted it. Cranmer thought this was a flaw in his argument: if he did not condemn the conscience of others, he could not condemn his own for remaining loyal to the state. But More refused every offer of loopholes, looking beyond the English laws to the wider laws of Christendom. None of his hearers wished to be drawn into this debate, and he was sent to the Tower, to await his formal trial.

He had his personal servant to attend to his needs, and was allowed to write. Occasionally he ran out of ink; there are several letters written to his daughter Margaret with a stub of charcoal from the fire. They are tender letters, assuring her that she is in his prayers, together with the entire family, lovingly listed. The fact that his imprisonment was illegal troubled his scrupulous mind, but his health was better than when he was at home. The illness he spoke of when he

151

resigned the chancellorship had been no diplomatic ploy; he was subject to severe chest-pains and cramps. These had temporarily disappeared, as he hastened to assure Margaret when she was allowed to visit him. She had sworn the oath 'as far as it would stand with the law of God' – a concession Henry would not allow to her father.

He carried on a short correspondence with the king's confessor, who had been committed with him, and was now wavering. More would not influence him in his decision, but told him that he himself wished to go cheerfully to God. He even welcomed the return of his illness, because it made the thought of death more pleasant.

He had to endure a great deal of talk from his family about saving his life by taking the oath. When he teasingly rallied Margaret for taking the part of Eve, tempting her father Adam with the fruit she had tasted herself, she told him that even his jester advised him to take the oath.

Dame Alice was also allowed to visit him. When she heard the sound of the bolts on the door, she looked round the fairly spacious room, with its high vaulted roof and deep window, exclaiming that she couldn't have slept there – the locked door made her feel she couldn't breathe. Her husband pointed out that she always locked the doors at home each night, and slept easily there – what difference did it make to her breathing whether the bolts were on the inside or the outside? She remained unconvinced: it was the argument about the flat earth all over again. She may have been unreasonable and obstinate, but in this case she had right on her side – it did make a difference.

Thomas entered into correspondence with his fellow prisoner, Cardinal Fisher, counselling him not to say anything damaging to his cause when he came to trial, or use any phrases similar to his own, in case they were accused of collusion. For the most part, their correspondence consisted of cheering one another and exchanging presents.

One day when Margaret was visiting her father, they saw from the window a little band of Carthusian monks going to their deaths. The brothers had prepared themselves well for the barbaric rites of their sentence, and went with joy, but father and daughter were reminded that More would probably share their fate, as he had once shared their austere lives. He said over and over again that he was not afraid of death, but he was afraid of torture and prayed constantly that he would not weaken if he were called upon to endure it.

Both More and Fisher underwent further examinations by the authorities, and six days after the Carthusians' martyrdom, Fisher was tried. A statement he had made, denying Henry's supremacy of the Church, though protected under a pledge of secrecy, was used against him; and he was condemned to death. Despite an offer of pardon on the scaffold, he remained true to his faith, begging the bystanders for their prayers that he would not deny his Lord at the last instant when the axe was poised.

More's trial followed within ten days. Lawyer to the end, he had given no reason for his refusal to speak at his examinations about the king's second marriage, which he denied he had resisted maliciously. He preferred to keep silence, and think about Our Lord's passion, and his own death. Indeed, he had written two very moving devotional works during his fifteen months' imprisonment, one of them a meditation on the Passion.

There were other articles in the indictment; one he had foreseen, about collusion between himself and Fisher, for they had made similar statements at their examinations. More explained that this was due to their comparable education and cast of mind. The most damaging evidence concerned More's having denied to Rich, the solicitor general, that the king could be head of the Church. More denied this charge, but it was his word against Rich's, and though Rich certainly committed perjury, his word prevailed. The jury took only a quarter of an hour to reach their verdict of 'Guilty'.

It seemed that More would be sentenced without being asked if he had anything to say in his defence, but he reminded his judges that a prisoner should be allowed to speak. Then he broke his long silence, denying the right of Parliament to pass a law contrary to the law of the Church, and reaffirmed that the king could not be head of the Church in England, which was only part of a wider Church, owing allegiance to the See of Rome.

He cited Magna Carta and the king's coronation oath to

back his case for the freedom of the Church, and proudly claimed that the centuries-old traditions of Christianity and the bishops and laity of the universal Church would approve his stand. He ended by recalling that St Paul, who had condoned the martyrdom of St Stephen, was now a saint with him in heaven, adding that he prayed that those who were now his judges would merrily meet with him there – 'to our everlasting salvation.'

As he went out of the court, his son John begged at his feet for his blessing, and at Tower Wharf Margaret embraced him again and again, ignoring the guards and the crowds. He tried to comfort her, his favourite daughter, who had shared all his secrets – even the hair-shirt, which she had washed for him. This he sent back to her with one of his letters written in charcoal; it was the last he was to write, leaving his few possessions to members of the family – a handkerchief, a parchment picture, a counting-stone. To the rest he sent his blessing and his prayers; all he had left to give. He said he wanted to die the next day – his name day, the feast of St Thomas within the octave of St Peter.

His wish was granted. Early in the morning of the 6th of July, he was told he would die before nine. The savage sentence of disembowelling had been mitigated, as in Fisher's case, to beheading. The bringer of the news was a man called Thomas Pope, with whom he had a mutual interest in learning. Pope was moved to tears when More asked if Margaret could attend his burial, and replied that the family had permission to be present. It was typical of More that he should comfort him with the hope that they would share the joys of heaven together. Pope persuaded him not to wear a costly silk gown a friend had sent him, that More wanted to give to his executioner; instead, he left him a gold angel.

On his way to Tower Hill, a woman in the crowd offered him wine, which he refused, saying that his master had vinegar and gall to drink, not wine. Another called him a 'hard friend', for giving a judgement against her, and he replied that he stood by his judgement. A man from Winchester, whom he had talked out of suicidal depression, asked More to help him, as he had relapsed into illness. More assured that he would pray for him, and asked for his prayers.

The ladder to the scaffold was rickety, and More asked to be helped up, adding: 'As for my coming down, let me shift for myself.' From the scaffold, he made a speech, which the king had ordered to be as brief as possible. After begging the crowd to pray for him, he asked that they should also pray for the king: 'That it might please God to give him good counsel.'

And he added that he died: 'The king's good servant, but God's first.'

Kneeling, he repeated part of Psalm 51, then got up briskly, and when the executioner asked his pardon, embraced him. He had brought a linen cloth to bind his eyes, which he insisted on doing for himself, and rearranged his beard on the block so that it should not be cut when the axe fell, since his beard had not committed treason. So he died, with a joke on his lips.

His body was buried in St Peter ad Vincula in the Tower, attended by three faithful women from his family circle. His head was exposed on London Bridge, but Margaret Roper obtained it before it was thrown into the Thames, and kept it safely for her lifetime. The likelihood is that it eventually found a resting-place in St Dunstan's, Canterbury.

When the news reached Europe, his many friends there were devastated. Erasmus, old and ill, wrote to a colleague that he felt he had died himself – 'There was only one soul between us' – and he did die in the following year.

More was a proud Londoner, an English patriot, and a great European: his life, with its brilliant achievements, his writings, and his rise and fall from high office, attracted many biographers – the Protestants claiming on the strength of his humanism that he was one of the first Protestants, the Catholics that he was one of the first martyrs of the Counter-Reformation. His wit, courage, courtesy, his love of peace and the humility of his spiritual life make him live on in the hearts of his countrymen. Four centuries after his death he took his place with his friend and fellow-sufferer, Cardinal John Fisher, among the saints of the Roman calendar; their feast is celebrated on the 22nd of July.

＊ ＊ ＊

The programme was over. Kate searched for the remote control button, asking:

'Do you want to see the news?'

'Let's have a rest from it,' he said slowly. 'I know the news.'

'Another riot?'

'Yes.'

'Many people hurt?' she asked anxiously.

'Some. I couldn't really tell,' he replied.

There was a long silence.

'You know we were talking about St Thomas More —' she began.

'You were,' he pointed out, smiling.

'He got involved in a riot. He tried to stop it – he couldn't, but when it was over, he asked for a pardon for the rioters.' She sat down by his feet and hugged his knees. 'When I said he was a lot like you, I meant it.'

'Then you'll understand why I've got to stay here. You can go to Oz; take the children – I'd be happier if you did. But this is my country, and I couldn't live with myself if I went ex-pat. Not while there's still something I can do to keep the peace.'

There was another long silence, then she turned her face to his. It was an effort for her to speak.

'Even if it kills you?'

'Your mind's still on that saint of yours,' he rallied her. 'I'm no saint – you know that.'

'He didn't think he was... Of course we'll stay with you, whatever happens. I promise you that... But it isn't sensible, you know.'

'I know,' he said, and kissed her. 'Thank you, Kate.'

St Margaret Clitherow

 middle-aged woman presided over the till of a baker's shop in the city of York. She was deferred to by the two girl assistants, neatly dressed in white caps and overalls, wrapping bread and cakes. She inspected the girls every morning before the establishment opened its doors, and if their hands were other than pristine, they felt the cutting edge of her ready wit. She sharpened her wits on the customers too – most of whom she knew by name.

Her husband, the master baker, plied his trade at the back of the premises. He was a convivial man, with a thirst that his work engendered, and when the first baking was over, he would repair to the pub on the corner to satisfy it. He was immensely proud of his wife, who organised the business and the family, leaving him free to indulge his more masculine pursuits – pigeon-fancying, and the growing of rather large vegetables. But perhaps he was proudest of her when she was singing and dancing in the chorus of the local dramatic and operatic society. He appeared in the front row of the audience on first and last nights, and his applause was for her alone. For her part, she rose when he did in the early hours of the morning, and he never went out without breakfast. Then she did the work of the house, roused the last of her five children, who still lived at home, then trudged off – rain or shine, snow or fog – to attend the earliest mass. In her childhood she had

157

attended a convent school and had been so impressed by the nuns amongst her teachers that as a young woman she had become a convert. Her husband did not share her religion, and the children as they grew up had ceased to practise. She was the last person in the world to be suspected of having a secret sorrow, but sometimes her husband's and children's purely secular view of life made her fear for their immortal souls.

It was at such times that she sought out the shrine of St Margaret Clitherow, in the Shambles. There in the dark oak-panelled room, usually alone, she prayed earnestly, commending her family to the intercession of the saint with whom she had so much in common.

* * *

The story of the Reformation in England had begun with the desire of Henry VIII for a male heir, and the refusal of Pope Clement VII to allow him to divorce his wife, the emperor Charles V's aunt; the pope had an alliance with the Holy Roman Empire, and the Reformation took hold because there had always been an anti-clerical party in England, and it was now finding an articulate voice among scholars who were using the new texts of the Scriptures, the Desert Fathers, and the ancient Greeks, when the great Eastern libraries were made available. Although the king himself spoke against the doctrines expounded by Martin Luther, he was only too anxious to profit by his criticisms of the monasteries, and he encouraged the propaganda against them. Although there was no doubt that in some of the houses the vows of poverty, chastity and obedience were not observed, as the visitations ordered by Pope Paul III had shown, the charges were greatly exaggerated to make their suppression popular.

Their lands enriched a whole generation of gentry, and were in fact a gigantic bribe to make these gentlemen accept the king's policies, and acknowledge him as having the juridical, though not the spiritual, powers of the pope. The lurch toward Protestantism continued during the minority reign of Henry's son Edward VI, when his mentor Warwick saw through the institution of the Book of Common Prayer and the end of the celibacy of the clergy. Every parish church in the land was stripped of the last vestiges of Catholicism – the old missals, the altars, statues of the saints and stained-glass windows – the whole inheritance of the Middle Ages.

When Edward's half-sister Mary, the daughter of Henry VIII's first wife, acceded to the throne in 1553, she restored the mass, but could make little headway against the tide of popular opinion, owing to a disastrous marriage with Philip of Spain which enraged her people. Insular as always, the national pride had been given a resurgence by freedom from the papacy, and this alliance with a Catholic European dynasty was a backward step. With the encouragement of Philip, she further weakened her position by her savage persecution of the Protestants. She made the fatal mistake of providing the new Church with martyrs, who showed great courage in its defence.

In 1556, the fourth year of Mary's reign, a daughter was born in the city of York to Thomas Middleton and his wife Jane. She was baptised Margaret in the Church of St Martin-le-Grand, of which her father was church warden, and so responsible for the restoration of the old services in the parish. He was a wax chandler by trade, and no doubt welcomed the greater use of votive lights that accompanied the old devotions. This gain was not enough to keep him faithful when, on the accession of Elizabeth in 1558, the Protestant religion was reinstated. He was running with the tide; England was strongly nationalistic, and the national Church represented freedom from the rest of Europe. It was now that the English sea-captains were free to pillage the Spanish ships coming back laden with treasure from the New World. Poets and dramatists were fulsome in their praise of the young queen. The mercantile and artistic life of the nation was entering a rich new phase.

Back in York, prosperous with its farming and the profits from the wool trade, young Margaret was brought up as a Protestant. She was a bright, lively child, though her father was ailing. When his daughter was only four years old he made his will, leaving her some silver plate and the right of inheritance of the family home after her mother's death. Ill as he was, Thomas Middleton was made a sheriff, though he was

159

suffering so badly from gout that he had to take the oath of office on his sick-bed. He lingered on until 1567, when Margaret was eleven. It was not considered necessary for girls of her class to learn to read and write, but no doubt she learned from her mother housewifely skills and something about running a business.

Her mother did not mourn for long. A scant four months after her husband's death, she had married an innkeeper called Henry May. He was ambitious to rise in the city hierarchy, and ended by becoming the Lord Mayor of York. Margaret may have been uncomfortable as a step-daughter for in 1571, when she was only fifteen, she married a widower with two sons. He was much older than she was; a butcher called John Clitherow, with a prosperous wholesale and retail business. After the marriage ceremony in her native parish, St Martin le Grand, she moved to her husband's home, over his shop in the Shambles.

It was a noisy, smelly place. The street was used as an abattoir, and the slaughtered animals were dismembered and carried into the shop and displayed for sale. The air in the narrow street must have been stifling in summer. It was not an atmosphere for the squeamish.

Somehow Margaret flourished. She quickly became the mother of two children and, young as she was, ruled the household with a firm hand, keeping her servants and the journeymen in order. Yorkshire women are noted for their toughness and resilience even today, and Margaret Clitherow was their worthy ancestress. Although she was quite capable of hanging meat alongside her husband, she enjoyed the feasting and dancing and singing that accompanied his progress up the ladder of civic responsibility. From bridgemaster, a member of the committee overseeing the upkeep of the bridge over the River Ouse, he progressed to special constable, charged with routing out Catholic suspects. By 1574 he achieved the rank of gentleman by becoming a chamberlain of the city of York.

He was not without Catholic relatives, and his brother William later became a priest, but he himself conformed to Anglican worship. By 1573 those who did not were fined, and if over the age of sixteen were forbidden to move more than five miles from their own dwelling. A year later his wife was to be subject to these restrictions.

It is not known what exactly made Margaret take instruction to become a Catholic. In 1572 the city had been shaken by the execution of Thomas Percy, the Catholic Earl of Northumberland. His family was so powerful that although convicted of treason he was offered his life if he would turn Protestant. His refusal made a great impression upon the people, most of whom had conformed to the religion professed by those in power. Whatever the reason for her conversion, Margaret was to be faithful until death.

But she was not isolated in her adherence. She was always popular with her neighbours, and in the Shambles she had a next-door neighbour who was a convinced Catholic, and had a mass centre in her house. It was a room on the top floor, and Margaret had constructed a narrow entrance from the adjoining chamber so that she could creep through and receive the forbidden sacrament. In that close society not much could be kept secret. Her husband knew of her change of heart, and to his eternal credit allowed her to imperil his fortune. When she was made an official recusant in 1576, and became liable for fines, he paid them uncomplainingly. As a mere wife in those days, in spite of her unremitting work for the business, she had no money of her own.

But the house next door was raided, and the worshippers imprisoned. Margaret was taken to the new prison on the Ouse Bridge, which had been built to house Catholics who disobeyed the new laws against hearing mass. There she started to follow a very different way of life. It was her first taste of enough leisure to learn to read and write. Amongst the cross-section of the faithful were some from the old Catholic families, who could teach her. The original mass centre in York, the town house of the noble Vavasour family, flourished, and much aided the Catholics of the city. Through them no doubt books of devotion became available. Margaret learned to love Thomas á Kempis's *Imitation of Christ*.

With her fellow prisoners she evolved a regime very much like the life of the early Christians. They had food, clothing, and everything else in common, encouraged each other in the singing of psalms and hymns, and vied for the post of servant

161

in the community. At intervals some of the priests and lay people were taken away to suffer martyrdom. Margaret was in no doubt where her own way might lead.

After a year she was released, but the Margaret Clitherow who returned to the Shambles was very different from the one who had left. Her voice, known for its sharp wit, was gentler. She could no longer stomach the rich foods at the civic feasts to which her husband's position procured invitations. She attended to his wants as dutifully as ever, but her own were simpler – rye bread, milk, pottage and butter. Her neighbours loved and trusted her, bringing her their problems – and in a close-packed community, disagreements often broke out in those narrow streets. The citizens found her presence calming: out of gratitude and affection, they did not betray her.

For she was harbouring seminary priests in her home, which had taken over from her neighbour's as the local mass centre. Priests were arriving in ever-increasing numbers from Douai on the continent. After 1580 they brought with them the translation of the New Testament which Margaret learned to love. Especially vivid to her must have been the Acts of the Apostles, and the Epistles to the persecuted in the early Church, which were so very applicable to the scattered remnants of Catholic England. On the feast of the Assumption, 1581, the worshippers at Dorothy Vavasour's town house suffered a surprise raid by the authorities. Mrs Vavasour was given a sentence of life imprisonment in a damp cell in the prison on the Ouse. Many more paid for their devotion with their lives.

This left Margaret as the only person with the will and ability to organise a mass centre in the city; a task she set about without delay. The penalties for hearing mass now became more severe. This was partly due to the fear with which the authorities regarded the arrival of the first Jesuits in England. They were the shock troops of the Counter-Reformation, owing their allegiance directly to the pope, and known for their zeal for martyrdom. In this fierce climate of persecution, Margaret was arrested again, but released this time after only six months. She was pregnant with her third child, and it was the custom to ensure that the innocent baby should be born outside prison.

Her husband John continued with his ambiguous behaviour. He was genuinely devoted to his wife, admiring her courage, and never reproaching her for conduct which must have embarrassed him. He was anxious for his position as a civic dignitary, and could not see why such a fuss was made about devotional rites. He belonged to the unthinking majority who took the line of least resistance. When indulging his appetite for alcohol, he was said to be abusive about Catholics, but in his wife's company he was sober and industrious. He was not the first or the last to express one opinion during a night out with the lads, and another when restrained by a determined spouse.

It was about this time that Margaret parted with her eldest son, sending him to Douai to be educated. She was determined that one of her children at least should be free from the tormenting secrecy of the conditions under which she practised her faith. It was no doubt her wish that he should have a vocation to the priesthood, though it was a hard time for those who had. Between July 1582 and May 1583 five of those who ministered to the York community were taken to the castle prison. One by one they were dragged through the city and executed upon the gallows at Knavesmire with the barbaric savageries of those days. Margaret would make her way by night to meditate at the scene of their deaths, returning before dawn to her house, for she was constantly watched. In the summer she was imprisoned again – this time for eighteen months – and released on condition that she was kept under house arrest.

She had declared that she would never turn a priest from her door, and her confessor told her she should prepare for her own death, anticipating an Act that was passed by Parliament in 1585, making it high treason for anyone born in England to go abroad and take holy orders, then return to his native country. Anyone who succoured such a person was also liable to the death penalty. In spite of this she allowed her confessor to live in the house.

In March 1586 a young Flemish boy of twelve was staying with the family. His fear and ignorance were played on by those whose work it was to hunt out Catholic transgressors of the law. Terrified, he led them to the secret room recently vacated by the priest – so recently that a meal was still on the table. Mass vestments and altar plates were discovered in the Shambles, and traced to Margaret. She was arrested, and her trial fixed for the 14th of March.

The Guildhall, with its stout wooden pillars and vaulted roof, was crammed for the event. The place was familiar to her as the scene of those feasts she had attended reluctantly with her husband. Today her judges faced her from the high table; two from the Assize court, supported by four members of the Queen's Council of the North. Calmly and firmly she denied that she had ever harboured enemies of the queen. Her demeanour impressed everyone present, not least one of her judges. He asked her how she wished to be tried.

'Having made no offence, I need no trial,' was her reply.

This was sensational, since a refusal to plead carried an automatic sentence of pressing to death. The kindlier of her judges, John Clinch, urged her to plead.

'If you say that I have offended and must be tried, I will be tried by none but God, and your own consciences,' she persisted.

Like the clowning of devils in a mystery play, two men were then paraded in the mass vestments. If their rough humour was meant to disconcert her, the intention did not succeed. When asked how she liked the use to which the vestments had been put, she commented that she 'liked them very well when they were on the backs of those who know how to use them for God's honour, as they were made.'

Clinch redoubled his efforts to get her to plead, but his companion on the bench became hostile, and accused her of immorality with the priests. At that time it was a common charge, fuelled by Protestant propaganda. Neither approach moved her. She had made up her mind not to risk a trial in which her family and neighbours might have been called on to give evidence against her. She wished to die without leaving her death on anyone's conscience except her judges. The trial was held over for a second day, Judge Clinch hoping that a night's reflection would alter her mind.

Given Margaret's determination, it was a forlorn hope. Next day the crowded court heard her pour scorn upon them, challenging them to find witnesses against her – apart from 'children who with an apple or a rod you may make to say what you will.'

This enraged the judge who had been against her from the first. He called her a 'naughty, wilful woman', and pronounced the most cruel form of punishment provided in the law, involving three days of torture by pressing with weights before death was allowed to end her sufferings. Margaret merely commended her judges to a better sentence, when they came to the judgement of God.

Her husband was distraught, and suffered a severe haemorrhage from his nose as he cried out that she was the best wife in England, and the best Catholic. But not even the offer of all he had could save her now. For ten days, while her cause was discussed in every house in York, and her popularity grew, she languished in prison. Attempts were made to blacken her name: stories were circulated of infidelity to her husband, and that she and the priests she harboured lived in luxury, while her children starved. Hardly anyone believed them. The final indignity was to try and get her to renounce the faith, but she firmly repulsed their efforts.

Her execution, considering the state of public opinion in the city, could not be long delayed, and was set for the 25th of March. She spent the night before in prayer, and then donned a linen shift she had made for herself. The sentence had called for her to face death naked, and it troubled her. From her few possessions, she sent her hat to her husband, to signify her loving acknowledgment of him as head of the family, and her stockings and shoes to her daughter Anne, indicating that she should follow in her footsteps.

Bareheaded and barefoot she was taken the few yards from the prison to the Tolbooth. There, within sight of the river by which she had been born, sentence was carried out. As the weights were piled upon the door under which she lay, she was heard to say:

'Jesu, Jesu, Jesu, have mercy on me.' Her last agony took a quarter of an hour.

The burial of her body was performed hastily, near a dunghill. Six weeks later, loving Catholic hands disinterred it, found it without a trace of putrefaction, and gave it an honourable resting-place. It was not until four hundred years later, on the 25th of October 1970, that she was declared a saint, along with thirty-nine other English martyrs. At St Peter's in Rome, a crowd of fifty thousand roared their approval; and the devotion to her continues to this day in her native city of York.

* * *

It was late at night. Her husband had forsaken the pub, to view the snooker on television. She hoped his temper would not suffer for it in the morning. As she scrubbed the cooking-pots from supper, she thought about her children. The youngest was in his room, studying for his A-levels, and expected to get a university place. Her two daughters had married well-to-do farmers in the county. Her remaining sons were in London – one a lawyer with a flourishing practice and political ambition; the other had joined the City rat-race, and thrived on it. Though all had climbed the social ladder, they reverted to their native accents when they came home. They were fond of their parents – yet still the hurt remained... She stifled a sigh, and tackled the potato saucepan.

There was a step on the stairs. Expecting that her youngest had come down in search of coffee to refresh his labours, she started to fill the kettle. He came in and watched her preparations: a typical man, she thought – waiting while she made it. As she crossed the kitchen to get the Nescafe, she caught sight of his face. There was something different about him – a kind of inner excitement. Previous experience made her suspicious.

'What have you been up to, son?' she enquired brusquely.

'Nothing, mum,' he muttered self-consciously.

'You can't tell me. Have you failed your mocks?'

'I haven't heard, but I don't think so,' he returned mildly.

'You've got a new girl,' she accused at random.

'No, mum. What made you think that?'

He refused to meet her gaze, and took the cup of coffee she handed him. She resigned herself to her usual state of maternal ignorance. You gave birth to them, you fed and clothed them, but what went on in their heads was a mystery.

As he left the room, he turned in the doorway.

166

'By the way – I went into St Wilfred's today. Father Hunter was there, and we got talking. I only meant to light a candle for the mocks, but he had me making my confession... Trapped me, he did.'

She was about to cry out with pleasure, but he was gone. Instead, she polished the saucepan until she could see her face in it.

St Teresa of Avila

t was a shaft of moonlight through the uncurtained window that had woken her. Instantly her senses sang, as they always did, avid for the sight and sound and smell of the beautiful world that surrounded her. She sprang up, hurried to the door, and opened it. Beyond the strip of garden where she grew the vegetables that formed the basis of her simple meals, were the dales, free and open, miles upon miles of them. The fresh wind was like a cold bath and she shivered with delight.

Hers was no dream cottage; it was more of a shack, with pre-fabricated walls and a corrugated iron roof. The heating was provided by an ancient and temperamental stove, on which she cooked. There was a single tap, and no electricity. The old lady in the house next door, too poor to install any modern improvements, was glad to rent it to her in exchange for help in the garden, which had become overgrown since her husband died.

For the woman at the door, it was the fulfilment of a dream that had haunted her from her childhood in the big city, where her father had been a successful businessman. She had been lively and intelligent, popular with her brothers and sisters; a practical girl, who had helped with the smaller children, mopping up their messes, and dealing with their tantrums. She had a taste for folk-music, and the writings of Tolkien, and raced with her contemporaries to adopt the latest fashion in clothes. Yet alongside this, when the clamour of a busy household was at its height, she longed for the quiet of the country; to be solitary, and to feed the spirit she felt to be within her.

A pious uncle had introduced her to a poem by Richard Crashaw: the Hymn to the Adorable St Teresa – in which he used the eagle and the dove as images of her. She began to feel an affinity with the great saint, and started to read her writings; such a singular blend of the practical and the divine. She found that St Teresa too had used the beauty of nature as a stepping-stone to union with its creator. Now, as she looked at the rolling heights picked out in the moonlight, the valleys velvety black beneath, with here and there the flash of a late traveller's headlights to remind her that she was not a lone viewer of this magnificence, she felt she was almost physically borne upward and outward into the heart of the scene.

Then a torrent of words of praise and adoration poured into her mind. She strained to retain them, holding on to their glowing phrases. Later on, in tranquillity, she would call them to mind, and painstakingly reconstruct them, for she was a poet...

* * *

The last decade of the fifteenth century was a golden one for Spain. In 1492 Christopher Columbus discovered America, and began the march of the conquistadors across the north and south of the continent, providing a poor country with the wealth of the New World. Although the Spanish kings let this influx go to their heads, giving them ambitions to rule in Europe as well, a little of it remained to enrich the nobility and merchant classes. The poorest, as is always the way, remained as poor as ever; many indeed being tied to the land as serfs. Also in 1492 the last Arab emir of Granada was conquered, ending the Moorish occupation that had lasted from the Dark Ages. It had left a divided country, half of whose population, and the most successful and industrious half, was Arab or Jewish in origin. Many of its nationals had been received into the Christian faith, and were indispensable to the life of the country. The Spanish kings looked to Catholic Christianity, with its universality of law and dogma, as the one hope of unifying their diverse peoples. They were guided by the Inquisition, the clerical court that could impose its will upon all Catholics. Later on it would be used to combat a new heresy coming down from the north, but as yet Martin Luther was only a child of nine.

The Inquisition reflected the Spanish character, which owed much to the blended practical and spiritual quality of Judaism, and the military prowess and pride of their Moorish conquerors. In the fierce punishments handed out by the clerics there is an echo of the uncompromising severity of those in the Koran. When the Inquisition came to Toledo in 1485, specifically to examine Jewish converts accused of backsliding into Mosaic observances, many rich men holding high position in the town had cause to be afraid. One of them, Juan Sanchez, married to a member of the noble Cepeda family, decided to take advantage of a period of grace during which it was possible to confess to trivial crimes like eating meat in Lent, in order to escape the burning that was the final solution to obduracy in more serious offences.

Accompanied by his young sons – Alonso, one of the youngest, was only five years old – he joined the penitential processions, wearing a yellow tunic with green crosses back and front, and carrying a green candle. The humiliations attendant on a lack of orthodoxy made their mark on him; he never lapsed again. For years he kept his head well down, and changed his name, taking that of his wife's family, Cepeda. His sons followed his example. Toledo held the memory of his shame, for in his parish church the badge of his humiliation, the yellow tunic, hung with the fading record of his lapse. First he sent his sons to a relative in Avila, and then, as they started to build their businesses and make advantageous marriages, he joined them.

Alonso grew up and married a well-born lady, who, after having three children, died within two years. She had lived long enough to bring him a handsome dowry. He scorned the family business in silks and other textiles, and went into tax-farming and the manipulation of money. He was no financial genius, but did not need to be. He married again, a girl of fourteen – a cousin of his first wife, Dona Beatriz de Ahumeda. Her parents were glad, once a dispensation had been obtained, to keep her considerable fortune in money and land within their extended family. She quickly entered upon the round of housekeeping and childbirth. After the birth of two sons, her third child – born on the 28th of March 1515, within half an hour of dawn – was a daughter, Teresa.

More were to follow; by the time the family was complete it comprised nine boys and three girls. Teresa was devoted to her brothers and sisters, and they to her. Don Alonso must have expressed his love for Teresa very judiciously, for there is no evidence that her siblings were ever jealous, although she was her father's favourite. She was lively and intelligent, and when she was old enough to be let loose in her father's library, she devoured the Lives of the Saints, with which it was liberally supplied. This pious reading fired her childish imagination, and led to her first great adventure.

She persuaded Roderigo, the brother nearest to her in age, to emulate the martyrs by running away to North Africa, so that they might be beheaded by the Moors. Ever practical, even when most loftily inspired, she insisted that they should save crusts of bread to sustain them on their long journey. The two children set out with high hopes, but were soon missed, and their uncle was despatched on his horse to find them. They had not reached the first bridge across the river that divided Avila from the inhospitable plateau of Castile; the crusts remained uneaten, and the children were returned to their anxious mother. After that, their youthful piety was confined to building hermitages from the stones in the garden – which had a disconcerting habit of falling down.

Teresa's mother liked to read the popular romances of the day, based loosely on the Arthurian legends, and concerned with the amours and adventures of mythical knights – the appeal of which was not unlike the bodice-ripping historical fiction of our own day. The taste did not diminish, although Cervantes was to pillory it later in *Don Quixote*. Surreptitiously – for her father disapproved – Teresa shared her mother's taste, though she was careful to point out in later life that her mother only read them as a distraction from the cares of her household, and never neglected her duty.

Teresa, however, was completely absorbed by them. They gave her a liking for fine clothes and jewels; she became worldly and rather vain. The catalogue of her charms – nice hair, dark eyes, a fresh complexion – gives no direct explanation of the attraction she had for all sorts of people. That she possessed that elusive quality, a magic personality, there is no doubt. She even prevailed upon Roderigo to assist her in concocting a romantic novel of their own, circulated within the family. She may have gained from this juvenile exercise (which did not survive) some of the confidence to write her later works.

At the critical age of fourteen, when Teresa was flowering into womanhood, her mother died, worn out with the childbearing she had embarked upon when she was scarcely older than Teresa was now. Grief-stricken, her daughter had recourse to Our Lady, mother of us all, to take her place. Don Alonso became a single parent; his only assistant in overseeing his high-spirited second daughter was her half-sister Maria, already in the long process of negotiations to be married. The extent of Teresa's involvement in worldly pleasures at this time is unclear. Probably, what she described vaguely in the light of her later ambitions to complete detachment, was nothing we would regard as very terrible. Traditionally, Spanish girls have always been well-protected; their chastity and piety a matter of family honour. But she was much in the company of a female cousin, less strictly brought up, whom Teresa's father regarded as a bad influence. To protect his daughter, he removed her to the care of the Augustinian nuns at the convent of Our Lady of Grace, where she spent the next eighteen months as a boarder.

This was a very different sort of life. Her father, for all his piety, liked to live well. Possibly because of his early shame, he enjoyed the trappings of wealth, fashionable clothes and a good table. Now Teresa lived in a poor congregation, glad enough to make a little extra money from the boarders. Her brothers, now growing into men, talked robustly of making their fortunes on the battlefields of the New World. Her sole masculine influence was confined to the glimpse of a visiting priest.

For a week she pined, then her natural resilience reasserted

173

itself, and she set out to win the hearts of her companions. She was popular with everyone, especially the mistress of the novices, in whose charge the youthful boarders remained, night and day. She seems to have been a simple soul, totally dedicated to God. She had a short way with notes and messages from the cousin – who was convinced that Teresa had been confined against her will – and supervised her conduct with visitors. As if she were longing for some sort of direction, Teresa took to conventual life like a duck to water, though as yet she felt no vocation. Then all was ended, when she developed what might have been some form of malaria (since it was to recur later) and she had to return to her father's house.

She was now nearly eighteen, and would soon have to make the choice between the only two careers open to a woman of her rank – marriage, or the religious life. Her mother's history had been no great advertisement for the attractions of the marital state, and she doubted her ability to stand the rigours of life in the cloister. While she was still undecided, her half-sister Maria and her husband invited her to convalesce on their country estate.

She broke her journey there, at the house of an uncle, a widower who lived in seclusion, only waiting until his children were off his hands to adopt the life of a friar. Together they discussed the books of devotion she read to him, and she developed a revulsion against the shallowness of the world. Weakened by her illness, she feared the approach of death, and felt totally unworthy of heaven. The influence of her uncle's favourite reading, the writings of St Jerome, who had called on high-born women to leave their father's houses and become warriors of Christ, appealed to her. After spending a scant two weeks with Maria, she returned to acquaint her father with her decision. It was not to enter the stern convent of the Augustinians, but to follow the more indulgent rule of the Carmelites at the convent of the Incarnation, where a friend of hers, Maria Suarez, was already a nun. She still held back a little of herself. Hers was no total abandonment to love of God; it was a fear of hell that drove her on.

Whether she prepared the ground badly, or whether her father had his own ideas for her future, the news was a shock to him, and he met it with a blank refusal. He needed a female head of the household. There was a young daughter, Juana, who needed guidance, which after Teresa's convent schooling, she would be able to supply. He may not have abandoned hope of a brilliant marriage for her; she was still young and attractive enough for that. Teresa persisted, already showing signs of the strength of purpose that was to distinguish her later life. It took courage for a girl to stand up to her father, in the sixteenth century. She was absolutely dependent on his approval of her resolution. Father held the purse-strings, and a dowry to take to the convent was essential to her plans.

He gave way a little, saying she could enter after his death. But having made her decision, she was unwilling to have it delayed to an uncertain future. How could she tell if her enthusiasm would survive the temptations of the good living her father's house provided? She had to make the move now or never. She enlisted the help of her brother Juan, whom she had fired with a desire to become a Dominican monk, and who was sympathetic to her cause. One chilly November morning before dawn they walked the silent streets of Avila to the Convent of the Incarnation. Her distinguished name and known talents gained her entry. She waited, having staked everything on the fact that she was her father's favourite – and that he was always careful to preserve his family honour in the eyes of the world. She had read him rightly: he bowed his head to the inevitable, and gave way. The dowry would be forthcoming.

The poorer nuns at the Incarnation slept in a dormitory. Don Alonso's wealth ensured that Teresa would acquire the use of a suite of rooms, comprising her cell, a guest-room, a small kitchen, and an oratory – to be furnished and decorated as she pleased. Although her mood on entering was one of surrender rather than a joyful advance to embrace the life – indeed, her departure from her family cost her great pain – once she became a postulant, she determined to be perfect in her observance of the Rule. Against her own proud and ardent nature, she strove to cultivate humility and subservience.

She became enthusiastic in penance, flogging herself with nettles, and fasting prodigiously. Later she would describe these excesses in scathing terms. Characteristically, she did

175

not neglect the good works that go hand in hand with faith, and volunteered to nurse an elderly nun whose terminal illness had particularly revolting symptoms.

All this took toll of her own fragile health. She had been professed for barely a year when her father became seriously alarmed. He consulted the best doctors in Avila, but it was a herbalist enthusiastically recommended by her sister Maria who was chosen to treat her. This alternative practitioner only operated in the country; and she left the convent, accompanied by her old friend Maria Suarez, for the foothills of the Gredos mountains. There grew the special herbs that were required for her treatment; but they only grew in spring. This was autumn, and she had a winter to get through. In great distress she turned to a little book that her pious uncle had given her when she called on him, on her way to the hoped-for cure. It was *The Third Spiritual Alphabet* by Francisco de Osuna, a Franciscan friar.

This volume dealt with a subject rather neglected in the convent of the Incarnation – contemplative prayer. The author was correct enough in his attitude to the Church, but had become popular in Spain among those influenced by the Lutheran wind blowing from the north. No less an authority than St John of Avila had counselled that it should be studied with discretion. Despite this warning, Teresa absorbed the book with all her abundant energy. Her body was the frail lamp through which a great spirit glowed and burned. For the first time in her life, she found a release for her genius. Slowly, and with some difficulty, she forged a relationship with God in prayer. It brought her rich rewards, moments of bliss in which she could look down with contempt on the earthly things that had given her pleasure. It altered her life at the very moment when it was most threatened.

She lost no opportunity to talk of the great new love that was consuming her. Her natural confidant was her confessor. On the face of it, he was not a worthy recipient: he was a sensual man, and kept a mistress. He was also attracted to his penitent, for love begets love, and her deep spiritual love spilled over to him. She assured him earnestly that she could never be trapped into mortal sin, and received his assurance that such a thing was far from his thoughts. She set out, as many good women have done before and since, to reclaim the man from his wicked ways. Unlike most, she was successful, without destroying herself in the process, and claimed her first convert outside her own family. She fastened on the symbol of an amulet his mistress had given him, which he wore round his neck. She would always seize on concrete symbols, claiming that her imagination was 'sluggish'. Using her influence over him, she persuaded him to part with the amulet, and flung it into a nearby river. This certainly seemed to do the trick. His mistress's power to charm him waned, and he gave her up.

Came the spring, and the herbalist started her treatment. She seems to have been particularly inept, because her frequent purgings, and the vile concoctions she forced her patient to take, all but killed her. She was unable to swallow any food, and was racked with pain in every part of her body. Eventually, at death's door, she was taken back to Avila. When she fell into a coma it was decided she should end her days at the Convent of the Incarnation. She received extreme unction, and a grave was dug. Her father wept over her seemingly lifeless body, insisting: 'The girl is not dead...!'

He was right: she did not die. For eight months she was paralysed, reduced to communicating by moving the fingers of her right hand. For three years she was bedridden. When she was able to move at last, she was so weakened that she crawled through the little suite on hands and knees. She attributed the saving of her life to the intercession of St Joseph, to whom she would always have a special devotion. Her recovery was widely held to be miraculous, and there was no shortage of friends and relatives to congratulate the recipient of such a favour. She had lost none of her gift for charming people, and they flocked round her, some of the more privileged invading her suite. She regarded this as a chance to gain converts to the practice of mental prayer. One of them was her own father, who was turning more and more in his declining years to spiritual consolations.

This pleasant way of life lasted more than a decade, but there were dangers in it of which she was only half aware. She lost her taste for prayer, and began a close relationship with someone who had the same sort of influence over her as her frivolous teenage cousin once had. In her autobiography, this figure is so shadowy as to be sexless, but seems to have absorbed her attention, whether man or woman, and made her love of God less central. But Our Lord had marked her for his own, and gave her the first vision of himself that she ever received.

She relates how he appeared to her, an image that she perceived with the eyes of the soul, and let her know that this friendship displeased him. She dismissed it as a figment of her imagination, brought on by an over-sensitive conscience; but when a large toad appeared while she was in the company of her friend, she was convinced that this was a further sign that she should not persist in the friendship. As yet she was very young in her experience of heavenly communications.

In 1554 a copy of a Spanish translation of St Augustine's *Confessions* came into her possession, and struck an immediate chord with her. She had always considered herself a great sinner, and identified with the saint's struggles to detach himself from the pleasures of the world. While she was still in great distress over this, she came across an artist's depiction of the wounded Christ, no doubt losing nothing by being in the realistic Spanish style of the period. She broke down in tears before it, vowing never again to offend the Saviour who had suffered so much for her.

Henceforward she began her meditations by thinking of her Bridegroom when he was most lonely and forsaken, trying to make up by her devotion for his rejection by others. She was to be richly rewarded. Another source of inspiration was the contemplation of the beauties of the natural world – a stretch of water, or a single flower – which led her straight to their creator. Few saints have had such a feeling for gardens, which she used as an image for the soul in her description of the life of prayer. But all her images are simple and vivid, and drawn from everyday things. She deplored her lack of learning, and one of her greatest compliments was to describe a person as 'learned', but this very lack makes her accessible over the centuries. She speaks to all souls – even those with no experience of the spiritual life.

Her own spiritual life became intense. She passed from the Prayer of Quiet, the passive attendance on God, to the Prayer of Union, when God invades the soul and possesses it. Then she began to hear voices, and that really scared her. While she heard them – with the ear of the soul, for they did not come to her external sense of hearing – she was convinced that they came from God. But she knew too that such voices had a bad name amongst her contemporaries. Too many pious women had been deceived into thinking they were receiving messages from heaven, and ended up in the arms of the Inquisition.

Despairing of certainty, she appealed to a succession of confessors, who were of little use to her; they either lacked experience of mental prayer, or regarded it as dangerous if not heretical. There was one Jesuit who seemed to be sympathetic, but he was only passing through Avila. He recommended the Spiritual Exercises of St Ignatius before going on his way. She found them helpful, but they did not solve her problem.

Her distress became acute, fuelled by the reaction of the community, amongst whom rumours about Teresa became rife. It was hard to know which gave her more anxiety – those who were excited by her mystical gifts, or those who could not understand why she should have been so favoured, and expressed their scepticism.

Then Dona Guiomar de Ulloa, a wealthy widow, became oppressed by her empty life, and pleaded with Teresa to become her companion. Such was the laxity of the rule of enclosure at the Incarnation, that Teresa's poor health was considered reason enough for her to be allowed to accept the invitation. For a considerable time, all went well; during nearly three years she enjoyed the peace and security of Dona Guiomar's home. She found another sympathetic Jesuit confessor, who was prepared to believe her when she said she was experiencing the actual presence of Christ when she prayed. But then he fell ill, and after being nursed by his penitent and her benefactress, he was posted away from the town.

His successor, Father Alvarez, was of a different stamp altogether. He was completely out of his depth in dealing with Teresa, and swung violently between supposing her to be possessed by the devil, and considering her to be suffering from too great a religious fervour. Teresa was again deeply unhappy, and went back to the Incarnation. She was forty-four years old – aging by the standards of the time – but treated by Father Alvarez like a novice who could not be trusted to know her own mind. She had her number of communions cut down, and her books were taken away. Her precious solitude was frowned upon, and she was urged to seek company. She strove in vain to make Father Alvarez understand the quality of her visions. But the tables were turned when he himself had a vision, while meditating; when he told her of it, she teased him, and after that they were on better terms.

Gradually she was granted the favour of seeing Our Lord. To the inner eye of her soul appeared first his hands, then his face, and then the whole beauty of his resurrected body. Her ecstasies became frequent and public. They possessed her so entirely that she began to dread the presence of other people. She was generally regarded as a pious peep-show, pursued about the convent in the hope that she might be seen apparently insensible, or levitating. The harder she fought to achieve anonymity in the community, the more singular she became.

Her young sister Juana, who had once taken the guest-room in Teresa's suite, was now married, and her place had been taken by two nieces, Maria and Beatriz. They entertained pious ladies in the evenings, and Teresa would join them – the central figure in the group. She talked with great wisdom, and spiced her conversation with her ready wit. One autumn evening in 1560 she was talking of the hermits of Mount Carmel, whom the Order had been founded to emulate. Maria, half-jokingly, regretted that she could not follow the old rule of austerity and complete enclosure that had existed before the mitigation of 1432. There were some orders of friars who had become Discalced (or barefoot) but there was no similar order of nuns. Dona Guiomar, who was of the company, offered with her usual generosity to endow a house once it had been started, and Maria offered a thousand ducats from her dowry.

Teresa smiled at their enthusiasm. It occurred to her that a small convent run according to the primitive rule would be very much to her taste, but the atmosphere seems to have been light-hearted and almost frivolous, and she did not take the discussion seriously. But not long after, having received communion – a time when she was most prone to have revelations – a project for the foundation was completely disclosed to her: even the name – St Joseph's. She was bidden to tell her confessor straight away. Father Alvarez took up his usual position of fence-sitting, saying he would refer the matter to the Father-Provincial of the Carmelites. This did not satisfy Teresa. She sought other advice, and was happy enough to get a favourable opinion from a very holy friar; Fray Pedro de Alcantara, who was the founder of the Reformed Franciscans. They had succeeded in rekindling the true spirit of St Francis himself.

Despite – or perhaps because of – his great holiness, Fray Pedro's advice proved to be very practical. He had great insight into the psychology of the authorities. He insisted that Dona Guiomar should do all the negotiating with the provincial of the Carmelite order, and that the legal papers for the purchase of a suitable house should be in the name of Teresa's sister Juana and her husband. This was necessary, because not only were Teresa's religious superiors liable to look askance at an attempt by a nun to leave her convent and set up one of her own, but there would be opposition from the civic authorities who had suffered a proliferation of religious foundations, which when insufficiently endowed became dependent on the alms of the townspeople.

For six months they were kept in a state of suspense. Dona Guiomar even appealed to Rome, and Teresa persuaded her to have the new foundation put under the protection of the Bishop of Avila, thus bypassing the Carmelites who had shown some opposition to her plans. Builders of 'dream homes' in Spain will not be surprised to learn that the legal proceedings were protracted, or that a wall collapsed during its construction. A young son of Juana, no doubt watching with interest as small boys will, was badly injured. His aunt Teresa took him to her room, and appeared hand in hand with him an hour later. This may or may not have been a miracle; Teresa would neither affirm nor deny it.

Then, when the plan seemed on the point of fruition, the Carmelite provincial had other orders for her. A friend of his, Dona Luisa de la Cerda, had been recently widowed, and was utterly crushed by her bereavement. Descended from the ruling houses of France and Spain, and married to a nephew of the cardinal archbishop, she had lived a life of wealthy security, and was unused to deprivations of any kind. At her home in Toledo, still an imposing city despite being superceded as the capital by Madrid, she had heard of the humble nun of Avila, and asked for her as a companion.

At first Teresa was disappointed. Her heart was with the new foundation; she was inclined to take her friends' advice and beg not to go. But one of her revelations came to stop her, saying that God would be served by her journeying to Toledo. Life in Dona Luisa's household was quite different from any she had known before; yet she found that the widow, who speedily became a friend, was surrounded with protocol by which she was as closely bound as a nun to the rule of her order. It was mitigated by fine clothes and jewels certainly, which Dona Luisa paraded for her companion's distraction; but Teresa now had, through her visions, glimpses of the jewels of heaven, and was unimpressed.

She welcomed any chance to escape to her own room, where she was spied upon by the numerous hangers-on of the household, hoping to catch her in ecstasy. A chance encounter with an old acquaintance, Father Garcia de Toledo, a Dominican, led to one of the great documents that was to enrich the Church, and make her celebrated as one of its Doctors. This was the more remarkable because at first she had hesitated to enquire about the state of his soul – but they soon found themselves engaged in a deep, searching discussion. He was so moved by the experience, he asked her to write her own account of her spiritual journey. Now she had an opportunity to write, free from the cares of her work as the foundress of the Reformed Carmelites. She set about her task at once, and before she left Toledo in June 1562, the first draft of her greatest work, the guide to the life of prayer – the spiritual inspiration for countless souls – was complete.

Meanwhile visitors came and went, including Fray Pedro, and a forty-year-old widow called Maria Yepes. She had entered a Carmelite convent on her husband's death, and remained attached to it though not professed. Although she could neither read nor write, she knew the ancient Carmelite

Rule by heart, and had felt called by Our Lady herself to found a reformed community. Travelling to Rome to obtain permission, she had experienced in a Mantuan convent what it was like to live under the strict Rule. It seemed incredible that Teresa had never known that this involved an absence of even communal possessions and endowments, but she learned as much from this pious lady. She straightway started seeking counsel about whether it would be advisable for her own foundation.

From his sickbed, Fray Pedro was eloquent in his championship of Lady Poverty; others put strenuous arguments against her attempt to launch her frail boat without provisions. Her great confidence demanded that she and her sisters should abandon themselves utterly to Divine Providence. So on the 24th of August 1562, Teresa, two of her cousins who had been Incarnation nuns, and four novices – orphans without dowries – settled down in the simple house that had been prepared for them. Almost immediately Teresa was assailed by doubt. She had obtained permission for the foundation by devious means: how could she hope to keep the sisters faithful, when they never knew where their next meal was coming from? Would she herself, with her poor health, be able to stand the austerity of the life? Had the devil, or her own pride, deluded her into thinking that she could do more for God at St Joseph's than she could at the Incarnation? Her wonderful gift for prayer deserted her. She knelt before the Blessed Sacrament, flinging herself on the divine mercy. As suddenly as they had come, her doubts vanished. Calm and serene, she faced the storm that was growing in Avila about the little vessel.

The civic authorities were becoming concerned, and so were the nobility, the shopkeepers who depended for their livelihood on getting a share of their wealth, and other religious orders, also anxious for their slice of the communal cake. Grumbles with a familiar ring were heard, about 'taxpayers' money'. A meeting of the town council ordered an assembly of all the interested parties. Some of them did not wait for its deliberations, but gathered outside St Joseph's to close the new foundation by force. The situation was worse because Teresa had been ordered by the Prioress of the

Incarnation to appear before her, and, faithful to her vow of obedience, she complied. Her beleaguered nuns stood firm; they barricaded themselves in, and defied the invasion. The town councillors, finding the four defenceless but determined novices more than a match for them, withdrew to plot anew.

Meanwhile at the Incarnation Teresa, confined to her cell, remained equally firm. She freely admitted that her life had been imperfect, submitted to the prioress's authority, and was unfailingly pleasant and polite to everyone. But she still had her trump card – the bishop's jurisdiction over her convent – and she was only biding her time before playing it. When she did so, the bishop backed her to the hilt. Her opponents appealed higher, to the royal council, and a lawsuit began. Lawyers then were no less reluctant to line their pockets than they are in our own day, and Teresa had no money. But she had friends in Avila who rallied to her cause.

The town councillors eventually suggested a compromise. If Teresa would agree that the convent should be endowed, they would offer no opposition to it. She was sorely tempted: all she and her nuns wanted was to be free to live for God. Surely it would be better to give way, and end the disagreement with the authorities? The dilemma was ended by one of her revelations. Fray Pedro appeared to her from beyond the grave, pleading for his Lady Poverty, as he had in life. Teresa acted at once. There was a higher authority than the royal council, and she sought it. She appealed to the pope himself. It was becoming obvious that the reformed orders were a powerful weapon in the Counter-Reformation, and a papal rescript was forthcoming. The nuns of St Joseph's were to be allowed to live as they wished, without any possessions, on the alms of the faithful.

There followed three and a half years of calm such as Teresa was never to know again. Day after day the Rule was followed. She laid down a strict regime for her nuns that accounted for every minute of their day. The liturgy, private prayer and meditation, the work of house and garden, spinning and weaving took up much of it. But recreation was not neglected. Teresa considered it a healthy exercise to combat the melancholy which she regarded as a hazard in the religious life. She encouraged the writing of verse, and singing and dancing were not unknown. Some of the more serious-minded nuns considered it was beneath them, but she had stern ways of making her displeasure felt at these lapses in perfect obedience.

On the whole she had a poor view of female intelligence, and thought book-learning for her nuns a waste of their time. In this she may have been remembering the romances that she considered had corrupted her youth. The petty jealousies and vendettas that grew up between women living in a small enclosed community she dealt with firmly. She seemed to be unaware that men were subject to the same weaknesses, and compared her situation bitterly with that of her male counterparts. But her problems were not theirs. She was running a powerhouse of prayer; they were free to be active in the world. Her nuns were striving to be the backbone of the Counter-Reformation, the bankers of the spiritual riches that the rest of the Church could draw upon. She appealed to her nuns for heroic strength, and the measures she took, though severe, were necessary for the end in view.

But the time was coming when she would be called to the active life. In the meantime she added the history of the founding of St Joseph's to her autobiography, and wrote other works for the edification of her nuns. These must have been composed at odd moments, because she took her turn at the work of the house; she was rather a good cook, and her spindle was not idle even when the inevitable visitors, attracted by her fame, called her to the parlour. She was not deprived of heavenly consolations, receiving many visions.

The move to a wider sphere of activity came in 1567 when the Father-General of the Carmelite order reached Avila on a visit of inspection of all the houses. He came with reform in mind, but he was so impressed by St Joseph's and its foundress that he gave her a patent authorising her to found convents of Reformed Carmelite nuns in any part of Castile. Before he left Spain, he had also given her permission to found two priories for friars – a great concession. The friars undertook the important office of confessors to the nuns, and Teresa had suffered grievously from unsympathetic confessors.

It was taken for granted that Teresa's energy, united to

Divine Providence, would look after their finances. Such indeed proved to be the case. At critical moments, benefactors appeared with gifts of money or property for the foundations. In four years Teresa established seven convents in various parts of Castile. The material of the foundations was often shaky, but her nuns took physical discomfort in their stride. Along with the communion vessels, often borrowed, and the statue of St Joseph from the mother-house, she took a quantity of straw so that her nuns should always have bedding. She travelled by mule or cart, ever since the day when she had consented to use the Princess of Eboli's coach, and had been admonished by a hostile priest for doing so. Her nuns were indignant, but Teresa accepted the rebuke, saying:

'He is the only one with the courage to tell me my faults.'

Her frail health seemed to improve on these gruelling journeys. She managed to find two friars who wished to help her adapt her rule to fit their different circumstances. One was the prior of the Carmelites in Avila, who had helped her in her setting-up of the convents. He resigned his post to join a tiny priory in Duruelo, thirty miles from Avila. It was so cramped that the two chapels were only large enough to sit in or lie down, not to stand. He found there a young man whom Teresa had persuaded to stay with the Carmelites when he thought he might try his vocation as a Carthusian. He appears to have been an art student at some stage in his career; at any event he had all the artist's practical ability, and could turn his hand to anything – even being in demand as a stone-mason, in spite of his diminutive stature which made him look younger than he was. This young friar was called John of the Cross.

But Teresa was still technically a member of the community of the Incarnation, and in 1571 their nuns elected her prioress. She went there with deep misgivings, fearing that it was an attempt to impede the reforming movement. However, she had permission to live as a Discalced wherever she was, and the apostolic delegate had given her the job of organising the affairs of the Incarnation. From the security of St Joseph's she gave an order that all the lay people who used the convent as a convenient refuge should remove themselves. Such was her authority that she was obeyed – albeit grumblingly. There was a hard core of opposition to her election, and she disarmed it with a master-stroke. On the first day she assumed the office of prioress, with all eyes upon her, she took her old place in the choir. The seat of the prioress was occupied by a statue of Our Lady, with the house-keys in her hands. The symbolism was instantly and vividly apparent.

She put the finances of the convent on a more solid basis. There had been a great deal of bungling with meagre resources. On the spiritual side she announced to her nuns that she was giving them a saint for their confessor. It was the young John of the Cross – and in the fullness of time her prophecy was justified, when his feast joined the calendar of the universal Church. He was wise beyond his years, and even chided the foundress herself with the gentle admonishment:

'When you make your confession, Mother, you have a way of making the prettiest excuses.'

His other talents included exorcism, and firm and confident cures for the melancholy that Teresa regarded as the curse of conventual life. They were very close, and we would have had a great treasure if her letters to him had survived, but he considered them too intimate, and destroyed them.

Her term of office was three years, and after it was over she took to the road again, visiting her foundations, and seeing that the constitutions under which they had been set up were adhered to. There were some notable incidents. The Princess of Eboli, a colourful character noted for her beauty, which was enhanced rather than impeded by the black eye-patch she wore, lost her husband, who was the one restraining influence on her flamboyant personality. Always capricious, she decided to take the veil, and elected to try her vocation at Teresa's convent at Pastrana.

This unlikely postulant resisted all attempts to fit her into the narrow mould of the primitive rule, and insisted on being bowed and scraped to, as she imagined fitted her rank. The king used his influence to get her to return to the young children she had left in order to satisfy her whim for the spiritual life. She blamed Teresa and the order for this, and harassed the nuns so that they had to flee the lands on which their house was built, because they were under her jurisdiction. At one stage she had read Teresa's autobiography and laughed over it with the ladies of her court. Her final act of revenge was to denounce it to the Inquisition, and only powerful friends and Teresa's irreproachable orthodoxy saved her from the clutches of that institution.

One of the Reformed friars in her original foundation was a young man called Father Jeronimo Gracian. Though only thirty, he had been entrusted with the office of Carmelite Provincial in Andalusia. Teresa was very impressed by his gifts and his personality. Their respect was mutual, and ripened into a deep friendship. They were both charming and spontaneous, and delighted in each other's company. Teresa had found at last a spiritual director very much to her liking. It was confirmed by a vision in which Our Lord joined their hands in a pledge of unity. This might have been extremely dangerous to the equilibrium of a less balanced sixty-year-old than Teresa, but she cared for him with a mother's love, and he reciprocated as a son. She was becoming tired; her health was precarious, and she needed help in the care of her foundations. Father Gracian provided that help.

But this idyllic state of affairs was not to continue. Far away in Italy, forces inimical to the Reform were acting to deal with its future in Spain. Teresa paid the penalty of too much success. The permission to set up new houses was revoked, and the ones that had been founded in Andalusia were to be disbanded. Teresa herself was to return to Castile and be confined to one convent. The only concession was that it could be one of her own choice. Poor communications ensured that this edict reached her some nine months late; time enough for her to open a new convent in Seville. Much against her inclination, it was a grand occasion, which pleased Father Gracian. Her book of autobiography was again denounced, this time resulting in an investigation by the Inquisition. She passed this examination with flying colours, even taking a certain satisfaction in the event.

Gratefully she left Andalusia, having found that its hot climate was an obstacle to her nuns' devotions and their peace of mind. The order of seclusion in Castile caught up with her; it was very much to her taste. She was weary of the battles between the Calced and Discalced wings of the order, and happy to leave the politics in the capable hands of Father

Gracian, although she sent many letters espousing the cause of the Reform.

There had been one consolation in Andalusia; she was surrounded by her family again. Her brother Lorenzo and his three motherless children had come home from Peru. Her young niece Teresita was eight, and the apple of her aunt's eye. She lived in the convent, dressed in the Carmelite habit, and made the elderly woman's heart so glad that she suspected it might be a sin against detachment – until she was reassured by one of her visions.

She lived for the first year of her seclusion in the convent at Toledo where she spent a great deal of time in writing, completing her *Book of the Foundations* and another epic of the spiritual journey; *The Mansions of the Interior Life*. This was in obedience to Father Gracian, and a labour of love on that account. She also wrote almost a quarter of her surviving letters to him, full of solicitude for his difficulties with enemies amongst the Calced, and homely advice for his health and well-being.

The letters chart a kind of holy love affair; the names were coded to guard against scandal if – as was only too possible – they should fall into the wrong hands. We have little conception of the viciousness of the quarrels in religious life at that time.

Gossip was rife about their relationship. In the struggle, no holds were barred. Then the deaths of two protectors of the Reform meant that persecutors in high places were free to act against it. Father Gracian went literally to ground, living as a hermit in a cave outside Pastrana. St John of the Cross fared worse, and was actually imprisoned in Toledo in conditions that appalled Teresa when she heard of them. He later escaped, but his health was much impaired. All Teresa could do for her dear ones was to continue to pray for them, and petition the king on their behalf. Then the worst happened, and Father Gracian, emerging against his will to resume his duties as visitor to the Discalced in Castile, was arrested by his enemies, and confined to a monastery where he had to undergo rigorous penances.

During all this turmoil, Teresa, now at her beloved St Joseph's, was utterly wretched. It seemed that her work was being systematically destroyed. But her prayers were answered. The king, who had never ceased to back her, managed to prevail on the papal nuncio to order Gracian's release, and he was allowed to resume his previous position in Andalusia. As for Teresa, who was now sixty-five, the period of waiting and watching was over, and she was called upon to begin her travels once more.

She had fallen downstairs a few months earlier, and was still in pain from the injury; but, as ever, travelling to old-established convents and founding new ones proved a tonic, and she began to feel as if she had never been ill. On these journeys, she was less liable to ecstasies, which she found so taxing, she almost regarded them as another form of illness, often being overcome by exhaustion for several days afterwards. But rattling along in a cart on perilous mountain roads, with guides who were unreliable and often left her party in the lurch, seemed to stimulate her. These journeys were by way of being a triumphal progress, with the townspeople turning out to welcome one whom they counted a saint already.

Then her brother Lorenzo died, and this flung her into grief. To add to her troubles, he had made her executrix of his will, and so prey to an unruly collection of relatives who were also beneficiaries. She began to feel the full weight of her sixty-five years, but this did not prevent her from taking charge of her niece Teresita – now fifteen – who wanted to join her order.

Father Gracian had been chosen to head the newly-formed province of the Discalced Carmelites – separating them from the jurisdiction of the Calced at last – but her hope that he would join her to establish the new foundations was dashed. A pathetic letter survives, regretting this, and describing her desolation and loneliness.

The journey from Avila was horrendous; it poured with rain all the way – a deluge worse than anything within living memory. They were quite a large party, including the lay sister who was the nurse-companion Teresa sorely needed – Ana de San Bartolome – her niece Teresita, the prioress-designate of the new convent, and several others, both lay and religious. Father Gracian and a friar companion acted as outriders on mules. Everywhere the roads were flooded, and the marshy ground near Burgos could only be traversed by pontoon bridges over raging water.

Teresa rallied the party, calling on them to be martyrs if necessary; particularly stipulating that if she should be swept away in the torrent, they must not try to rescue her. On one occasion she believed that Father Gracian had fallen into thick mud, and was relieved when the figure of one of the muleteers emerged, quite unharmed.

It was on this journey that she was reported to have complained to God about the perils they had to face, and received the answer:

'That is how I treat my friends.'

The saint is said to have replied tartly:

'Yes, Lord – and that is why you have so few of them.'

The foundress was very ill by the time they reached the town, spitting blood and vomiting. She recovered a little, but had to keep to a liquid diet. Worse still, there was opposition to the foundation by the local archbishop, but they made so many friends amongst the townspeople that he was forced to give permission for the establishment of the convent. Like many people who began by opposing her, he was won over by her personality, and attended the dedication. His intervention had held up the work for many months, and it was summer before Teresa could return to Avila. She said goodbye to her beloved Gracian, and set out with the faithful Ana and her niece. She was never to see Gracian again, and her tender farewell to the nuns had a quality of finality about it.

At Medina she broke her journey, only to be told that she must make a detour to Alba, where a new prioress was to be installed, and to add her prayers for the safe confinement of the duchess' daughter-in-law. Her nuns urged her to plead ill-health, and proceed straight to Avila, but she put her adherence to her vow of obedience before all other considerations. She set off on another nightmare excursion in a draughty and badly-sprung coach. Her companions had difficulty in finding anything to eat in the barren region, and her condition deteriorated. On the way to Alba the little party learned that the ducal heir – a son, for whom Teresa had never ceased to pray – had been born prematurely. Her comment was: 'Thank God, now they have no further need of this old saint!'

On the 20th of September 1580, they reached Alba – Teresa admitted that she felt she had not a sound bone left in her body. She was grateful for the fresh white linen sheets provided only for invalids, and sank into them at – for her – an unprecedentedly early hour. Next morning she was up, and though leaning heavily on a stick, she insisted on inspecting every aspect of the convent. For the next nine days she contracted business on its behalf, until a severe haemorrhage made her retire to the infirmary. There was a grille overlooking the chapel, and she was able to see mass celebrated. Her last confession was heard by one of her earliest friars, who was reduced to tears. She then gave her nuns her final message, to observe the Rule and Constitutions, telling them this was all they needed to obtain eternal glory. She begged their forgiveness for providing a bad example as a nun.

On the night of the 3rd of October she was racked with pain, and clung to the psalms for comfort, repeating them as an antidote to her suffering; but at dawn her face became peaceful and serene. She only lost her tranquillity when Ana, the devoted peasant she had taught to read and write, and who was to chronicle her last days, was sent away to take food and rest. Her niece Teresita noticed her agitation, and Ana returned to cradle the dying woman in her last hours. Death came gently at nine o'clock, on the evening of St Francis of Assisi's feast – a saint with whom she had much in common. Everyone remarked on the curious fragrance which penetrated the rest of the house, from her room.

To the sixteen convents and fourteen priories she had founded, her death brought mingled grief and joy. Her own sons and daughters were certain of her sanctity. This was acknowledged in Rome when she was canonised in 1622. Alba and Avila vied with each other for the privilege of owning the remains of her mortal body. No less than five times it was disinterred, venerated, and dismembered, to supply the relics on which so much store was set in those days. These found their way all over Europe, and even into the New World.

What would please her more was that six years after her death a papal bull made her order completely independent;

and it has remained so until the present day. Her feast is kept on October 15th.

* * *

She was harvesting apples when the postman – her first visitor of the day – arrived on his bicycle. She offered him a glass of dandelion wine, but he declined it on the grounds that it was too potent a brew, and he would not trust himself on the highway after imbibing it. They both knew that he didn't care for it, but the laws of hospitality had been observed.

She glanced down at the letter he gave her. He hovered expectantly, hoping for an item of news to add to the store he took round the remote farms of the area.

'It's from my publisher,' she said, and opened it, trembling a little. She scanned the typewritten lines, and struggled with a new and terrifying thought. 'They want me to go and read my poems in London... Of course I can't.'

'But you must, miss,' he urged. 'We'll have you on the telly in no time!'

'I've got nothing to wear.' It was the age-old female cry.

He surveyed her speculatively. 'You're about the same size as our Sandra; she'd fix you up with something.'

'Thank you so much – I'll think about it,' she assured him.

After an exchange of gossip he left, impatient to spread the news. She hadn't the heart to swear him to secrecy. Turning back to her task, removing the apples with a neat twist and placing them carefully in her basket, she turned over in her mind this call to go into the outside world.

The last time she had been in the city, she had hated it. She remembered the barren pavements and the press of the crowds milling about her, each person wrapped in a private world of greed and anxiety. It was impossible to leave her oasis of quiet... But how if she were being called to share it with those poor people, so poverty-stricken in their pursuit of riches? God had not given her the gift of language to keep it to herself. What would her favourite saint have done?

What she had done, of course. When the call came, St Teresa of Avila went on her travels. Slowly she took up the basket, and went indoors to write her letter of acceptance.

193

St Clare of Assisi

A diminutive figure stood on a windy corner in the town centre. The first thing that would strike a passer-by was that she was exceedingly thin – almost emaciated. The second, on coming nearer, that for a small person she was making a great deal of noise. That was necessary, of course, to penetrate the tumult of traffic and the conversations of people shouting to be heard above it. Her guitar, playing flamenco music, was equal to the struggle, and so was her voice, which seemed to burst from her thin frame, resonant and passionate.

In spite of the unfamiliarity of the sound, it made its impact. Every few minutes some coins were dropped into the guitar-case at her feet, mostly of small denominations. The old contributed their mites because she looked as if she could do with a square meal, and something more substantial to wear than a faded sweatshirt and ragged jeans; the wind was cold, and they knew all about the expense of food and clothes. The children dragged their mothers to listen to the exciting music, and pestered them for pennies.

When she was not singing, she rewarded them with smiles that lent great radiance to her dark eyes.

A sudden shower cut short her efforts. People hurried by with their heads down. The girl shook her short, fair hair, put her guitar back in its case, and set off. She was soon soaked to the skin, yet seeing a group of people huddled under an awning she gave them an impromptu concert, this time of Irish folk-tunes. They seemed to catch light from her, and lost their hangdog expressions. Someone requested 'Danny Boy', and she obliged, ending with 'Raindrops Are Falling On My Head' – laughter followed as she introduced it. A man in plaster-stained overalls gave her a pound coin. She thanked him, and added it to the rest, then walked off into the rain, leaving a welded group of cheerful acquaintances wondering who she was.

She made her way to a building that had once been a chapel. It had been deconsecrated, but the girl had carved a rough crucifix and hung it where the altar had been. There was also a picture of Our Lady drawn in felt-tip pen on brown paper. The furniture was composed of armchairs with broken springs that betrayed their scrap-heap origin, and grouped round a calor-gas stove was a line of mattresses with ragged blankets. On these six men were lying; the youngest about sixteen, the oldest at least seventy. They greeted her as she walked in.

'How did you do?' asked the boy

'We'll eat tonight,' she assured him.

She was a member of the Third Order of St Francis, and sister and mother to these derelicts. Her inspiration was the founder of the Second Order – St Clare of Assisi.

* * *

Early in the twelfth century, northern Italy was in a state of conflict. This had been going on for nearly a hundred years, and was to drag on for a century more. The reason for it was the tension between the Holy Roman emperors, and the papacy, under some popes who had political ambitions. It became a question of which was to be the guiding influence. It was in the emperor's interest to preserve the fabric of feudal society, governing with the help of the nobility, himself at its head. The popes promoted a freer system; the city states to provide a more democratic government, with the clergy and the monasteries as the guardians of culture and civic works. Needless to say, there was good and bad on both sides;

not all the feudal lords were devils, nor all the bishops saints.

But by any reckoning, Corrado of Lutzen, Duke of Spoleto, who ruled the town of Assisi from his citadel of 'The Rock' that loomed above it, was one of the viler characters. He was ruthless and had a temper that exploded into near-madness: his nickname was 'Fly-in-the-Brain'. In 1198, on the accession of a dynamic new young pope, Innocent III, he was summoned to Narni to surrender his dukedom to the papacy. The townspeople of Assisi took advantage of his absence to sack his castle on the Rock, and those of his dependent nobles on the surrounding hills. They set up a commune, and declared for the papacy.

There is not much doubt that Francis Bernardone, a young man of sixteen, was involved in the uprising. He was brave and high-spirited, and had some aspiration to becoming a knight, though his father was a cloth-merchant, and not a member of the nobility. His mother, who came from Provence, and probably taught him some of the French songs he was so fond of, used to complain that he behaved 'more like a prince than our son'. When peace came, he was a leading figure in the festivities that the gilded youth of Assisi delighted in, now they no longer had to pay the loathsome taxes to their feudal lord. It was for older and wiser heads to worry about the expense of running the town.

There can be no apologies for beginning the story of Clare Offreduci by mentioning Francis Bernardone first; he is an integral part of her history. She might have become well-known even if she had never met him, for she was beautiful, intelligent, and of strong character, but she would certainly have been different. She was twelve years his junior, but must have known him by sight as a child, because everyone in Assisi knew him. His doings were the talk of the place. Her family was a cut above his, upper-class and military, as opposed to being in trade, however prosperous; but it was a small town – they had been baptised in the same font, and walked the same narrow streets.

It was not until he was twenty-five and she was thirteen, that the great scandal broke. Francis had become increasingly discontented with his frivolous existence. A spell as a prisoner after a battle with the neighbouring city of Perugia, and a

mysterious illness, had contrived to make him more thoughtful. And he had been foiled in his ambition to become a knight
by powerful dreams that first offered him glory, and then
commanded him to abandon all thought of arms, and go back
to Assisi. In his perplexity he went to pray in the ruined church
of St Damian, where he claimed that the figure on the crucifix
above the altar spoke to him, asking him to rebuild the church,
and turn his back on his former luxurious life. He showed the
impetuosity that was always to characterise him. Requiring
money, as he thought, to carry out his task, he went to the
usual source of it – his father's shop in the market-place. There
he took a bolt of red cloth, rode to a nearby town and sold it,
then brought the money to the surprised elderly priest at St
Damian – who wisely refused it, but consented to accept
Francis as an oblate; a servant of the church.

His father, who was a fiery character, pursued him as a
thief. Francis hid in a dark cavern, but his father caught up
with him. Pleading his new status as a religious, he was
brought before an ecclesiastical court, presided over by
Guido, Bishop of Assisi. By this time Francis had only the
clothes he stood up in, having given all his possessions to the
poor. When his father went over the story of the theft, he
stripped off his garments and flung them at his feet. Bishop
Guido, won over by the magnificence of the gesture, covered
his nakedness with his mantle, and bade him go in peace. He
went out into the cold countryside, new-born to poverty,
singing in French.

Assisi must have been ringing with the news, and the
townsfolk took sides in discussing it, mostly coming down
against Francis, because when – in obedience to one of his
voices – he returned to Assisi a year later dressed in rags, he
was the object of almost universal derision. He went about
begging for stones to restore St Damian – a sort of pious
'brickie'.

One of Clare's characteristics, like his own, was that she
was no respecter of persons: she treated all alike. When she
saw him at work while she was out riding with a companion,
she spoke to him. Something about the tattered, thin figure,
full of enthusiasm for his task and the love of God, appealed
to her. He confided to her that St Damian would one day

house a company of those wise virgins who keep oil in their lamps for the coming of the bridegroom. Young as she was, she understood him, and an idea began to dawn.

Over the next two years he repaired another church, and moved on to that of the Blessed Virgin, called the Portiuncula (the 'Little Porch') where he was joined by others, both laymen and clerics, who were attracted to the life of poverty. Without intending to at all, he had stumbled into a situation which needed a rule by which they could all live together. During this time Clare still visited him. They were falling in love; not with each other, but with Poverty. The necessity for a rule remained, and having decided on one which reflected the gospels, commanding that true disciples should go out without purse or staff, Francis – impetuous as always – upped and went to Rome.

The ragged band of travellers must have looked very odd at the papal court. It was a time when the princes of the Church really were princes. After the austerity of the Dark Ages when the spirit of penance had reigned to cleanse the world of pagan luxury, a wave of laxity had settled in. Francis had felt it as a young man in Assisi when he was the king of feasts and admirer of chivalry. So in the Church there were bishops who wielded political power, and abbots who armed their monks.

Pope Innocent III was a reforming pope, but he had only just begun to make inroads on his immense work. Moreover, he was cautious by nature, and set his face against what he considered excesses of zeal that would leave the Church even more vulnerable to the heresies that crept in with them. And what Francis proposed seemed like an excess of zeal: all very well for the early Church when men still living had been contemporaries of Our Lord in his life on earth, and believed that the second coming was imminent, but not for modern man over a thousand years later. When Francis approached him he would not make an instant decision, impressed though he was with Francis's sincerity.

While he was mulling it over, he had a dream. There are good scriptural precedents for taking notice of dreams. Even if they are the images conjured up by our subconscious of truths lying deep within us, Pope Innocent's dream was certainly a striking image. It was of the Lateran Basilica tumbling down, and being upheld by a small figure in a torn habit, whom he recognised as Francis. It is not too much to say that this dream altered the history of the Church. On the strength of it, Innocent III gave Francis the backing he needed for his rule, and set free his genius for religion to permeate the whole body, wherever his friars went.

As yet there were only twelve companions, and they returned to Assisi with the pope's blessing. Their reception was much more welcoming than the one given to Francis when he returned alone and empty-handed three years before. More men offered themselves to the order, from Assisi and from further afield. Amongst them was Clare Offreduci's cousin Rufino. In the Lent of 1211, Francis preached in the church of San Rufino, and Clare heard him. Like everyone else who listened, his message of poverty and simplicity, peace and reconciliation, went to her heart. With a female companion, Buona di Guelfuccio, she went to the Portiuncula escorted by her friar cousin, and talked to Francis about her vocation.

These visits were in secret, like lovers' trysts. Her family – her proud and arrogant father Favarone, and his equally patrician wife Ortulana, who always backed him to the hilt – would have been scandalised to know that their daughter was consorting with a man like Francis. This, despite the fact that Ortulana had herself made a pilgrimage to the holy places of Jerusalem in her younger days (a mark of great piety) and when she had prayed during her pregnancy with Clare for a safe delivery, she had felt some divine reassurance.

The secret novitiate lasted for a year. It was not a formal instruction; Francis was incapable of being formal with anyone. The man who kissed a leper as one of his first acts of heroic charity, called the sun his brother, and addressed meetings of thousands as if they were one person, took a far from conventional line with this young girl. He spoke with lively fervour of his devotion to the gospels and the way of life they preached, and of his love for his 'Lady Poverty', in the language of the troubadours. Clare, who had been brought up in luxury, had a generosity of spirit to equal his. Her resolve to abandon the wealth of her background grew as the year passed. The question remained: how and when it should be done.

We cannot blame her parents for their opposition. They may have had dreams of a great marriage for her. If she had to be a nun, she could have joined an order where the rule was light and relaxed, and this might have led to a career as an abbess, exerting control over a rich community. What Clare was proposing was something quite new for a woman; to be poor as the friars were, and live a life totally enclosed and prayerful. But there was one person in the family who was with her – her younger sister Agnes, in whom she confided her ambitions; and Agnes came to share them. She too resolved to abandon the world at the first opportunity. Yet even from her, Clare kept the exact moment of her departure from the family home. That was known only to Francis and the faithful chaperone of her novitiate, Buona di Guelfuccio. What they had planned with Francis was no less than elopement.

The two romantics had chosen their moment carefully. Clare was to begin her life as the bride of Christ in the week that begins with his triumphal entrance into Jerusalem. On Palm Sunday she went to the church of San Rufino as usual. According to custom, the bishop blessed the palms, and sat beside the altar as people lined up to receive them. Whether Clare had, like many brides, an attack of shyness – she was certainly on this last public appearance dressed with extra magnificence – or whether the bishop was privy to the plot and used this as an occasion to give her a signal, is not quite clear. Certainly when, for whatever reason, she remained in her place, he left the altar to go to her, and pressed the palm branch into her hand.

That night when the moon shone – 'Sister Moon', as Francis with his trick of personalising everything had called her – Clare and her companion stole down to the seldom-used 'door of the dead' in the family house, in order to escape detection. It was cluttered with beams and disused furniture, and her wedding finery must have suffered as they tugged to clear it. They made their way out of the town by the narrow streets, then through the woods to the Portiuncula where the friars were waiting with flaming torches to welcome them. They conducted her to the simple altar, where she exchanged her bridal gown for a rough homespun habit tied with rope, and sandals. Francis cut off her beautiful blonde hair, and covered her head with a veil. The hair itself was preserved as a relic, and still exists.

The two lovers had not really thought out their next move. They knew that Clare would eventually live in the perfect poverty of the Franciscan ideal, but at the moment no place existed in which she could do it. A temporary refuge was found for her with some Benedictine nuns, and she prepared to join with them in the celebration of Holy Week. Very soon her peace and joy were shattered by the appearance of her father, mother and Uncle Monaldo – a fierce and warlike character, accompanied by a band of armed men. Surprised by them in the chapel, Clare took refuge at the altar, clinging to its cloths in order not to be dragged away. Then with a gesture worthy of Francis himself, she took off her veil, revealing her shorn head. At least that made the intruders realise that she had gone too far in her renunciation of the world ever to turn back. After a day or two of wrangling, they left her to her devotions.

But Agnes was not to be left behind. Only fifteen, she showed the same resolution as her older sister. On Low Sunday, no doubt taking advantage of the distractions created by Clare's defection, she too escaped to join her sister. This was too much for the Offreducis, who arrived in force, resolved to terrorize her into returning home, where they had made an attempt to betroth her in order to thwart her vocation. As they tried to remove her by force, she made herself into a dead weight that was impossible for the strongest to carry. As her Uncle Monaldo, exasperated, raised his hand to strike her, it was reported that his arm felt a shock of pain so acute that he was unable to complete the action. Eventually the Offreducis gave up and left the sisters to comfort and sustain one another.

Later in the year the friars made St Damian ready for them, and the second Franciscan order came into being. They were known as the Poor Ladies, and were closely associated with the friars, who gave them spiritual counsel, and begged for their frugal needs. It was not until much later that they begged for themselves, when the roads were less fraught with danger than they were in the early thirteenth century. Clare was not to leave St Damian until her death forty years later. She was made Abbess in 1216 when she was just twenty-two years old: Agnes became abbess of the Poor Ladies in a house in Florence.

In spite of their enclosure, they were not entirely cut off from the world. Indeed, when Clare heard from the friars of the martyrdom of some of their number in Morocco, she thought seriously of becoming a missionary. It might well have been Francis who persuaded her that she was in greater demand as the head of his 'storehouse of prayer' which kept the friars nourished as they travelled about the world. The wisdom he had about her vocation was balanced by hers about his. He became troubled as his order grew, and the need for greater organisation became apparent. He was tempted to leave this to others, and revert to an earlier love, the life of a hermit. It was then that Clare told him he should live for others rather than himself; and he took her advice, carrying his apostolate of reconciliation and love into the very camp of the Saracens in the Holy Land.

As Clare's personality matured, and more houses were set up, Francis gradually withdrew his presence, fearing that they would become too mutually dependent. This must have cost them both much anguish, as their love for one another, rooted though it was in Christ, gave them great joy in each other's company. Late in his life, Francis once said that he had only looked into the faces of two women. One was probably his great friend the widow Jacoba, who was allowed to see him on his deathbed, but the other must surely have been Clare.

Some ten years after the foundation of St Damian, his Brothers, feeling that he needed consolation, prevailed upon him to invite Clare for a meal at the Portiuncula. Legend has it that as they partook of the repast – truly Franciscan in its simplicity – the warmth of their communication appeared as a glow above the house, and agitated peasants arrived with buckets of water, fearing that the building was on fire and determined to save the lives of their beloved friends.

The austerities that Clare practised in the name of poverty were endless. She kept some heroic fasts, and slept on vine branches until she became ill, when Francis prevailed upon her to use a straw mat. She was always the last in the house to go to sleep, making the rounds of her nuns to ensure that they were warmly covered. She was the first to wake, and light the candles in the choir. Her youngest sister Beatrice joined the community, and – after her stern husband died – her mother, Ortulana. Clare had great faith in the efficacy of the sign of the cross as a cure for illness, and delegated its use to her mother and sister, so that they might receive thanks for it, rather than receiving thanks herself. She always led in selflessness, and earned the love and respect of the whole community. Francis's pope, Innocent III, was the first to grant her – verbally – the privilege of living in total poverty. Some time later, by an oversight, the friar who acted as chaplain to St Damian was withdrawn. She countered by rejecting the alms that the friars begged for them, saying that if their spiritual needs could not be met, they would do without the physical needs too. After this early example of a hunger-strike, the chaplain was hastily reinstated.

The Poor Ladies had houses in Austria, France, Spain and Bohemia, where the daughter of the king, Anne of Bohemia, became abbess. There are letters extant (formerly supposed to have been written by Clare, though they were probably penned by Pope Gregory IX) welcoming her vocation and profession, and outlining the life of a Poor Lady. They are full of Clare's spirit, and we know that Pope Gregory consulted her frequently. His was the second papal assent to her idea of total poverty – verbal again, but while she lived that was enough to ensure its adoption by the whole order.

Francis still made rare visits to St Damian, usually at the insistence of his vicar, for he would not indulge himself in the delight they took in each other's company. Thomas of Celano has left us an account of an occasion when he went to preach a sermon to them. It took the form of a symbolic pantomime. He made a circle of ashes round himself in silence, sprinkled some on his head, recited the 'Miserere' (Psalm 50) and left. At this demonstration of the message of Ash Wednesday, they were reduced to penitential tears.

Yet toward the end of his life, prematurely aged and in great pain because of an illness that affected his eyes, he sought the consolation of Clare's near presence. He stayed in a hut in the garden of St Damian. One night when the rats that infested it were unusually noisy, disturbing his sleep, he composed his *Canticle of Praise*. Clare always regarded herself as 'the little plant of our Father Francis', and there could be no more clear example of their spirit than this. How many poets would have cursed the rats for disturbing their muse, making all thought of writing impossible? But Francis, to whom the rats were brothers like all living things, used their scratchings and squeakings to accompany his hymn of praise to their creator. He and Clare turned worldly values upside down, and found in the depths of what most people would consider misery and deprivation, a holy joy.

One of the letters to Anne of Bohemia speaks of the Poor Ladies as being mirrors of the poverty of the manger and the poverty of the cross. It is almost impossible to believe that Clare did not write this. Holy Week was the anniversary of her profession – the Resurrection, of course, was the Good News of the first disciples, the heart of Christianity. Francis had a special devotion to the passion of Our Lord, and mirrored it with such devotion that he bore in his own body the Five Wounds. A legend grew up that Clare had tended them, but Francis was exceedingly shy of his great honour, and only allowed his Brothers to glimpse them, and that accidentally. Clare did have great devotion to the wounds of Our Lord, and there exist five meditations on them that have been attributed to her. In the last months of her life, she certainly said the Office of the Passion composed by Francis, every day.

Like Francis, who fashioned the first crib, she truly celebrated Christmas. It was not considered such a great feast at that time, but they celebrated it long before Prince Albert and Charles Dickens got their hands on it and launched the great commercial boom that now sickens some Christians. The Christmas of Francis was a holy season. The institution of the crib brought home to its mediaeval audience the reality of the manger in Bethlehem by using live animals, and real straw. With true Franciscan frugality the straw was saved to feed the animals, so that they could share in the feast. (It was said that a little of it laid on a woman having a difficult labour resulted in its rigours being eased.) Francis allowed himself to eat meat on Christmas Day, even when it fell on a Friday; with his usual extravagance, he smeared the walls with fat, saying that the very stones should eat meat if they could! Clare would certainly have allowed her Daughters to share in this relaxation.

Eventually a message from Francis came to St Damian that his life was ending, and that they were not to grieve. Clare had once said that she would obey any command of his, but this one she could not carry out. Thomas of Celano gives a moving account of how the Poor Ladies received the body of their father in Christ, and as it lay in the church at St Damian, they mourned the loss of his wise counsel and example. It seems that the Poor Ladies must have heard of the canonization of St Francis from the lips of Pope Gregory himself: he certainly visited them when he was in Assisi, finding much joy in being with them. It was to him that Clare said:

'No suffering has ever troubled me, no penance has ever burdened me, no sadness has ever been too arduous.'

So she survived even the blow of Francis' departure from this life. Indeed she carried his memory with her, and it influenced every one of her actions.

She showed that she shared in his courage quite late in her life, when the Saracen mercenaries of the emperor Frederick II attacked Assisi during one of his conflicts with the papacy. They were approaching St Damian, and Clare ordered the chaplain to bring the pyx with the Blessed Sacrament reserved in it, then stood with him at the gate, facing the mob of soldiers who were famous for their unrivalled brutality. For a tense moment she pitted her will against theirs, fortified by the Sacred Host, no doubt remembering that she was the child of soldiers. A late portrait shows a gaunt and patrician countenance. Whatever it was about the sight of these two figures holding the pyx aloft, the seasoned troops were terrified; they turned and fled.

When Pope Innocent IV succeeded to the papacy, he too enjoyed the friendship of the Poor Ladies. When she was well enough, Clare wove articles used in the celebration of mass, for churches too poor to afford them. In 1253, when she was already ailing, there seems to have been some sort of accident with a door that fell on her as she made her nightly rounds. She consented to rest on a couch, which argues that she knew she was near her end.

At once there was a series of visitors to witness her passing and make their farewells. Her sister Agnes came from Florence, and all the earliest companions of St Francis who were still alive, including Brother Juniper – jocund as always, of whom she enquired what toys to amuse her he had up his sleeve? An old friend, Cardinal Reynaldo, Bishop of Ostia, came and gave her communion, and to him she entrusted her testament, calling on him to bring it to the attention of the pope.

In it, she called upon her nuns to know their vocation. She recalled the days when St Francis had been rebuilding the church of St Damian on his own and had prophesied that it would be their home. She rallied them to be:

'Models and mirrors, not only for other faithful, but also for our sisters called to the same vocation, so that they be models and mirrors for others living in the world.'

Next came the clauses concerning poverty in perpetuity, including the provision that they must never own land except what might be used for a vegetable garden. In a lengthy passage she spoke of St Francis again, and the debt owed by the Poor Ladies to the friars Minor. Superiors were reminded that they should guide their sisters by example rather than the dignity of their office, and she ended by entrusting her testament as a sign of the blessing of Our Lord and St Francis, to which she added her own. She signed it:

'Your mother and handmaid.'

She need not have enlisted the help of the Bishop of Ostia, for Pope Innocent IV himself came to see her. As he drew near her couch, she made a supreme effort of courtesy and kissed his feet. She begged for plenary absolution for her sins. His humble reply was:

'Would my need was as yours.'

Before withdrawing, he left in her hands the written permission for her Order to be vowed to perpetual poverty.

As she drifted into death she called her sister Agnes, asking if she were sharing her vision of the king in glory. A little later she saw angels in the corner of her cell, with Our Lady radiant in their midst. Legend tells that it was Our Lady who came over and welcomed her into heaven with a kiss. It was August 11th, 1253: she was in her sixtieth year.

When her old friend the Bishop of Ostia became Pope Alexander IV, he presided over the ceremony of her canonization. Her feast is celebrated in the Roman calendar on the 12th of August. She was accredited during her last illness with receiving a vision of a mass she was unable to attend physically, on the wall of her cell. So a thirteenth-century nun, St Clare of Assisi, became the patron of the newest of the media, television.

* * *

Later the same night, having cooked supper for her charges on a tiny stove in the corner of the vestry, our young troubadour performed with her guitar again for their benefit. She was called upon to adjudicate over an accusation of cheating at cards, and helped the youngest to learn to read. She waited until the last one was snoring on his mattress, and then went back to the vestry.

After an hour spent in prayer and meditation, she spread a sleeping-bag out on the bare boards, and slept like the child she was.

St Francis of Assisi

he psychiatric social worker looked at the unkempt young man before him with professional compassion.

'How have you been getting on since we last met?' he enquired. The thin brown face lit up with a radiant smile: 'Very well.'

'You look as if you might be sleeping rough again,' observed his interrogator.

'Oh, I don't mind. It's nearer to heaven, isn't it?' said the young man with complete confidence.

'But you can't get anything from Social Security if you have no address.' He felt irritation mounting, and tried to suppress it. 'Didn't you like the hostel we found for you?'

'It was very nice. I made some good friends there.'

'Then why — ?'

The young man reached into a gaping pocket and pulled out a single cigarette, proffering it with a gesture of exquisite courtesy:

'Would you like a cigarette?'

'Thank you, I don't smoke,' said the social worker hurriedly.

'Neither do I.' The young man returned the cigarette to its former resting-place. 'Some of my friends do. I find that if they're angry, it gives them something else to think about.'

'But I'm not angry,' said the social worker defensively.

'I think you are. People often get angry with me,' said his client simply, without resentment.

'It's not that we're angry...' The social worker took refuge in the first person plural. 'But you don't seem to do a lot to help yourself. When you left hospital we gave you a perfectly good set of clothes, and the best accommodation we could, and within a week you've lost both.'

'Not lost,' corrected the young man. 'Exchanged.'

'Exchanged?' echoed the social worker. 'What for?'

He looked more closely at the young man. His clear eyes showed none of the tell-tale signs of addiction.

'Peace of mind,' replied his client. 'When I came out of the hostel the first morning, I went for a walk in the park. It was the most wonderful day, a real gift from God, and there was a poor man sitting on a bench. Then I saw him rummaging in a litter bin. So I thought: "How can I be so comfortable when he's in want?" I got him to take my new suit, and my place in the hostel. He didn't want to at first, but after a bit he said he'd give it a go.'

'Luckily for us he didn't stay. He was an alcoholic... Don't you see that these charitable impulses of yours get out of hand? Wasn't it enough that when you stole your father's hi-fi equipment and sold it to give money to anyone you saw on the street, it landed you in court?'

'But I hadn't any money of my own to give,' said the young man, very reasonably.

'Look...' The social worker took a deep breath: 'I don't deny that some people slip through the social net, but it doesn't help if you persist in trying to join them. Smarten yourself up and get a job, and then you can do something for them. In the meantime, leave it to someone else. There are all sorts of agencies –'

'But it's sharing their lives that helps them,' the young man interrupted. 'When I'm as poor as they are, they talk to me. I can tell them they're loved and wanted, and they'll believe me.' The social worker glanced at his watch; it was not unnoticed by his client.

'You're busy,' he said. 'I don't want to waste your time.'

'You're not wasting my time. We've got off on the wrong foot, and I'm not sure what to do about it.'

210

'But it's my fault –' persisted the young man.

'I've broken all the rules. I've practically lost my temper with you... The fact is, I've had a terrible day. My wife told me she's pregnant, and she'll have to give up work, and I don't know how I'm going to pay the mortgage...' His voice trailed away.

The client smiled: 'Don't worry – babies bring their own luck with them... You are pleased about the baby?' he added, anxiously.

'I'm not sure at the moment.'

'I'll ask St Francis about it. It's funny, when I ask for anything, he always gets it for me. And you'd think he'd be so busy, too.'

'Is he?' said the social worker, baffled. Suddenly a thought struck him: 'You don't think you're St Francis, do you?'

'No.' His client smiled slowly. 'There's only one of him.'

And then the telephone rang.

* * *

Francis Bernardone was born in 1183, in the small Umbrian town of Assisi, in northern Italy, at a watershed in the history of the Middle Ages. A great series of crusades in the Holy Land had had a limited success; Jerusalem itself was still in the hands of Saladin. Genghis Khan was on the threshold of a career that would establish an empire stretching from the Black Sea to the Pacific. Frederick Barbarossa, whose reign as head of the Holy Roman Empire had extended from the Ebor to the Elbe, was in his declining years. Richard I was king of England, which he rarely visited, leaving it to the inept management of his brother John; his fighting temperament led him to join the crusades, which the popes had declared to be holy wars, saying that all who died in them would save their souls.

In Francis's youth, the crusaders' tales must have been told over and over again, gathering glamour as truth receded, and suppressing their sordid side – the political wrangling between the leaders, the disease that laid waste the camps, and the carnal licence among their followers – yet the idea of chivalry persisted. It had an even earlier origin, in the legends of almost mythical characters like Arthur and Roland. Francis heard the songs of the troubadours from his Provencal mother, praising the virtues of courtly love in a Never-Never-Land where knights would dare incredible adventures for a favourable glance from their chosen lady.

As he grew up, his appetite was whetted by the tournaments between members of the local nobility; a necessary part of the great festivals. It was an opportunity for showing off horsemanship and skill in the martial arts, with palatial banquets afterwards and the victor in the place of honour. The tournaments did not come to an end when the town of Assisi threw off the tyranny of their overlord, the Duke of Spoleto, and his adherents. The middle-class tradesmen – among them, Francis' father, a cloth-merchant – gained power from their success, and helped to finance these popular pastimes. At the time of the uprising, Francis was sixteen, and well able to take part. The excitement, and the conviction of the rightness of the cause, helped to inflame his enthusiasm for the life of a soldier.

All his aggression went into the battle itself; he was renowned for his courtesy. When he led the young men of Assisi on horseback through the narrow streets at night, shouting and singing after a drinking bout – kin to youths on their motor-cycles in our own day – he apologised with disarming charm and paid for any damage with lavish generosity. It was, of course, his father's money. We only hear of one brother in his family; there were probably more children, but Francis was treated by his parents as an adored only son who could do no wrong. If his nature had been spoilable, he would have been spoiled; as it was, he went along with his father's ambition for him – that he should break out of the merchant class into which he had been born, and enter that of the nobility.

There was a route by which this could be arranged. If a merchant was prepared to become a wholesaler instead of a retailer, and cease to trade personally, he could set his son up with a horse, and armour, and send him with a servant into the field. But Pietro Bernardone does not appear to have done this, preferring that his son should take his turn at serving in the shop. He continued to go off on buying-trips to France, and probably further afield. Some of the stock found its way to adorn his son, who gained a reputation for being a dandy. His contemporaries describe him as being on the small side, with thin, regular features, straight dark brows, and brown eyes – ordinary enough, but the real compliments were for his voice, which was low and sweet. And he was always singing.

Francis seemed to be on the road to realising his ambitions. He was accepted among the young nobles in the town, not quite as an equal, for they could not overlook his day-job as a shop-assistant, but he could still hope to become a knight. He might easily have settled down to become the rather overweight, cynical father of a family, his dreams forgotten. At nineteen there was no sign that his character, unremarkable except for its frivolity, held within it a genius for religion that would change man's thinking for centuries to come.

The wealth of the burghers of Assisi, and their ostentatious parade of it, began to pall on the common people who did not share their riches, and there were angry demonstrations. Hearing of these difficulties, the rival city of Perugia sensed an opportunity for gain, and marched upon Assisi. The alarm bells rang, calling out the townsfolk in its defence. Internal strife forgotten, they marched to meet the Perugians, and Francis rode with the cavalry. The armies met at Collestrada, and the men of Assisi were beaten by their well-prepared neighbours.

Francis's rich clothes ensured that when he was captured, he would be held for ransom, not killed out of hand. But conditions in the dungeon he shared with his fellow cavalrymen were squalid to say the least. The Perugians did not intend to lessen their profits by leniency towards their captives. The prospect was bleak, and Francis's companions slumped into apathy, as negotiations for their release dragged on.

But not Francis. He showed that his natural gaiety did not depend on favourable circumstances. When he sang his favourite Provençal songs, the gaolers jeered at him, but they could not put him out of temper. Such resolute cheerfulness may have irritated his fellow-prisoners at times, but their real resentment was saved for one of their number, who was remarkably cantankerous. We know him – there's one in every school, and pub, and place of work – overbearing, always looking for offence, and perhaps a bore as well. Francis set out to charm this unlovely character, who began to show a better side of his nature under this treatment. Because Francis accepted him with a generous spirit, the others began to accept him too.

After their release, they went back to Assisi. It often happens that people who have shown courage and resource at a time of stress collapse when it is over. Something like this seems to have happened to Francis, for he developed a debilitating illness that involved extreme physical weakness and mental depression. Nowadays it would be attributed to a virus infection, contracted in the dungeon. We may be sure that his mother devoted herself to nursing her favourite, and was delighted when he progressed to walking with a stick from room to room, and later going out into the countryside. Eventually he recovered sufficiently to resume his old life, but the illness had left its mark on him.

One day he was working in the shop, with customers demanding attention, all wanting to be served first, when one of the beggars who abounded in the mercantile part of the town chose that moment to ask for money. Francis brushed him aside, and went on serving his customers; then, out of the corner of his eye he saw the beggar's retreating back. Struck with remorse, he left the shop and rushed after the beggar, overwhelming him with a generous gift of money.

An impoverished knight also aroused his sympathy, and he gave him the fashionable clothes he was wearing. Having experienced hardship himself, he resolved that he would never turn away anyone who asked for his help.

He was still looking for a direction in his life. It would not be enough to be the leader of the feasts in provincial Assisi for ever. He loved his friends, but although he bought their admiration with his father's money, he longed to move on to a wider world. One night he had a dream that confirmed him in his wish to become a knight. He dreamed that he was in a magnificent palace, surrounded by the armour and trappings of knighthood. Better still, there was also a beautiful girl, dressed as a bride. Francis felt certain, as if a voice had told him so, that all this was meant to be his. Almost immediately, he was offered a post as squire to a knight who was travelling to Apulia, to fight for Pope Innocent III. He busied himself in acquiring the most costly uniform, a magnificent horse and weapons. He was a fine sight as he bade farewell to his friends, and rode from the gates of Assisi. He certainly sang on his way; he always did.

That night was spent in Spoleto. It had been a hard ride, and he had become so tired that his sleep was uneasy. Again he had the dream about the magnificent palace and the knightly accoutrements, but this time he found himself wondering who they belonged to. Then he heard a voice that asked him:

'Francis, who can do more for you – the Lord or the servant?'

He found himself replying: 'The Lord.'

'Why do you leave the Lord for the servant, and the Prince for the vassal?' enquired the voice.

Francis thought he had made a terrible mistake, and asked what his next move should be. The voice advised him to go back to Assisi, where he would be told what to do. He knew in his heart who the greater Lord was: he had left God out of his plans. Next day he returned to Assisi, expecting derision from his friends.

Instead they welcomed him back; his colourful figure brightened the town for them. He decided to give them a banquet that would outdo all the rest. The food was doubly delicious, the wine flowed freely, and they ate and drank until they felt sick. Then they went out into the street, making the walls echo with their drunken singing. He followed behind, the staff denoting him to be the master of the revels still in his hand, knowing that it was for the last time. He dropped back, and further back, until their singing was muffled by distance. A great peace came to him; he could neither move nor speak. He saw his previous life as empty and worthless, leading him nowhere. It was as if, in that moment, he had grown up.

But if 'growing up' means weighing things in the balance and proceeding cautiously, in another sense he never grew up. He would never lose his directness and simplicity, never be soured by cynicism. His instant obedience, born of a wish to please – his impetuosity, his literal interpretation of the message delivered to him, all these belonged to the innocent

215

world of a child. His vision of the way forward was painted in the vivid primary colours that children are fond of; he was filled with a childlike wonder and sense of discovery.

He set off again, not weighed down with armour, but on a pilgrimage to Rome. He must have hoped to find, at the centre of Christendom, something to feed his new awareness of religion. He ignored the pomp and ceremony about him, and threw in his lot with the poor in the outer vestibule of St Peter's, changing clothes with a beggar, becoming one of the crowd, and sharing their food. He was scandalised by the meagre offerings at the altar, and made one of his magnificent gestures, tossing down a handful of coins. He reverenced all the clerics he met, as men set apart, but his favourites were the poor ones, to whom he gave lavish donations for their churches.

When he went home again, his faith was ready to be tested. He had a nightmare in which the devil said that one of the bogeys of his childhood – a local woman, hideously deformed – was to be his bride, unless he abandoned his new way of life. The devil in person was a very real presence in the Middle Ages, but Francis was quick to choose the misshapen bride if it were God's will, and he must have been comforted to wake up and find that it was a dream.

The next trial came when he was awake. All his life, he had a phobia about leprosy; he found even the most remote contact with lepers repulsive. While he was out riding alone, one of them approached him with outstretched hand. Not content with giving him money, Francis jumped off his horse and kissed the man's ravaged face. Once he had done this, he felt joy and relief, as if the burden of fear had been lifted. He got back on his horse, and looked round to see where the leper had gone, searching the wide landscape – but there was no one to be seen. Francis saw the hand of God in this experience, beckoning him on to an apostolate among the poor and outcast. His previous feeling of repulsion was turned inside out, and became an attraction to those who suffered; he sought out lepers in their wretched hovels, not only attending to their material needs, but also kissing their hands and mouths, assuring them of his love.

Assisi had many churches, and some of them had been

allowed to fall into disrepair. In his solitary wanderings Francis developed a habit of visiting these half-ruined places. The fashionable churches were crowded; they served as meeting places, and court rooms, and at their doors relics of highly dubious origin could be bought. Francis, trying all the time to deepen his relationship with God, was impatient of distraction. One day he was moved to visit a church dedicated to St Damian. Though it was tumbledown, a very old priest was saying mass at the altar, before a striking crucifix. It was like an icon, with attendant angels, and the holy women and St John depicted in bright colours, heaven and earth mourning together; and the pale body of Jesus with arms outstretched, looking down sorrowfully on the world he was redeeming. Francis meditated before it, becoming more and more deeply involved with the mystic figure, body and soul united in an intense act of supplication. The pale lips moved, and said:

'Francis, repair my house, which is falling into ruin.'

A less impetuous character might have taken this to mean that it was the whole Church of Christ on earth that was meant, and that his mission was to renew its vision in a spiritual sense, but Francis had a child's literal obedience. The suffering figure had asked him to repair a church; he was in a church that needed repair, and he would set to with stone and mortar to do the job, for which he had no experience whatever. As a first step, he gave the old priest his remaining money to buy a lamp and oil, so that the image which had become so precious to him should be honoured by a light, continually burning before it.

Then he hurried out, and met a friend, and tried to tell him what had happened. Moved by pity for his wounded Lord, the tears sprang to his eyes, and such was the power of his sincerity, the friend shared his emotion.

After this there came the misunderstandings and bunglings that led to Francis's appearance in court before the Bishop of Assisi, his rejection by his family, and his acceptance of God as his father.

He spent the next two years as a labourer, adopting a habit of a kind – a rough tunic cast away by its previous owner, which he embellished with a cross in white chalk, and tied with a thin rope. The old priest who served St Damian looked

217

on with pity at the slight figure, toiling away at his back-breaking task and, fearing for his health, he shared his food with Francis. It was hardly luxurious, but Francis – though courteous and grateful as ever – felt he should not become accustomed to it; after all, he would not always be able to rely on someone else to provide him with food – so he made a begging trip into the town. The resulting mixture of scraps revolted him, but he made himself eat it, and soon began to enjoy it as a gift from God.

When the light before the crucifix began to fail, he had no more money for oil, but he knew the more noble houses in Assisi from visiting them as a guest. He selected one where he thought he might be given some oil, but was overcome with self-consciousness when he saw a crowd of young men playing games outside, and retreated in confusion. Angry with himself, he took refuge in prayer, then advanced on the house a second time. He threw himself on the mercy of the owner, finding it easier to express himself in French, and got what he came for. At this time, he seems often to have used his second language; it was the language of poetry and song for him, and in spite of all his hardships, he was supremely happy.

But his solitary life was not to continue for long. On the feast of St Matthias – the apostle chosen to replace Judas, after the resurrection – Francis went to hear mass in the chapel of the Portiuncula. It was dear to him, for he had laboured to repair it too, and he knew it better than the Benedictines who came occasionally to say mass there, from their monastery on Mount Subasio. He always cherished what was neglected and despised by other people. Within him, a great fountain of love welled up for the whole of creation, and spilled out, washing away what made it unattractive to ordinary men and women, and making them see the world anew, as if it had just come from the hands of God.

On this February morning, the priest read the appointed gospel, which happened to be St Matthew's rendering of Christ's call to his disciples to go out and preach the Good News. He called on them to heal the sick, taking nothing that was not strictly necessary – no shoes, no extra tunic, no staff, and no money – especially no money. Every word went straight to Francis' heart, where increasingly over the past two years he had come to enshrine poverty as a direct route to God. His idea of poverty was not abstract – he never dealt in abstractions, which made him quite different from the orthodox theologians, with their lists of vices and virtues. Francis gave them identity; to him, poverty was 'Lady Poverty', the most beautiful woman in the world, whose knight he had become.

He could barely wait until the end of mass, so impatient was he to answer the call to action. The first disciples could hardly have been more ready with their response. Off came his shoes, the small satchel at his waist, and he cast away his stick – we can almost see them, flying in all directions. The other command was to preach the gospel. He had no training as a preacher, and not much experience of being preached at. At that time, sermons were not considered important; as long as the priest administered the sacraments, he fulfilled his mission. As a layman, Francis was not supposed to preach at all, but as we have already seen, when on fire with a new idea, he had scant consideration for the rules of canon law.

He went off to the square, where most people gathered, and started to try and communicate the stupendous discoveries he had made. The Assisians had become used to the small figure in the brown tunic, which seemed almost a caricature of a monk's habit, but not since the scandal of the bishop's court had they heard him speak. Curiosity probably led them to give him a hearing. He poured forth his love through his eyes and his voice; and when he ran out of words, and the townspeople returned to their own concerns, three men from the crowd stayed behind, moved to seek him out.

Their names were Egidio, Pietro, and Bernardo di Quintavalle; the first followers of what came to be known as the Franciscan ideal. Bernardo was rich, and when he asked Francis what he should do to share his way of life, Francis gave him Our Lord's answer to the rich young man in the gospels:

'Sell all you have and give it to the poor.'

Bernardo felt able to be more generous than Our Lord's would-be follower, and made an instant response. The four of them spent the night at his house, still a little uncertain of their next step.

In the morning Francis led them to the church of San Niccolo, and after prayer, he opened the book of the gospels, having agreed to follow the direction indicated by whatever he read there. The first text that caught his attention echoed the message he had given Bernardo, the previous day:

'If you would be perfect, go and sell all you have and give it to the poor.'

Reinforced in his convictions, he opened the book again, and these words leaped to his eye:

'Take nothing for your journey.'

There had to be a third attempt – three for the Trinity – and he found:

'If anyone wishes to follow me, let him deny himself.'

Across the centuries, many other people have found that a random opening of the Bible would give them a message, but few have felt as bound by it as the brothers of Francis.

They had to find somewhere they could be together. Francis was clear that they should not be hermits, committed to solitary improvement in their spiritual lives. He wanted them to go out into the world and share the riches of their poverty with everyone. He made it plain that they were not to be tied to bricks and mortar; it was only by belonging nowhere that they could belong everywhere. But he had found inspiration in the little chapel of the Portiuncula, dedicated to Our Lady of the Angels – and Our Lady was a pattern of poverty and humility. Putting up rough huts of branches, they gathered round the chapel, making it the first of their temporary resting places.

During the following few months, more brothers arrived; first three, then five more, until they were the same in number as the apostles. The only requirement to newcomers was to abandon everything they owned in the world. All the established orders had a vow of poverty, but they gave what they had to the order, and it was used to finance their communal life. Francis' followers did not keep anything for themselves; the brothers lived by begging – earning alms when they could by menial tasks, tending livestock or using the skills they had acquired in the world. Francis was a firm believer in manual labour as an aid to prayer. So the simple rule was worked out, step by step and day by day, as new circumstances arose. By the middle of April, the structure was apparent, and the sixteenth of that month is celebrated as the birth of the Order of the Friars Minor.

However, the formal naming and approval of the rule could only come from the Church. It was all very well for the enthusiastic band, living in a heady atmosphere of religious fervour, to seek a new way of evangelising the world; there was an establishment that regarded them with suspicion. They were not the first movement to have that aim, and some had the seeds of heresy sown in their teachings. To his superiors, Francis appeared to be the self-appointed leader of a ragged troop which owed no allegiance to anyone. Though he wanted to follow the dictates of the special call he had from the lips of Our Lord, he had the greatest respect for priests – even the most lax and immoral among them – by virtue of their office; they had the power to administer the sacraments and give absolution.

The abbot of Monte Subasio offered to rent the Portiuncula to them in exchange for a basket of fish to be given each year. When this was discussed by the brothers, they decided to accept the offer, as they would not actually own the land. A previous attempt to settle in a disused leper hospital had ended when a farmer moved them out, to house his pigs there; and they were anxious to avoid such risks in the future. But this contract brought them to the notice of the Bishop of Assisi, who had known Francis at all the various stages of his career.

He invited Francis to a meal – which he refused, saying that he only ate when he had earned his food. Despite this rebuff, the bishop tried again, carefully suggesting that Francis and his friends should join an established monastic order. This was the last thing Francis wanted; he saw his mission as being a mobile force that would travel widely because it travelled light. Neither man could understand the other's point of view, and they reached a stalemate.

After this encounter Francis resolved to bypass the bishop's authority, and make a direct appeal to the pope, Innocent III. If he had known the man, he might have settled for the devil he knew; Innocent III was a great administrator and reformer. He had made the papacy a force to be reckoned with among

221

the secular rulers of his time, and he had a short sharp way of dealing with heretics – amongst whom he might well count Francis and his ragged little band. After much deliberation they produced a document setting out their rule, which would show the prelates in Rome that they derived their inspiration directly from the teachings of Jesus, as set forth in the gospels. Francis had no intention of discrediting the established orders; he merely begged leave to be different.

Before the twelve set out on their travels, they elected a leader. Interestingly enough, in the democratic election, Bernardo gained the most votes. Although there is no doubt that Francis was the heart of the enterprise, Bernardo was judged to have the better head. So they set off, singing on their way.

They arrived in Rome, knowing no one. Pious people made food available to them, and they waited, and prayed. Their own bishop chanced to be visiting the city on business, and met them. By now he wanted to be rid of any responsibility for them, and so did what many people might have done in similar circumstances – wished them on to a friend. As it happened, he was a powerful friend: Ugolino, Bishop of Ostia, and the pope's nephew. Ugolino agreed to see Francis, and was impressed by his humility and the good manners which seemed so much at odds with his tattered clothes. He saw to it that the brothers did not starve, though the procedures leading to an audience with the pope took time; but he promised that their rule would reach the eyes of the pontiff.

Eventually the day came when Francis was summoned to appear at the Lateran. Innocent told him bluntly that the rule as it stood would not do. It was beyond human endurance to live in absolute poverty. From Innocent's point of view as an expert administrator, he was absolutely right; in fact in later years it caused a rift that all but wrecked the Franciscan order – but that was still in the future. Francis the romantic would not abandon his Lady Poverty, and he pointed to the homelessness of Our Lord during his ministry. Such was his shining humility, it never occurred to anyone to make the obvious retort – 'You are not Jesus'. Instead the pope urged him, as his nephew had done, to try his vocation within a monastery.

In papal circles, the prelates whispered against Francis.

Being the man he was, he did not hear them. It was more important that the brothers should not be disheartened. Even their leader Bernardo thought they should leave the city, but Francis held firm. He could not leave without the pope's blessing on their work, otherwise their preaching and their works of mercy could be banned from the diocese of any bishop who took a dislike to them.

True to the injunction in the gospel not to take no for an answer, he approached the pope a second time. On this occasion he was armed with a parable about a great queen who had taken her sons to live in the desert as soon as they were born. When they grew up, she brought them back to the king, their father, and he received them with joy. In that spirit Francis offered his little family, schooled in the hard desert of poverty, and begged the pope to accept them.

His ingenuity in presenting his case, his firmness in holding to his principles, overwhelmed the pope. He gave Francis permission to preach where he was approved by local bishops, and appointed him leader of the brothers; no more was said about confining them within the framework of monasticism. However, it was not a complete capitulation to Francis's requests, for the question of the rule was quietly ignored. But Francis was not the man to refuse a gift that would further the glory of God, and he seemed quite unaware of the authorities' guarded attitude towards him. His childlike trust in people was one of the most moving things about him. The brothers knew that any bishop they approached would hesitate to go counter to the wishes of St Peter's successor; their work could begin in earnest. Songs of joy lightened their journey back to Assisi.

There followed a springtime of growth, of hope and enthusiasm. Francis marshalled his tiny force, and standing at a crossroads he sent them forth in pairs – north and south, east and west – to preach the new vision of the gospels. It was a gesture typical of him, and no one else could have done it. When they reported back to the Portiuncula, they brought tidings of many souls saved, and a new regeneration of the faithful. They brought new companions too, swelling the numbers of those who were flocking in to join the order.

The brown-clad army began to swarm along the roads

throughout central Italy, and beyond. They were not always welcome; ragged and not over-clean, they often slept rough, and in the eyes of the staid townsfolk, they were little better than gypsies. They received a warmer welcome in villages, for the country people were starved of novelty, and what began as a search for something to enliven their days of toil often ended in a resurgence of their spiritual lives. On the whole, the people were not catered for by the orthodox clergy; in the thousand odd years since the birth of the Church at Pentecost, religion had become a specialist pursuit by a few. That was why Pope Innocent III, a reforming pope, welcomed the Friars Minor. They were the heralds of a great return to the values of the evangelists and St Paul.

All this was summed up in the person of Francis himself. Stories began to circulate about him, of his extraordinary cures and fulfilled prophecies. There is no doubt that he had singular powers, which came from his close observation of nature and his instinctive affinity with it. He personalized the landscape he moved in, translating inanimate objects into living beings. He greeted the sun as 'Brother Sun', the moon as 'Sister Moon'. Fire and water also acquired personalities – yet somehow he stopped short of the pagan view of the elements. They were strictly revered as the work of God's hand.

The creatures of the natural world were treated with special tenderness. The friars were encouraged to walk with downcast eyes, so they might not be seduced by the sight of worldly treasures – but that meant they missed nothing on the ground. Francis was known to have moved to safety some worms, which had strayed on to the path in wet weather, so they should not be trampled on. He once expressed a wish that the emperor should issue a decree forbidding the killing of larks, then considered a delicacy. The story of his sermon to a flock of birds, who remained silent when he spoke to them, is well-known in our own day; and the troublesome wolf of Gubbio, tamed by the courage and gentle words of Francis, has left an unforgettable picture in our minds.

He could be moved to anger too. He had an almost pathological hatred of money, and his penances for any of the brothers who handled coins were humiliating and revolting.

He equated it with dung, and saw to it that the brothers did so too, by association. But his care of them was infinite. He had tamed his body, which he christened 'Brother Ass', to an extraordinary degree of spiritual fitness. He hardly ate, or slept, and could endure any amount of hardship without losing his joy in life. But he never lost sight of those brethren who found the subjection of bodily appetites difficult.

When a brother could not sleep because he was hungry, Francis plied him with food, and even ate with him, to make him feel better about breaking his fast. When the men of the Portiuncula went overboard in their use of iron hoops and corslets, scourgings and fasts – mediaeval practices to achieve spiritual growth at the expense of the body – he was firm in his command to curtail such extravagances. He was exquisitely sensitive to the psychological difficulties of any of the brothers: diffidence, and feelings of unworthiness, vanished under the warmth of his regard. He was accessible to all – as, like his Master, he was a servant to all.

The year 1213, when he was just thirty years old, marked a further expansion of the order. Through the reception of Sister Clare, the door was opened to women. The Second Order gave the friars a storehouse of prayer to call upon in their missionary work, and practical help in patching their poor garments, and producing medicines from their herb-gardens. Since the beginning of Francis's mission, some of his most attentive listeners had been married people, or followers of professions that could not be abandoned to make the full sacrifice to the Franciscan ideal – but Francis had room for these too, and instituted the Third Order, to accommodate those who could not withdraw from their worldly responsibilities. It would not be formalised for some years, but he was always careless about organisation.

He realised that meetings would have to be arranged for his extended family, and the first general chapter took place at Pentecost, 1215. The gatherings had to be held outdoors, to cope with the great numbers, and the townspeople of Assisi provided food for the visitors. Missionary journeys were discussed, plans made for future ones, and difficulties were aired. Francis had never insisted on having control over recruits to the order; he allowed the missionary friars to admit anyone to their company who seemed to conform to the rule of absolute poverty – but not all those who were admitted understood what was meant by that. The missions had reached university cities like Padua and Bologna, and men of learning responded to the call. They regarded their books not as possessions, but as extensions of their minds, and were horrified to hear that Francis expected them to give up their books. They had a champion amongst the earliest companions of Francis – Elias of Cortona. There were also those who were zealous enough at first, yet slid back after a while into idleness and gluttony. Without a novitiate to weed out these unsuitable candidates, they remained within the order, fomenting discontent.

Yet for the moment they could be united as Francis spoke to them all, pouring out his love for them, and for the whole of creation. The chapter ended with a *Te Deum* that echoed from the surrounding hills. When it was over, Francis pursued a plan he had been cherishing for some time. As a youth, he had thrilled to the call of the crusades; now he wished to go to the Holy Land, not as an armed knight, but as a messenger of peace. The humblest of men, he believed that if he could talk to the Saracens they would see how much the Holy Places meant to Christians, and vacate them of their own free will. He had experienced the power of the words of Christ in his own life, and thought that if he put them to the infidels, they must capitulate before them.

He set out for the Middle East by way of France and Spain, and there succumbed to a serious illness. It sapped his strength so much, he had to return to Italy; 'Brother Ass' was to prove an unruly beast for the rest of his life.

This was not his only disappointment. In November 1215, his friend and patron Pope Innocent III put a ban on new religious foundations. Francis's rule had never been formally approved, and the new decree meant that now it never could be. Francis, and twenty of his friars, went to Rome to find out where they stood.

During the visit, his old friend Cardinal Ugolino of Ostia introduced him to Dominic, founder of the Order of Preachers. Though their temperaments were very different, they liked one another. Ugolino hoped much from the friendship between them; Dominic was a brilliant theologian and superbly orthodox, and readily agreed to his own order being subject to the Augustinian rule. Francis remained in frustrated silence when the question of his adoption of a rule came up. He had no intention of abandoning what he had received from Christ himself; no amount of learned argument or political trafficking made any impression on him.

Still, he was interested in Dominic's missionary work in Germany, and saw a fruitful field there for his friars. While Dominic appealed to the learned and sophisticated, Francis's brothers reached the hearts of the common people. On his return to Assisi, he planned to send out a mission. When Pope Innocent died, his successor Honorius was reported to look favourably upon the Franciscans – nevertheless, the mission to Germany was a disaster. The German bishops were hostile; the Dominicans could converse with the learned through Latin, but the Franciscans were mostly unlettered Italians, and could not get their tongues round this unaccustomed language. Even the common people failed them, rejecting their message. The order also had trouble in an attempted mission to Hungary; and in Spain – where the Spaniards, recently liberated from their Muslim conquerors, were more orthodox than the pope – they were accused of heresy. The friars fled to Portugal, where the queen offered protection. It began to look as if the Franciscan ideal was unsuitable for export.

Yet the Chapter held at Whitsun 1218 appeared to be a triumph. Thousands of friars were present. Dominic was a guest, and Cardinal Ugolino sang the opening mass. Another attempt was made to get Francis's consent to putting the order under a monastic rule or even to unite with the Dominicans. Behind the scenes, even some of his own friars were agreeing that this would bring their troubles to an end, but Francis remained steadfast to his original inspiration. The cardinal did not lose his affection for him, however much he regretted his obstinacy, and advised Pope Honorius to give the Franciscan missionaries a document stating 'To whom it might concern' that they had the papal blessing upon their work. Francis deplored the fact that an important document had to have a wallet for safe-keeping; he did not want his friars to diverge from their strict rule of poverty, and felt that they were losing their freedom, bit by bit.

He prevailed upon Cardinal Ugolino to allow him to preach before Honorius and the assembled cardinals. Ugolino was nervous lest his protégé might shame him in this illustrious company. Francis may have looked eccentric, swayed by his fervour into a dancing step to accompany his words, but where the cardinal expected discreetly concealed laughter, he found that the distinguished listeners were moved to tears. Francis' naked vulnerability and sincerity touched their hearts.

After that, Francis put all his doubts behind him. His health had improved sufficiently to make another attempt upon the Holy Land. He left the direction of the order to two deputies, and sailed from Ancona for Accra, taking eleven companions with him, working their passage.

The Christian forces were laying siege to Damietta. Like all soldiers, when not actually fighting they sought entertainment, and there were not many innocent pastimes so far from home. From the highest to the lowest, drink and women were their usual diversions, but they were not all vicious, and Francis in his charity embraced them, even making some converts.

He carried his own holy war to the enemy, crossing the lines to preach to the Saracens. This took enormous courage, for the tales of their cruelty had been rife in Europe since his childhood. He knew he risked martyrdom, and went singing to meet it. The Saracens were disarmed by the ragged beggar with princely manners; he found his way into the presence of the Sultan of Egypt, who felt there was nothing to fear from someone so obviously mad, and welcomed him as an amusing novelty. Francis offered to enter a fire with the Muslim priests, to make a trial of their different faiths, but the sultan refused the contest. However, Francis gained the goodwill and finally the respect of his hearers, and was sent back to the crusading army under guard, before – as seemed quite possible – he should make any converts.

Then the Christians attacked Damietta and sacked it, with a barbarity that shocked Francis, who had idealised the crusaders as knights of chivalry. He realised at last that he did not fit into the framework of modern war; this was no place for his master, the prince of peace. He set out for home, a child whose dreams had been shattered by grim reality.

When he arrived in Italy, there was bad news from the Portiuncula. In his year-long absence, another chapter had been held. During it, the rule had been debated, and despite a spirited defence by his loyal friends, it had been demolished, clause by clause. The rule of poverty was to be eased, and the friars were to adopt the rule of the monastic orders. Cardinal Ugolino, in whom Francis had trusted, had approved the revisions. Within the order, Elias of Cortona was emerging as a leader for the party of change.

A rumour had spread throughout Europe that Francis had been martyred in Egypt; his dissatisfied brothers felt they were free to go to Rome and gain favours from the Curia for their innovations. When Francis reached Bologna, he found the friars had lapsed from perfect poverty, and were living in what he considered luxury. He lost his temper and cleared them out of their fine house; even the sick had to leave their beds. It was the confirmation of his worst fears.

He went to meet Cardinal Ugolino at Orvieto. Ill and dispirited, he agreed to discuss the conditions under which the order should be governed, now that his band of followers were numbered in thousands. Finally he consented to put his life's work under the cardinal's protection, and embarked on a course designed to reconsider what he thought most important. It was agreed that the revisions should be debated at the Michaelmas chapter of 1220.

His return to the Portiuncula was welcomed. Whatever the dissensions, he was still loved by everyone. The bond between Francis and his brothers – even the most wayward, from his point of view – was as strong as ever. After all, they had believed that he was lost, and although a martyr's crown would have set a final seal on his brilliant life, they were happy it was not yet won. But while he sat on the ground amongst them, his vision was voted into the past. At last he rose, and proved that his ability to make a gesture – princely in generosity, yet touched with divine humility – was as fresh as ever. He named Pietro di Cantana the General of the order, kneeling at his feet to offer him obedience.

The new general incorporated the qualities of the new

Franciscans. He was of noble birth, and a scholar; yet there were still men who were faithful to Francis. They banded together and eventually found a name for themselves – the Strict Observants. Their opponents became known as Conventuals. Francis attempted to frame a new rule, which took him most of a year. He was not used to the niceties of clerical jargon, and it drifted off into expressions of his mood of the moment, hovering – unusually for him – between hope that something might be saved from the wreck, to despair that the divisions could ever be healed. It was not calculated to please the official mind, and it failed to do so.

One of the new men was Anthony of Padua, the first theologian of the Franciscan Order. On his appointment, Francis sent him a letter – affection for Anthony vying with his distrust of learning. He must be amused today by the irony of a Doctor of the Church becoming the object of a cult invoking his aid when making frantic searches for lost socks, or missing car keys...

It was a relief for Francis to leave politics aside and resume his missionary journeys. He did not spare himself, visiting up to five villages in a day. In the towns he was mobbed, the citizens so anxious for relics that they tore pieces of his patched tunic from his back. His tenderness for members of the animal kingdom was not diminished, especially those connected with Jesus in the gospels. Lambs were dear to him on this account; he saw one pastured with some goats, and wanted to buy it from its owner. Of course the brothers had no money, but a passing merchant purchased it, and gave it to them as a gift. They were bound for the bishop's palace at Osimo, and although the bishop was delighted to see Francis, the lamb he was leading was an embarrassment. Francis, suspecting that his new pet might end up in the episcopal kitchen, preached a moving homily on the parable of the lost sheep, and made the bishop see the animal through his eyes. A solution was found to the problem of its future by sending it to some nuns at a nearby convent; they wove its wool into a tunic and sent it to Francis as a present.

There are stories about a rabbit who found shelter in his lap, and only left him with great reluctance, and a fish that he rescued from a net and returned to the water, where it showed the same tenacity, playing beside the boat that carried him. Bees he loved for their industry, and the beautiful order of their lives, and he insisted on their being given sugar and the best wine in the winter. Flowers overwhelmed him with their beauty, and he talked to them as if they were capable of understanding his words – and who knows that they did not? Every stone, tree and hill seemed to Francis a hymn to the Creator: in the history of the Church, many have renounced the world, but no one loved it as much as Francis.

But the constant, unstinting giving of himself took its toll. He was forced to ride instead of walking, and his companions urged him to give Brother Ass, that had served him so well, a respite from austerity. They tempted him with delicacies that he would never have looked at when he was well, and tried to see that he had warm clothes as winter set in. But however many cloaks he was given, he found poor men who had none, and gave them away again. At last he consented to nurse his ailing body, and retired to the hermitage of Fonte Columbo, near Rieti.

There he made use of his enforced leisure and produced a second rule to take the place of the one rejected as too vague and discursive. He was forty-one, but very frail, and he had to look to the future of the order after his death. He tried hard to be specific about details of how the order should be governed; the times of fasting and the rules of obedience to superiors, but he could not resist the old idealism breaking through.

The friars were still to own nothing, to labour for their alms, and where that was not possible, to beg for their bread. He sent it off to Brother Elias, now general of the order. It failed to reach him, and Francis patiently reconstructed it from memory. It is essentially the pattern of life for the friars Minor to this day, though the form had an official interpretation imposed upon it by Cardinal Ugolino when he became Pope Gregory IX, and inevitably some of the tone of Francis's own voice was lost.

To celebrate Christmas that year, he had one of his happy inspirations. Family life had always been an attraction to Francis – indeed a temptation. One winter night when he was younger, a bemused brother saw him by moonlight, first rolling in the snow, then making seven snowmen of it. He talked as he worked, calling one his wife, the others two daughters and two sons, and the remaining pair the servants they would need to wait on them. He urged himself to earn the money to clothe them all, as they were dying with cold. These were the cares he would have if he were married, and Francis knew he must serve God single-mindedly. But there was no harm in serving the Holy Family.

About a fortnight before Christmas, in the little town of Greccio, he contacted a good friend of his, a man of noble birth but simple piety, and asked him to fetch an ox and an ass, a manger and some hay, and bring them to the woods outside the town before midnight on Christmas Eve. Then he and the brothers went round, inviting everyone to celebrate mass with them.

Just before midnight the people came with candles and flaming torches to light their way. They were amazed to see before them the crib that Francis had arranged, out of the materials provided by his friend. Francis acted as deacon at the mass, and delivered the homily. No one can ever have forgotten how he told the story of the Nativity. A witness described the way he crooned the words, 'The child of Bethlehem' – moistening his lips with his tongue, as if savouring their sweetness. He insisted that the hay should be kept for the animals so that they too could join in the festivities, and it was said that it healed both animal and human illnesses. So the custom of making a Christmas crib, now universal throughout the world, was begun.

Many years before, Count Orlando di Chiusi had offered Francis an extraordinary present. It was nothing less than a mountain – Mount Verna – between the sources of the Tiber and the Arno, on the edge of Tuscany. It was so remote and difficult of access that it was rarely visited, and Francis had never spent much time there; but now he felt the need to be alone, away from the crowds who always seemed to find him and make demands on him – demands he never refused – away from the brothers, who also encroached upon him to solve their problems. He wanted to be alone with the Lord whose life and death and resurrection were as real to him as anything he encountered in everyday life.

He decided to make a retreat between the feast of the Assumption and Michaelmas. He took three companions, amongst them his faithful Brother Leo – secretary, cook, and if need be, nurse. Francis was very weak, and they progressed slowly to the summit of the mountain, where the black rocks made natural caves. There he selected a cave, and as his companions withdrew, he gave Brother Leo instructions that he should come every other day, bringing bread and any berries he could find in that remote region. There was the unspoken thought between them that he might die in this remote solitude.

A great deal that he experienced there, he never told anyone; it has only been conjectured from other, more articulate mystics. All that is certain is that on the 14th of September, the feast of the Exaltation of the Cross, during a meditation upon the sufferings of Jesus, a vision broke in on him which he described afterwards as the figure of one of the winged messengers of God, floating in the air before his eyes. Its wings were six in number; two extended above its head, two poised as if in flight, and two wrapped round its body, which was impaled upon a cross. He could not express the beauty and the sadness that came to him, rapt in contemplation, half in and half out of the world.

He did not at first know what the vision meant. Then he felt a searing pain in his hands and his feet and his side. He saw the marks of the nails and a bleeding wound, and knew he had the ultimate privilege of receiving the stigmata. He had followed Christ, his dearest friend, all his life, and now he was imitating the triumph of his death.

He showed his wounds to his superior, Brother Elias, as he was bound to do, and some of his closest associates had glimpses of them, but he was wary of pride in this great honour, and the secret was shared by very few. The Poor Ladies, whose superior Sister Clare was his ally through all his sufferings, washed his clothes and found blood on them. But his whole body was racked with infirmities that could have caused these stains, and like the rest of the world, they only knew the full truth when his body was prepared for burial.

The eighteen years of his ministry had left him ravaged by disease, particularly a chronic eye infection which gave him great pain, and he was threatened with blindness. Cardinal Ugolino offered him a consultation with the pope's own physician, but he refused. He went home to the Portiuncula, where he was tended by the brothers, and recovered enough strength to undertake a last missionary journey amongst his dear people. He rode among them, unable to distinguish their faces and almost too weak to talk, yet he did not spare himself. Then he made a last visit to St Damian's, living in a squalid hut made of wattles in the garden. Singing was heard coming from the hut; he was composing his *Canticle of the Sun* – a litany of praise to the Creator, for the world, the elements that surround it, and its people, all of whom he claimed as his brothers and sisters. In the final lines he praised God for his Sister, the Death of the Body, for which he must by now have longed. No part of his body was free from pain, and the skin was stretched like parchment over his bones.

Before his release, he went to Rieti. It had been decided that he should have treatment for his eye complaint, as a matter of obedience; the savage treatment at that time was cauterisation. Even Francis, used to pain though he was, dreaded the operation. Courteously, he addressed the fire that heated the irons as 'Brother Fire', saying that he had loved him in the past, and asked for his kindness now. His companions retreated, unable to watch, but no cry escaped him. The operation was unsuccessful, and he had to endure another, with the same result. There was nothing left but to take him back to Assisi, his birthplace, to await death. He was carried in a litter, by a circuitous route, to avoid any publicity that would bring out the crowds, anxious to pay their respects and make their farewells.

He was lodged in the bishop's house, as the Portiuncula could not provide him with privacy. He must have felt the paradox of seeking poverty all his life, yet spending his last days in a palace. He rallied sufficiently to write his will, with a final message to his beloved brothers and sisters, commending them to cherish his Lady Poverty. He dictated it slowly, while his strength permitted, to his faithful companions Leo and Rufino, who had travelled with him on most of his journeys. A friend who was a doctor came from some distance to see him, and in reply to Francis's question about the length of time he could expect to live, reluctantly admitted that it would not be long.

He insisted on returning to the Portiuncula, and joined in the singing that prepared his return to his Father God. He made one last gesture, requesting the brothers to lay him on the ground, naked but for a hair-shirt, and sprinkle him with ashes to show the meaning of the phrase: 'Ashes to ashes, dust to dust.' He was persuaded back to bed, and the brothers knelt to receive his blessing. As dusk fell on the 3rd of October 1224, his triumphant spirit left his broken body. And it was said afterwards that larks sang in the darkness that night.

All Assisi came to mourn him. As his coffin was taken to St George's Church for burial, it was halted at St Damian's for Sister Clare and her Poor Ladies to take their last sight of him. They disobeyed his injunction not to cry over his coffin.

Four years later a basilica was built, dedicated to Francis, and with great ceremony his coffin was transferred there; it became a place of pilgrimage for succeeding generations. Many wars have raged around it, but Assisi has kept its ancient peace.

Since his canonization, his feast has been kept on the 4th of October. In 1990, he was named as the Patron of Ecology, and so he intercedes for a world laid waste by bad stewardship, the very air polluted. Only now is man beginning to care for the world as Francis did, seven and a half centuries ago.

* * *

'I've told them I'm not to be interrupted,' said the social worker testily, picking up the receiver.

His client seemed to be in a dream, paying no attention to the one-sided conversation. At last the social worker rang off, and faced the young man squarely.

'I've got a good chance for you. The Parks Department want a gardener. It's hard work, but it might suit you. What do you say? They want to know right away.'

The young man's face lit up.

'You mean they'll let me look after the flowers, and clean up the litter, and talk to the people on the benches?'

'Amongst other things... Do you mean you'll take it?'

'Yes!' said the young man eagerly.

The social worker made arrangements for him to meet his future employers, and prepared to pass on to the next case, but the young man lingered.

'I won't forget to ask St Francis about the baby.' Then he said, with a smile that touched the social worker's heart: 'Thank you. You've been very patient with me.'

'Think nothing of it. That's what I'm here for' said the social worker brusquely. '...And God bless you,' he added, as the door closed.

Bibliography

Almedingen, E.M., *Francis of Assisi*, Bodley Head, 1967.

Armstrong, Regis OFM/Brady, Ignatius OFM, *Francis and Clare*, Paulist Press, Ramsey, NJ 1982.

Baldwin, Ann B., *Catherine of Siena*.

Bodo, Murray, *Clare: a Light in the garden*, St Anthony Messenger Press, Cinn. OH, 1979.

Broderick, Robert, *The Catholic Encyclopedia*, Thomas A. Nelson, New York, 1976.

Bougard, M. *The History of St Monica*, Augustine Publishing Company, Devon, 1983.

Brown, Peter, *Augustine of Hippo*, Faber and Faber, 1967.

Butler, Thurston & Atwater, *Lives of the Saints*, (complete edition in four volumes), Christian Classics, Westminster, Maryland, 1980.

Chambers, R.W., *Thomas More*, Jonathan Cape, 1935.

Chesterton, G.K., *St Francis of Assisi*, Hodder and Stoughton, 1923.

Clissold, Stephen, *St Teresa of Avila*, Sheldon Press, 1979.

Curtayne, Alice, *St Catherine of Siena*, Sheed and Ward, 1929.

Encyclopaedia Britannica.

Etienne Robe, *Two Portraits of St Therese of Lisieux*, Sands and Co., 1955.

Fernoud, Regina, *Joan of Arc*, Macdonald and Co., 1964.

Gallico, Paul, *The Steadfast Man*, Michael Joseph, 1958.

Gaucher, Guy, *The Spiritual Journey of St Thérèse of Lisieux*, Darton, Longman & Todd, London 1987.

Gibbon, Thomas, *The Decline and Fall of the Roman Empire.*

Hamlyn, Paul, *The Life and Times of St Francis*, A. Mondadori, Milan, 1967.

Hollis, Christopher, *St Thomas More*, Sheed and Ward, 1931.

Karper, Karen, *Clare: Her Light and Her Song*, Franciscan Herald Press, 1984.

Kavanaugh, K. OCD/Rodriguez, O. OCD, *St Teresa of Avila,* ICS Publications, Washington, D.C. 1976.

Knox, Ronald, *The Story of a Soul*, Fount Collins, London, 1977.

Longley, Catherine, *Margaret Clitherow*, Anthony Clarke, 1986.

Rupp, Gordon, *Thomas More, the King's Good Servant*, Collins, 1978.

Ryan, John SJ, ed., *Irish Monasticism.*

Sheed, F.J., *Collected Letters of St Thérèse of Lisieux*, Sheed and Ward, London, 1977.

The Confessions of St Augustine, trans. R.S. Pine-Coffin, Penguin Books, London, 1961.

Thomas of Celano, *St Francis of Assisi*, Franciscan Herald Press, 1962.

Trochu, Francois, *St Bernadette Soubirous* , Longmans, Green and Co., London, 1957.

Walsh, William Thomas, *St Teresa of Avila*, Bruce Publishing Co., Milwaukee, WI, 1943.

Werfel, Franz, *The Song of Bernadette*, Pocket Books, New York, 1940.